Despite the exponential growth of investors and FDI, still enforcement continues to lack the comprehensive engagement it deserves. This book acts as a multi-layered tool for investment audiences. It identifies and tackles existing difficulties at the enforcement stage, and explores and proposes solutions. In doing so, it examines ways to facilitate international investment arbitral awards faced with the obstacle of state sovereignty in an effort to also resolve excessive 'forum-shopping.' Various proposals aiming to enforce the winning party at the enforcement stage, are analysed.

Associate Professor Kyriaki Noussia
University of Reading

The question of enforcement of investment treaty awards is a perennial concern. Drawing on both domestic law and public international law, Esra Yildiz Üstün examines practical solutions to the question. Yildiz Üstün innovatively tackles issues of current importance, including enforcement of the decisions of the proposed multilateral investment court, and enforcement of costs awards against unsuccessful investor-claimants. She also analyses interactions between enforcement and international law on the responsibility of states and international organisations. Yildiz Üstün's new book is a valuable addition to studies of enforcement.

Associate Professor Jarrod Hepburn
University of Melbourne

INTERNATIONAL INVESTMENT DISPUTE AWARDS

LLOYD'S ARBITRATION LAW LIBRARY
Series editors: Robert Merkin and Hakeem Seriki

LLOYD'S ARBITRATION LAW LIBRARY

Arbitration Practice and Procedure
Interlocutory and Hearing Problems
Third Edition
Mark Cato, Julian Critchlow
and Robert Merkin

Rules of Evidence in International Arbitration
An Annotated Guide
Nathan D. O'Malley

Injunctive Relief and International Arbitration
Hakeem Seriki

Singapore Arbitration Legislation
Annotated
Second Edition
Robert Merkin and Johanna Hjalmarsson

The Practice of International Commercial Arbitration
A Handbook for Hong Kong Arbitrators
Anselmo Reyes

Transnational Construction Arbitration
Key Themes in the Resolution of Construction Disputes
Edited by Renato Nazzini

Rules of Evidence in International Arbitration
An Annotated Guide
Second Edition
Nathan D. O'Malley

Merkin and Flannery on the Arbitration Act 1996
Sixth Edition
Robert Merkin and Louis Flannery

International Investment Dispute Awards
Facilitating Enforcement
Esra Yildiz Üstün

For more information about this series, please visit:
www.routledge.com/Lloyds-Arbitration-Law-Library/book-series/LALL

INTERNATIONAL INVESTMENT DISPUTE AWARDS

FACILITATING ENFORCEMENT

ESRA YILDIZ ÜSTÜN

informa law
from Routledge

First published 2022
by Informa Law from Routledge
4 Park Square, Milton Park, Abingdon, Oxon OX14 4RN

and by Informa Law from Routledge
605 Third Avenue, New York, NY 10158

Informa Law from Routledge is an imprint of the Taylor & Francis Group, an informa business

British Library Cataloguing-in-Publication Data
A catalogue record for this book is available from the British Library

Library of Congress Cataloging-in-Publication Data
A catalog record has been requested for this book

ISBN: 978-1-032-10759-2 (hbk)
ISBN: 978-1-032-10762-2 (pbk)
ISBN: 978-1-003-21691-9 (ebk)

DOI: 10.4324/9781003216919

Typeset in Times New Roman
by Deanta Global Publishing Services, Chennai, India

CONTENTS

ACKNOWLEDGEMENTS

This book is based on my PhD thesis, which I defended at the University of Exeter in July 2017. I would never have been able to complete this research without support, encouragement and help from many people who deserve my sincere thanks.

Robert Merkin, QC, Lloyd's Professor of Law at the University of Exeter, planted the seed for this research and nourished its growth. I thank Robert for sharing his knowledge, for his unwavering support, and of course smiling face during the entire process of my thesis. I also would like to thank Dr. Kyriaki Noussia, who helped me to see the other side of the subject and gave me inspiration. I owe a debt of gratitude to her.

I gratefully acknowledge the generous financial support of the Turkish Ministry of Education during my LLM and PhD education in the UK. Of course I would like to thank my husband, Dr. Tayfun, needless to say for his priceless support and help. He was the best outcome of my PhD life. Also to my dear parents Ikbal and Ahmet Yildiz, who devoted their lives to my education. They always encouraged me to go further and prayed for me. Without their support, encouragement, and belief in me, I would not be here. I do not know how to repay them for their efforts. I am thankful to my mother-in-law, Leyla, for looking after my little daughter during the revising of this book.

Last but not least, this book is dedicated to my sweet daughter, Alçin Timsal; she makes me stronger in life.

It is impossible to enumerate everybody's name, so I simply express my sincere thanks to all.

TABLE OF CASES

ADC v Hungary (ICSID Case No ARB/03/16), 2006
AIG Capital Partners, Inc. v. Republic of Kazakhstan (AIG, Inc.), [2005] EWHC (Comm) 2239, [22], [2006] 1 WLR 1420
Air Service Agreement case <http://legal.un.org/ilc/texts/instruments/english/commentaries/9_6_2001.pdf>
AJT v. AJU, Court of Appeal, Singapore, 22 August 2011, [2011] SGCA 41
Alapli Elektrik B.V. v. Republic of Turkey (ICSID Case No ARB/08/13)
Amco Asia Corporation and others v. Republic of Indonesia, ICSID Case No ARB/81/1, Interim Order No 1 Concerning the Stay of Enforcement of the Award, (2 March 1991)
ATA Construction v. Jordan, ICSID Case No ARB/08/2, Award, 18.5.2010
Autobuses Urbanos del Sur SA, Teinver SA and Transportes de Cercanías SA v. Argentine Republic, ICSID Case No ARB/09/1, Award (21 July 2017)
AWG Group Ltd v. The Argentine Republic, UNCITRAL, Decision on Liability (30 July 2010)
Azurix Corp. v. Argentine Republic, ICSID Case No ARB/01/12, 2006
Banro American Resources, Inc. and Société Aurifère du Kivu et du Maniema S.A.R.L. v. Democratic Republic of the Congo, ICSID Case No ARB/98/7, 1998
Barcelona Traction, Light and Power Co. Ltd. (Belgium v Spain) (1970) I.C.J. Rep. 3
BG Group Plc v. The Republic of Argentina, UNCITRAL, Award (24 December 2007)
Bremen v. Zapata Off-Shore Co. 407 U.S. 1 (1972)
Cable Television of Nevis, Ltd. and Cable Television of Nevis Holdings, Ltd. v. Federation of St. Kitts and Nevis (ICSID Case No ARB/95/2)
CA Paris, 29 janvier 2019, n16/20822 [Paris Court of Appeal, 29 January 2019, n16/20822]
CDC Group Plc v. Republic of the Seychelles, ICSID Case No ARB/02/14, Decision on Whether or Not To Continue Stay and Order in CDC Group plc v. Republic of the Seychelles, (14 July 2004)
Cementownia 'Nowa Huta' S.A. v. Republic of Turkey, ICSID Case No ARB(AF)/06/2, 2006
Chevron Corporation (U.S.A.) and Texaco Petroleum Corporation (U.S.A.) v. The Republic of Ecuador, UNCITRAL, PCA Case No 34877, 1976
Chevron Bangladesh Block Twelve, Ltd. and Chevron Bangladesh Blocks Thirteen and Fourteen, Ltd. v. People's Republic of Bangladesh, ICSID Case No ARB/06/10, 2006
Compañia del Desarrollo de Santa Elena S.A. v. Republic of Costa Rica, ICSID Case No ARB/96/1, 1996
Compañia de Aguas del Aconquija SA and Vivendi Universal SA (formerly Compañia de Aguas del Aconquija, SA and Compagnie Générale des Eaux) v. Argentine Republic (I), ICSID Case No ARB/97/3, Award (21 November 2000)
Continental Casualty Company v. Argentine Republic, ICSID Case No ARB/03/9, Award (5 September 2008)
Cour de cassation, civile, Chambre civile 1, 12 mai 2021, 19-13.853
CME Czech Republic B.V. v. Czech Republic, UNCITRAL, Final Award (Mar. 14, 2003)
Creighton v. Ministre des Finances de l'État du Qatar, Cass 1 e civ 6, 6 July 2000
Crystallex International Corporation v. Bolivarian Republic of Venezuela, 2016 ONSC 4693
Crystallex International Corporation v. Bolivarian Republic of Venezuela, No 1:16-cv-00661 (DDC Mar 25 2017).
Crystallex Intl Corp v. Petroleos de Venezuela, SA, 879 F3d 79 (3d Cir 2018)
CMS Gas Transmission Company v. The Argentine Republic, ICSID Case No ARB/01/8, Award (12 May 2005)

Decision of the General Assembly of the Turkish Court of Appeals dated 8 February 2012, E. 2011/13-568 K. 2012/47
Decision of the General Assembly of the Turkish Court of Appeals dated 10 February 2012 E. 2010/1, K. 2012/1
Democratic Republic of the Congo v. FG Hemisphere Associates [2011] HKCFAR 41
Dirk Herzig as Insolvency Administrator over the Assets of Unionmatex Industrieanlagen GmbH v. Turkmenistan, ICSID Case No ARB/18/35, Decision on the Respondent's Request for Security for Costs and the Claimant's Request for Security for Claim (27 January 2020)
EDF International SA, SAUR International SA and León Participaciones Argentinas SA v. Argentine Republic, ICSID Case No ARB/03/23, Award (11 June 2012)
Elettronica Sicula SPA (ELSI) (USA v. Italy) [1989] ICJ Rep 15
Elsamex, S.A. v. Republic of Honduras, ICSID Case No ARB/09/4, Decision on the Continuation of the Stay of Enforcement of the Award, (7 January 2014)
El Paso Energy International Company v. The Argentine Republic, ICSID Case No ARB/03/15
Emilio Agustín Maffezini v. Kingdom of Spain, ICSID Case No ARB/97/7, 1997
Empresas Lucchetti, S.A. and Lucchetti Perú, S.A. v. Republic of Peru, ICSID Case No ARB/03/4, 2003
European Gas Turbines SA v. Sté Westman International Ltd, Paris CA, 1er Ch, 30 September 1993
Europe Cement Investment and Trade S.A. v. Republic of Turkey, ICSID Case No ARB 07/2)
Federation of Russia v. Noga, 128 JDI 116, 121–22 (2001)
Franck Charles Arif v. Moldova, ICSID Case No ARB/11/23, Award, 8.4.2013
Franz Sedelmayer v. The Russian Federation, UNCITRAL, Ad hoc arbitration rules; IIC 106 (1998)
Franz Sedelmayer (Germany) v. Russian Federation, Oberlandesgericht [Court of Appeal], Frankfurt am Main, 26 W 101/02, 26 September 2002
Franz Sedelmayer (Germany) v. State agency (Russian Federation), Oberlandesgericht [Court of Appeal], Cologne, 16 W 35/02, 6 October 2003
Franz Sedelmayer v. Russian Federation, Swedish Supreme Court of 1 July 2011—Mål nr Ö 170-10
Germany No 91 / W1, Franz J. Sedelmayer (Germany) v. Russian Federation, Federal Republic of Germany, Bundesgerichtshof [Federal Supreme Court], 4 October 2005
Germany No 92 / W2, Franz J. Sedelmayer (Germany) v. Russian Federation, Deutsche Lufthansa AG (Germany), Bundesgerichtshof [Federal Supreme Court], 4 October 2005
Impregilo SpA v. Islamic Republic of Pakistan, ICSID Case No ARB/03/3
Impregilo SpA v. Argentine Republic (I), ICSID Case No ARB/07/17, Award (21 June 2011)
Industria Nacional de Alimentos, S.A. and Indalsa Perú, S.A. (formerly Empresas Lucchetti, S.A. and Lucchetti Perú, S.A.) v. Republic of Peru, ICSID Case No ARB/03/4, 2003
Interhandel Case, (Switzerland v. United States of America) (1959) I.C.J. Rep. 6
Ioannis Kardassopoulos v. The Republic of Georgia, ICSID Case No ARB/05/18, Decision on Applicant's Request for a Continued Stay of Enforcement of the Award, (12 November 2010); Decision of the ad hoc Committee to terminate the Stay of Enforcement of the Award, (19 January 2011)
Ioan Micula and others v. Romania, ICSID Case No ARB/05/02, Decision on Jurisdiction and Admissibility, 24.9.2008, para. 166–168
Iowa Electric Light and Power Company v. Local Union 204, International Brotherhood of Electrical Workers, 834 F.2d 1424, (8th Cir. 1987)
IPCO (Nigeria) Ltd. v. Nigerian National Petroleum Corporation [2005] EWHC 726 (Comm), [2005] 2 Lloyd's Rep 326, [2005] 1 CLC 613
Joseph C. Lemire v. Ukraine, ICSID Case No ARB/06/18, Decision on Ukraine's Request for a Continued Stay of Enforcement of the Award, (14 February 2012)
Karaha Bodas Co LLC v. Perusahaan Pertambangan Minyak Dan Gas Bumi Negara, [2003] 380 HKCU 1
LG&E Energy Corp, LG&E Capital Corp. and LG&E International Inc v. Argentine Republic, ICSID Case No ARB/02/1, Award (25 July 2007)
Libananco Holdings Co. Limited v. Republic of Turkey, ICSID Case No ARB/06/8, 2006
Liberian E. Timber Corp. v. Gov't of the Republic of Liberia (LETCO I), 650 F Supp 73 (SDNY 1986), aff'd 854 F2d 1314 (2d Cir 1987)
Liberian E. Timber Corp. v. Gov't of the Republic of Liberia, 659 F Supp 606 (DDC 1987)
Liberian Eastern Timber Corporation (LETCO) v. Liberia, ICSID Case No ARB/83/2, 1983
Maritime International Nominees Establishment v. Republic of Guinea, ICSID Case No ARB/84/4, 1984
Metalclad Corp. v. Mexico, ICSID Case No ARB(AF)/97/1, 2000-2001
MINE v. Guinea, ICSID Case No ARB/84/4, Interim Order No 1 on Guinea's Application for Stay of Enforcement of the Award, (12 August 1988)

Ministry of Def. of the Islamic Republic of Iran v. Gould, Inc., XIV Y.B. Com. Arb. 763, 766 (1989) (C.D. Cal. 1988)
Mobil Argentina SA v. Argentine Republic, ICSID Case No ARB/04/16, Award (25 February 2016)
Motorola Credit Corporation, Inc v. Republic of Turkey (ICSID Case No ARB/04/21)
National Grid Plc v. The Argentine Republic, UNCITRAL, Award (3 November 2008)
NML Capital Limited (Appellant) v. Republic of Argentina (Respondent) [2011] UKSC 31
NML v. Rep. Argentine, Cass Civ 1, September 28 2011
Occidental Exploration and Production Co. v. Ecuador, LCIA Case No UN3467, Final Award (July 1, 2004)
Oil & Natural Gas Corporation Ltd. v. Saw Pipes Ltd., Supreme Court, India, 17 April 2003, [2003] INSC 236
Papel del Tucuman (in bankruptcy) v. Argentine Republic, ICC Case No 12364/KGA/CCO/JRF/CA/ASM/JPA, Award (5 March 2019).
Patrick Mitchell v. Democratic Republic of the Congo, ICSID Case No ARB/99/7, Decision on the Stay of Enforcement of the Award of 30 November 2004
Phulchand Exports Ltd. v. OOO Patriot, Supreme Court, India 12 October 2011, [2011] INSC 1038
Plama Consortium Limited v. Republic of Bulgaria (ICSID Case No ARB/03/24) Award (27 August 2008), paras 310, 312, 322–24
Ponderosa Assets, LP v. Argentine Republic, ICSID Case No ARB/ 01/3.
Pope & Talbot v. Canada, UNCITRAL, Award in Respect of Damages (May 31, 2002)
PSEG Global Inc. and Konya Ilgin Elektrik Üretim ve Ticaret Limited Sirketi v. Republic of Turkey (ICSID Case No ARB/02/5)
Railway Traffic between Lithuania and Poland (Poland v Lithuania) [1931] PCIJ Rep Series A/B no 42 108, 116
Repsol YPF Ecuador S.A. v. Empresa Estatal Petroleos del Ecuador, ICSID Case No ARB/01/10, Procedural Order No 1 concerning the Stay of Enforcement of the Award of Dec. 22, 2005; Procedural Order No 4 concerning the Stay of Enforcement of the Award, (22 February 2006)
Republic of Congo ('Congo') and the Congolese company Commissions Import Export SA ('Commisimpex') Commisimpex, Cour de cassation, Chambre civile 1, 13 May 2015, no 13-17751
Republic of Peru v. Caravelí Cotaruse Transmisora de Energía S.A.C. (ICSID Case No ARB/13/24)
Robert Azinian and others v. United Mexican States (ICSID Case No ARB(AF)/97/2)
Ron Fuchs v. The Republic of Georgia, ICSID Case No ARB/07/15, Decision of the ad hoc Committee on the Stay of Enforcement of the Award, (12 November 2010); Decision of the ad hoc Committee to terminate the Stay of Enforcement of the Award, (19 January 2011)
RSM Production Corporation v. Saint Lucia, ICSID Case No ARB/12/10, 2012
Rusoro Mining Ltd v. Bolivarian Republic of Venezuela, ICSID Case No ARB(AF)/12/5, Award (22 August 2016)
S.A.R.L. Benvenuti & Bonfant v. People's Republic of the Congo, ICSID Case No ARB/77/2, 1977
SAUR International v. Argentine Republic, ICSID Case No ARB/04/4, Award (22 May 2014)
Saba Fakes v. Republic of Turkey, ICSID Case No ARB/07/20, 2007
Scherk v. Alberto-Culver Co, 417 US 506 (1974)
Sempra Energy International v Argentine Republic, ICSID Case No ARB02/16, Decision on annulment, (29 June 2010)
Sempra Energy International v. Argentine Republic, ICSID Case No ARB/02/16, 2002
Sempra Energy International v. The Argentine Republic, ICSID Case No ARB/02/16, Decision on the Argentine Republic's Request for a Continued Stay of Enforcement of the Award, (05 March 2009); Decision on Sempra Energy International's Request for the Termination of the Stay of Enforcement of the Award, (7 August 2009)
SGS v. Pakistan and SGS v. Philippines (2004) 5(4) JWIT 555, 557
SIAG v. Arab Republic of Egypt (ICSID Case No ARB/05/15) Award (1 June 2009)
Société NML Capital (Iles Caïmans) v. Etat d'Argentine, Cour de Cassation (1ère Chambre Civile), no 10-25.938, 11-10.450 and 11-13.323, 28 March 2013
Société NML Capital Ltd v. République Argentine, Cour de Cassation (1ère Chambre Civile), no 09-72.057, 28 September 2011
Suez, Sociedad General de Aguas de Barcelona S.A., and InterAguas Servicios Integrales del Agua S.A. v. The Argentina Republic, ICSID Case No ARB/03/19, Decision on Liability, (30 July 2010)
1837–1842 Sicilian Sulphur Dispute, Great Britain, State Papers 1839–1840 Volume 28 (Harrison and Sons, London, 1857) 1163–1242
The Exchange v. McFaddon, 11 U.S. 7 Cranch 116 116 (1812)
The Russian Federation v. Yukos Universal Limited, the Hague District Court C/09/481619 / HA ZA 15-112

TMR Energy Ltd. v. State Property Fund of Ukraine and State Property Fund of Ukraine (ANTK Antonov), [2004] NLSCTD 244

Total SA v. Argentine Republic, ICSID Case No ARB/04/1, Decision on Liability (27 December 2010)

Turkish Supreme Court, 12th Civil Circuit, Decision 6469/13007 of May 24 2004

Uniprex S.A. v. Grupo Radio Blanca, Madrid Court of Appeal, Spain, 22 March 2006, case No. 178/2006-4/2004

United Parcel Service of America v. Canada, (UNCITRAL) 2 Award (24 May 2007)

Victor Pey Casado and President Allende Foundation v. Republic of Chile (ICSID Case No ARB/98/2)

Yugraneft Corp v. Rexx Management Corp, 2010 SCC 19, [2010] 1 SCR 649

Yukos Capital SARL v. OJSC Rosneft Oil Co, [2014] EWHC 2188 (Comm)

Walter Bau Ag (In Liquidation) v. The Kingdom of Thailand, UNCITRAL case

W Ltd v. M SDN BHD, [2016] EWHC 422 (Comm)

Wena Hotels Limited v. Arab Republic of Egypt, ICSID Case No ARB/98/4, Procedural Order No 1 of the ad hoc Committee concerning the continuation of the stay of enforcement of the award, (5 April 2001)

1837–1842 Sicilian Sulphur Dispute, Great Britain, State Papers 1839–1840 Volume 28 (Harrison and Sons, London, 1857) 1163–1242

TABLE OF TREATIES, CONVENTIONS, LEGISLATIONS

American Arbitration Association (AAA) Rules <https://www.adr.org/Rules> accessed 14 May 2017

Arbitration Act (UK) (1996) <http://www.legislation.gov.uk/ukpga/1996/23/section/69> accessed 9 May 2017

Charter of the United Nations (1945) <http://www.un.org/en/documents/charter/> accessed 26 April 2015

Convention Establishing the Multilateral Investment Guarantee Agency (1988) <http://www.miga.org/documents/miga_convention_november_2010.pdf> accessed 25 December 2016

Convention Establishing the World Intellectual Property Organisation (1967) <http://www.wipo.int/treaties/en/convention/trtdocs_wo029.html> accessed 24 September 2014

Convention on the Recognition and Enforcement of Foreign Arbitral Awards (New York Convention) (1958) <http://www.uncitral.org/pdf/english/texts/arbitration/NY-conv/XXII_1_e.pdf> accessed 10 December 2015

Convention on the Settlement of Investment Disputes Between States and Nationals of Other States (1965) <https://icsid.worldbank.org/ICSID/StaticFiles/basicdoc/CRR_English-final.pdf> accessed 18 December 2015

Draft Articles on Diplomatic Protection (2006) <http://untreaty.un.org/ilc/texts/instruments/english/draft%20articles/9_8_2006.pdf> accessed 28 February 2017

Draft Articles on Responsibility of States for Internationally Wrongful Acts (2001) <http://untreaty.un.org/ilc/texts/instruments/english/draft%20articles/9_6_2001.pdf> accessed 25 February 2017

Draft Articles on the Responsibility of International Organizations 2011 (DARIO) <http://legal.un.org/ilc/texts/instruments/english/draft_articles/9_11_2011.pdf> accessed 12 January 2017

Draft Convention on the Protection of Foreign Property (1967) <http://www.oecd.org/dataoecd/35/4/39286571.pdf> accessed 19 July 2015

Dutch Model Investment Agreement (2018) Article 20, available at <https://www.rijksoverheid.nl/documenten/publicaties/2018/10/26/modeltekst-voor-bilaterale-investeringsakkoorden> accessed 15 January 2019

General Agreement on Tariffs and Trade (1947) <http://www.wto.org/english/docs_e/legal_e/gatt47_01_e.htm> accessed 25 July 2015

Geneva Convention 1927 Convention on the Execution of Foreign Arbitral <http://www.newyorkconvention.org/11165/web/files/document/1/5/15939.pdf> accessed 22 June 2015

Havana Charter 1948 (full text) <http://www.worldtradelaw.net/misc/havana.pdf> accessed 28 July 2015

IBA Rules of Ethics for International Arbitrators 1987 <https://www.trans-lex.org/701100/_/iba-rules-of-ethics-for-international-arbitrators-1987/> accessed 30 April 2016

ICSID Additional Facility Rules <https://icsid.worldbank.org/en/Documents/resources/AFR_2006%20English-final.pdf> accessed 10 June 2015

International Chamber of Commerce Rules of Arbitration (2012) <http://www.iccwbo.org/ProductsandServices/ArbitrationandADR/Arbitration/Rules-of-arbitration/Download-ICC-Rules-of Arbitration/ICCRules-of-Arbitration-in-several-languages/> accessed 14 May 2017

International Chamber of Commerce's International Code of Fair Treatment of Foreign Investment (1949), the International Convention for the Mutual Protection of Private Property Rights in Foreign Countries (1957), a private effort known as the Abs-Shawcross Convention

International Law Commission, Draft Articles on Responsibility of States for Internationally Wrongful Acts (2001) Supplement No.10 (A/56/10), chp.IV.E.1 <http://untreaty.un.org/ilc/texts/instruments/english/draft%20articles/9_6_2001.pdf> accessed 12 February 2017

North American Free Trade Agreement (NAFTA) (1995) <http://www.nafta-secalena.org/en/view.aspx?conID=590> accessed 11 August 2015

Organisation for the Harmonisation of Business Law in Africa Uniform Act (OHADA) <http://www.ohada.org/index.php/en/> accessed 12 February 2016

Organization for Economic Cooperation and Development (OECD) Draft Convention on the Protection of Foreign Property (1967)

Rules—The Arbitration Institute of the Stockholm Chamber of Commerce (SCC) <http://www.sccinstitute.com/media/169838/arbitration_rules_eng_17_web.pdf> accessed 14 May 2017

The International Bank for Reconstruction and Development (IBRD) <http://www.worldbank.org/en/who-we-are/ibrd> accessed 22 March 2017

The International Development Association (IDA) <http://ida.worldbank.org/about/what-ida> accessed 22 March 2017

The International Finance Corporation (IFC) <http://www.ifc.org/wps/wcm/connect/corp_ext_content/ifc_external_corporate_site/about+ifc_new> accessed 22 March 2017

The London Court of International Arbitration Rules (LCIA) <http://www.lcia.org/Dispute_Resolution_Services/lcia-arbitration-rules-2014.aspx> accessed 14 May 2017

The new Enforcement and Bankruptcy Law (No 2004) <https://www.iiiglobal.org/sites/default/files/LawAmmendingtheExecutionoftheBankruptcyCode2004.pdf> accessed 9 May 2017

The United Nations Convention on Jurisdictional Immunities of States and Their Property 2004 (UNCSI) <https://treaties.un.org/doc/source/recenttexts/english_3_13.pdf> accessed 21 November 2016

Treaty Establishing the European Economic Community (EEC Treaty/ Treaty of Rome) (1957) <http://ec.europa.eu/economy_finance/emu_history/documents/treaties/rometreaty2.pdf> accessed 11 August 2015

Turkey-Iran BIT <http://www.ekonomi.gov.tr/portal/content/conn/UCM/uuid/dDocName:EK-018313> accessed 15 May 2017

Turkey-Saudi Arabia BIT <http://www.ekonomi.gov.tr/portal/content/conn/UCM/uuid/dDocName:EK-018298> accessed 15 May 2017

Turkish Private International Law Act 2007 / Turkish International Private and Procedural Code <http://jafbase.fr/docAsie/Turquie/Private%20international%20law%20Turkey.pdf> accessed 9 May 2017

UK State Immunity Act 1978 <http://www.legislation.gov.uk/ukpga/1978/33/pdfs/ukpga_19780033_en.pdf> accessed 9 May 2017

UNCITRAL Arbitration Rules (1976, amended 2010) <http://www.uncitral.org/uncitral/en/uncitral_texts/arbitration/1976Arbitration_rul es.html> accessed 14 May 2017

UNCITRAL Model Law on International Commercial Arbitration (2006) <http://www.uncitral.org/uncitral/en/uncitral_texts/arbitration/1985Model_arbitrati on.html> accessed 26 April 2016

United States: Foreign Sovereign Immunities Act of 1976 [21 October 1976] not official text <https://plone.unige.ch/art-adr/cases-affaires/6-klimt-paintings-2013-maria-altmann-and-austria/united-states-foreign-sovereign-immunity-act/at_download/file> accessed 11 May 2017

US Federal Arbitration Act (1925) <http://www.law.cornell.edu/uscode/html/uscode09/usc_sup_01_9.html> accessed 9 May 2017

Vienna Convention on the Law of Treaties (1969) <http://untreaty.un.org/ilc/texts/instruments/english/conventions/1_1_1969.pdf> accessed 3 March 2017

World Trade Organization Understanding on Rules and Procedures Governing the Settlement of Disputes (WTO DSU 1994) <http://www.wto.org/english/tratop_e/dispu_e/dsu_e.htm> accessed 23 October 2016

World Trade Organization's (WTO) Agreement on Trade-Related Investment Measures (TRIMs Agreement UNCITRAL)

LIST OF ABBREVIATIONS

AAA	American Arbitration Association
BIT	bilateral investment treaty
CETA	Comprehensive Economic and Trade Agreement
CJEU	Court of Justice of the European Union
DARIO	Draft Articles on the Responsibility of International Organizations
DRC	dispute resolution clause
ECTHR	European Court of Human Rights
EEC	European Economic Community European Economic Community
EFILA	European Federation for Investment Law and Arbitration
EU	European Union
FCN	friendship, commerce, and navigation
FDI	foreign direct investment
FET	fair and equitable treatment
FSIA	Foreign State Immunity Act 1976 (United States)
GATT	General Agreement on Tariffs and Trade
Geneva Convention	Convention on the Execution of Foreign Arbitral Awards
HKIAC	Hong Kong International Arbitration Centre
IBA	International Bar Association
IBRD	International Bank for Reconstruction and Development
ICC	International Chamber of Commerce
ICJ	International Court of Justice
ICS	Investment Court System
ICSID Convention	Convention on the Settlement of Investment Disputes between States and Nationals of Other States
ICSID	International Centre for Settlement of Investment Disputes
IIAS	international investment agreements
ILA Final Report	Final Report on Public Policy as a Bar to Enforcement of International Arbitral Awards

ILA Interim Report	International Law Association issued a Report on Public Policy as a Bar to Enforcement of International Awards in July 2000
ILC	International Law Commission
ILC Articles on State Responsibility	2001 International Law Commission's (ILC) Articles on State Responsibility
IMF	International Monetary Fund
ISDS	investor–state dispute settlement
ITO	International Trade Organization
IUSCT	Iran–US Claims Tribunal
LCIA	London Court of International Arbitration
LDCS	least developed countries
MFN	most favoured nation
MIAM	multilateral investment appellate mechanism
MIC	multilateral investment court
MIGA	Multilateral Investment Guarantee Agency
ML	model law
NAFTA	North American Free Trade Agreement
New York Convention	Convention on the Recognition and Enforcement of Foreign Arbitral Awards
NT	national treatment
OECD	Organisation for Economic Cooperation and Development
OHADA	Organisation for the Harmonisation of Business Law in Africa
PCIJ	Permanent Court of International Court
PILA	Turkish Private International Law Act 2007
SCC	Stockholm Chamber of Commerce
SIA 1978	State Immunity Act 1978 (England)
SIAC	Singapore International Arbitration Centre
SPF	State Property Fund
TIPPIC	Turkish International Private and Procedural Code
TIPS	treaties with investment provisions
TRIMS	Agreement on Trade-Related Investment Measures
TTIP	Transatlantic Trade and Investment Partnership
UN Convention	Convention on Jurisdictional Immunities of States and Their Property
UN	United Nations
UNCITRAL Model Law	UNCITRAL Model Law on International Commercial Arbitration
UNCITRAL	United Nations Commission on International Trade Law
UNCSI	United Nations Convention on Jurisdictional Immunities of States and Their Property

UNCTAD	United Nations Conference on Trade and Development
VCLT	Vienna Convention on the Law of Treaties
WIPO	World Intellectual Property Organization
WTO	World Trade Organization

INTRODUCTION

0.1 General background

When a transaction binds a national of one state and another state, a number of challenging questions arise, such as, Can a sovereign state restrict itself because of an investment contract between itself and a foreign national or corporation? Is there a sovereign state able to breach the contract for its public good? If so, do foreign investors have a right to be compensated? Can the home state interfere in a dispute between its national and another sovereign? If the investor is a corporation instead of an individual, which state is its home state under international law?

Over the history of modern civilisation, investment and trade have not been restricted to only within national borders. International law of foreign investment has gradually evolved to promote such investment and trade. Even though the attention of scholars on international investment law was in for much of the 20th century,[1] international law of foreign investment is one of the oldest parts of international law.[2] Despite its maturity, foreign investment law was a comparatively undeveloped field of international law until relatively recently. Foreign investment law has witnessed a period of rapid expansion, and the field is currently the fastest growing part of international law. Jackson describes the development of international economic law as being 'like trying to describe a landscape while looking out of the window of a moving train—events tend to move faster than one can describe them.'[3]

Investor–state arbitration is a dispute resolution method that enables a foreign investor to call a sovereign state to appear in a neutral forum and respond to investment claims. This brings binding awards that carry worldwide enforceability.[4] This generous concession to sovereign states, which allows for the waiving of immunity from jurisdiction and execution, can be traced back to the boom in foreign direct investment (FDI), a development which itself can be attributed to the increase in international investment agreements (IIAs).[5] This significant increase is clearly evidenced in a 2016 report from the United

1 Krista Nadakavukaren Schefer, *International Investment Law: Text, Cases and Materials* (Edward Elgar Publishing 2016).

2 Nicolette Butler, 'The State of International Investment Arbitration: The Possibility of Establishing An Appeal Mechanism' (PhD thesis, University of Leeds, School of Law September 2012).

3 John H Jackson, *Legal Problems of International Economic Relations* (3rd edn, West Publishing 1999) as cited in C Tietje et al, 'Once and Forever? The Legal Effects of a Denunciation of ICSID' (2008).

4 Campbell McLachlan, Laurence Shore, and Matthew Weiniger, *International Investment Arbitration Substantive Principles* (OUP 2007) 1.

5 Joseph M Cardosi, 'Precluding the Treasure Hunt: How the World Bank Group Can Help Investors Circumnavigate Sovereign Immunity Obstacles to ICSID Award Execution' (2014) 41 Pepperdine Law Review 3.

DOI: 10.4324/9781003216919-1

Nations Conference on Trade and Development (UNCTAD), which described the strong recovery in FDI in 2015.[6] Global (FDI) flows jumped by 38 per cent to $1.76 trillion.[7] In parallel, IIAs have continued to grow. In 2015, 31 new IIAs were concluded, bringing the total to 3,304 treaties [2,946 bilateral investment treaties (BITs) and 358 treaties with investment provisions (TIPs) by the year's end].[8] By the end of May 2016, close to 150 economies were engaged in negotiating at least 57 new IIAs.[9]

While FDI has increased due to the proliferation of BITs, it has brought some problems with it. In a dispute governed by an arbitration clause, this clause provides for an arbitral tribunal with jurisdiction over the disputing parties.[10] Although the consent in submitting to arbitration assumes a waiver of sovereign immunity from jurisdiction, winning investors may experience the obstacle of sovereign immunity from execution in the event of attempting to execute an award against a non-compliant state. In that circumstance, investors must seek to recover from the global assets of the losing state if it refuses to honour an award. In addition, if investors find the assets of a non-compliant state, they must also remove the bar of sovereign immunity laws governing access to those assets.[11]

In order to facilitate enforcement of arbitral awards, two conventions were drafted: the Convention on the Recognition and Enforcement of Foreign Arbitral Awards (the New York Convention, or NYC), and the Convention on the Settlement of Investment Disputes between States and Nationals of Other States (the ICSID Convention).[12] One of the aims of these conventions was to restrict state sovereignty power against foreign investors. The main advantage of the ICSID Convention is that its awards are final and binding, which means that it is like an enforcing state's court decision. Therefore, while the ICSID awards do not encounter a public policy obstacle, the New York Convention has not only an obstacle at the recognition stage but also a sovereign immunity bar in the enforcement stage. ICSID awards face only a sovereign immunity obstacle in the enforcement stage.

The essential stage in a dispute settlement proceeding is enforcement. Even if an arbitration has been won, if it cannot be enforced, then it is only a piece of paper. Furthermore, arbitration can be seen as a waste of time with high costs. In terms of ICSID arbitration, it may not be accurate to say that the ICSID awards are self-enforcing in all member states, which means that they are automatically enforced,[13] as there are a number of countries

6 UNCTAD 'World Investment Report 2016 Investor Nationality: Policy Challenges' (United Nations 2016) <http://unctad.org/en/PublicationsLibrary/wir2016_Overview_en.pdf> accessed 6 April 2017.

7 ibid 5.

8 ibid 8.

9 ibid. Of course 'the COVID-19 crisis will cause a dramatic fall in FDI. Global FDI flows are forecast to decrease by up to 40 per cent in 2020, from their 2019 value of $1.54 trillion. This would bring FDI below $1 trillion for the first time since 2005. FDI is projected to decrease by a further 5 to 10 per cent in 2021 and to initiate a recovery in 2022. A rebound in 2022, with FDI reverting to the pre-pandemic underlying trend, is possible, but only at the upper bound of expectations.' UNCTAD 'World Investment Report 2020 International Production Beyond the Pandemic' (United Nations 2020) <https://unctad.org/system/files/official-document/wir2020_en.pdf> accessed 25 August 2021.

10 Cardosi (n 5) 118.

11 Cardosi (n 5) 144.

12 Convention on the Settlement of Investment Disputes Between States and Nationals of Other States (1965) <https://icsid.worldbank.org/ICSID/StaticFiles/basicdoc/CRR_English-final.pdf> accessed 18 December 2015. Convention on the Recognition and Enforcement of Foreign Arbitral Awards (New York Convention) (1958) <http://www.uncitral.org/pdf/english/texts/arbitration/NY-conv/XXII_1_e.pdf> accessed 10 December 2015.

13 David A Collins, 'Towards a Grand Unified Theory of International Economic Law' (2015) 12 MJIEL 140–66.

which still insist upon separate authorisation by the national courts in order to allow enforcement of arbitral awards.[14] Non-compliance with ICSID awards may create a lack of confidence in the International Centre for Settlement of Investment Disputes (ICSID) to the point that it may lose its effectiveness and significance. In terms of the NYC, non-compliance of arbitral awards may cause people to lose confidence in the current investor–state dispute settlement (ISDS). In order to avoid non-compliance with investment arbitral awards, there are several practical solutions proposed by scholars and practitioners, but these suggestions have not yet been adopted in the field.

0.2 Central research questions

This book will mainly investigate the origin of enforcement issues in international investment arbitration and their practical solutions. Therefore, this research will be designed around the following questions:

1. What are the fundamental enforcement obstacles in investment arbitration awards?
2. How can such enforcement issues in international investment arbitration be overcome in practice? In doing so, how can a balance be struck between the interests of foreign investors and the host states?
3. Have any practical solutions been proposed by scholars and practitioners to resolve the enforcement issue? If so, why have these not been adopted in the field? Apart from previous solutions, are there any other practical recommendations for the issue?
4. How does the establishment of an international investment court overcome the issue of enforcement of investment arbitral awards?

Following these questions, the research will discuss the present solution proposed alongside new perspectives and possibilities for future development. In order to fully respond to these questions, a variety of secondary questions must also be considered:

i. Are international investment arbitration awards enforceable? Do problems occur when seizing a state's assets in an enforcing state?
ii. What are the reasons for non-compliance with investment arbitral awards in practice?
iii. Is there any convention to facilitate enforcement proceedings in member states?
iv. What is the relationship between the New York Convention and the ICSID Convention?
v. Which convention is better at enforcing investment arbitration awards in practice?
vi. Is it possible to totally exclude the home state when its national investor cannot enforce an arbitral award against the host state?
vii. If the non-compliant is a foreign investor, how will the non-compliance issue be resolved?

14 J Barratt and M Michael, 'The "Automatic Enforcement" of ICSID Awards: The Elephant in the Room' (2014) The European, Middle Eastern and African Arbitration Review <http://globalarbitrationreview.com/reviews/58/sections/202/chapters/2274/> in Collins 'Towards a Grand Unified Theory of International Economic Law' (n 13) 18.

0.3 Originality and significance of the book

Enforcement has become the crucial stage of a case in the investor–state arbitration mechanism, especially after Argentina's economic crisis and some states' reluctance to pay the award debts. As Cardosi states: 'Receiving an award is merely winning a battle, whereas receiving payment is winning the war.'[15] To date, enforcement of arbitral awards has been assumed to be voluntary because sovereign immunity has been restricted by the conventions and the area has been kept away from politicisation. Therefore, member states would honour arbitral awards voluntarily, without the need for intervention by a superior authority or other states. However, this has changed and some states have not paid awards by claiming state sovereignty. This is because, even though the conventions limit state sovereignty power, they do not completely remove state sovereignty as a possibility. Additionally, while the ICSID Convention explicitly allows the enforcing states to govern the enforcement process in accordance with their domestic rules, the New York Convention also does not mention state immunity in the text. Hence, after receiving the arbitral award, investors engage in extensive forum shopping to find any assets of the debtor states. This process uses a great deal of money and time. In terms of the host state as a creditor, it suffers from the non-payment of arbitral awards as well. Thus, the award is only a piece of paper without receiving the payment. More important, there has not been any practical solution applied to the issue and this may signal problems in the future.

Consequently, this book will analyse the origin of the enforcement issue of investment arbitral awards. Not only enforcement obstacles but also practical solutions will be explained from a new perspective by indicating the reason for not adopting proposals already suggested in the field. While doing this, the book will not only look at the enforcement issue in relation to foreign investors as creditors but also to the host state. While looking at the history of investment law, it is clear that its aim was only to protect foreign individuals or companies from the host state, but now it is also necessary to protect host states against foreign investors. This is because there is a considerable amount of investors who have more power to put pressure on investing countries around the world. The investors are more likely to be multinational corporations and they have a voice in the regulation of states as well. Investors continue to use the ISDS mechanism, with 696 publicly known up to 2015 and 70 new cases commencing in 2015 alone.[16] The total number of concluded cases reached 444 in 2015, with 36 per cent given in favour of the host state, 26 per cent in favour of the investor, and 26 per cent settled.[17] However, it should be asserted that the awards in favour of the states are mainly dismissed either on jurisdictional grounds or on the merits, and the awards in favour of the investor are with monetary compensation.[18] Therefore, a balance should be found when proposing solutions to the investment area.

15 Cardosi (n 5) 128.

16 UNCTAD, 'World Investment Report 2016 Investor Nationality: Policy Challenges' (n 6) 22.

17 UNCTAD, 'International Investment Agreement Issues' (United Nations 2017). <http://unctad.org/en/PublicationsLibrary/webdiaepcb2016d4_en.pdf> accessed 4 April 2017. See also Piero Bernardini, 'Reforming Investor–State Dispute Settlement: The Need to Balance Both Parties' Interests' (2016) 32 ICSID Review <https://academic.oup.com/icsidreview/article-lookup/doi/10.1093/icsidreview/siw035> accessed 10 April 2017. See the updated version of statistics from UNCTAD, 'World Investment Report: Key Messages and Overview' (United Nations 2019) <https://unctad.org/system/files/official-document/wir2019_overview_en.pdf> accessed 9 June 2021.

18 ibid 7.

It is expected that this book will have significant practical value and inspire the legislators of national sovereign laws and drafters of conventions and treaties regarding international investment arbitration. The originality of the book comes from three aspects.

Firstly, it will look at the issue not only from a foreign investor perspective but also from that of the host state in order to apply the most beneficial adjudication process to receive their payments. Until now, the enforcement issue has only been written about in relation to foreign investors in the literature. However, this research will also touch on the part of winning host states in the enforcement issue.

To date, two solutions have been proposed: drafting a hybrid sovereign immunity act and cutting the World Bank loans of the losing state. The reasons why these recommendations have not been adopted will be examined. This research will add further two proposals to the literature. One of these is whether the ICSID Administrative Council can play an active role by not accepting the next ICSID arbitration application of a non-compliant state or investor. This option will be debated as to whether the action can be justified under Article 22 of the Draft Articles on the Responsibility of International Organizations (DARIO). The other option is to use countermeasures against the host state by the home state on the grounds of Article 27 of the ICSID Convention. Article 60 of the Vienna Convention on the Law of Treaties (VCLT) may be another countermeasure to force the losing state to comply with the award.

Although there is no certainty about the European Union multilateral investment court proposal, it will be examined in detail how the proposal can recover the enforcement problems in the field.

There is no study which collects together the solutions to enforcement, so this book will contribute to future research as a source. Thus, the sustainability and promotion of international investment arbitration will be set out and made stronger by offering new perspectives.

This topic is also of great significance because FDI accounts for trillions of dollars every year. Therefore, it is important to ensure that any legal framework governing so many transactions operates in the most suitable manner that best serves its customers.[19] In addition to this, international investment law is gaining increased importance and so it is crucial to guarantee compliance with arbitral awards. The scope of investment disputes has extended to important issues such as human rights and the environment. Accordingly, foreign investment should be protected not only before the investment disputes with BITs and conventions but also after the dispute settlement by satisfying the arbitral awards. Otherwise, it may signal future problems in this area.

0.4 Structure of the book

In order to respond to the main research questions and secondary questions, this book is divided into six chapters, including the Introduction and Conclusion. An introductory chapter will provide a general introduction to the field, including background information, the central and the secondary research questions, the originality of the book, and the structure of the book.

19 Butler (n 2) 3.

The next chapter analyses the origin of the enforcement obstacles in investment arbitration under the ICSID. In addition to this, the extent to which host states can use their sovereign power over foreign investors at the enforcement stage will be considered. The chapter not only considers investors as the winning party but also will explore how the winning host state enforces investment arbitral awards against foreign investors.

The focus of the next chapter is the New York Convention and enforcement bar for the non-ICSID awards. This would be necessary to address enforcement issues under the New York Convention, which requires some engagement with the practice of domestic courts (such as the UK, USA, and Germany). Finally, the success of the conventions in terms of the practical enforcement of investment arbitral awards will be evaluated in accordance with the concrete cases.

The following chapter will examine the multilateral investment court (MIC) proposal regarding the potential enforcement system. It will be discussed whether the court needs a new international convention or if its decisions will be enforced under existing conventions such as the NYC or the ICSID. Also, this chapter will critically examine the potential risk of non-compliance of the court decisions with the possible sanctions for non-compliance party. This chapter will not only analyse the enforcement of MIC awards in the host state but also it will be demonstrated how the MIC decisions can be enforced in third states. As the United Nations Commission on International Trade Law (UNCITRAL) called the court proposal a radical reform for the field, it will be evaluated whether it can be a solution for the enforcement of international investment awards in practice.

In the next chapter, an attempt will be made to inspire others in the field so old and new proposals will be examined in detail. Since enforcement problems emerged in the investment field, scholars and practitioners have proposed solutions. The chapter will commence by evaluating these proposals and considering why they have not been adopted. Afterwards, the chapter will continue with a new perspective to facilitate enforcement of international investment arbitral awards by exploring the possibility of whether the ICSID Administrative Council can play an institutional role to comply with awards under the DARIO. Furthermore, another possible option is to take countermeasures under the law of state responsibility to persuade losing states to satisfy the awards. This option is plausible under the ICSID Convention and so it will be explained how it might be used and also why it has not been applied before. Article 60 of the VCLT will also be considered as a solution to this issue. Finally, the security for costs option will be discussed under the new rendered cases for both parties (foreign investor and the host state).

The last chapter is the conclusion, in which the research questions will be answered and the findings will be summarised.

Bibliography

Butler N, 'The State of International Investment Arbitration: The Possibility of Establishing An Appeal Mechanism' (PhD thesis, University of Leeds, School of Law, September 2012).

Cardosi J M, 'Precluding the Treasure Hunt: How the World Bank Group Can Help Investors Circumnavigate Sovereign Immunity Obstacles to ICSID Award Execution' (2014) 41 Pepp. L. Rev. 3.

Jackson J N, *Legal Problems of International Economic Relations* (3rd edn, West Publishing 1999).

Tietje C et al., ‘Once and Forever? The Legal Effects of a Denunciation of ICSID’ (Mar. 2008) 6 *Transnatl Disp. Mgmt.* 1, 5.

Mclachlan C, Shore L, and Weiniger M, *International Investment Arbitration Substantive Principles* (Oxford University Press 2007) 1.

Schefer K N, *International Investment Law: Text, Cases and Materials* (Edward Elgar Publishing 2016).

UNCTAD, ‘World Investment Report 2016 Investor Nationality: Policy Challenges’ (United Nations 2016) <http://unctad.org/en/PublicationsLibrary/wir2016_Overview_en.pdf> accessed 6 April 2017.

UNCTAD, ‘World Investment Report 2020 International Production Beyond The Pandemic’ (United Nations 2020) <https://unctad.org/system/files/official-document/wir2020_en.pdf> accessed 25 August 2021.

Convention on the Settlement of Investment Disputes Between States and Nationals of Other States (1965) <https://icsid.worldbank.org/ICSID/StaticFiles/basicdoc/CRR_English-final.pdf> accessed 18 December 2015.

Convention on the Recognition and Enforcement of Foreign Arbitral Awards (New York Convention) (1958) <http://www.uncitral.org/pdf/english/texts/arbitration/NY-conv/XXII_1_e .pdf> accessed 10 December 2015.

Collins D A, ‘Towards a Grand Unified Theory of International Economic Law’ (2015) 12(2) Manchester J. Intl Econ. L. 140–166.

Barratt J and Michael M, ‘The “Automatic Enforcement” of ICSID Awards: The Elephant in the Room’ (2014) *The European, Middle Eastern and African Arbitration Review* <http://globalarbitrationreview.com/reviews/58/sections/202/chapters/2274/> accessed 14 November 2016.

Bernardini P, ‘Reforming Investor–State Dispute Settlement: The Need to Balance Both Parties’ Interests’ (2016) 32 *ICSID Review* 38-57. <https://academic.oup.com/icsidreview/articlelookup/doi/10.1093/icsidreview/siw035> accessed 10 April 2017.

UNCTAD, ‘Investor-State Dispute Settlement: Review of Developments in 2015’ (2016) <https://unctad.org/system/files/official-document/webdiaepcb2016d4_en.pdf> accessed 10 June 2021.

CHAPTER 1

Obstacles in enforcement of ICSID awards

1.1 Introduction

As Waelde pointed out many years ago, a mere 10 per cent of disputes are actually about application and interpretation of the law; the other 90 per cent are entirely about evidence and enforcement.[1] The importance of being a winner in a case is to derive benefit from the court decision or tribunal award. Otherwise, the decision or award is just a piece of paper. Thus, it is vital to effectively enforce the award rather than just win the case.

Lawmaking and law enforcement are the cornerstones for 'the survival of a society governed by the rule of law.'[2] According to public international law, lawmaking is mainly focused on 'assessing the normative desirability, interpretation or application of substantive rules.'[3] Nevertheless, taking more regulatory measures does not necessarily lead to the well-being of society.[4] In other words, merely having a legal right does not make much sense in practice if such a right is not enforceable.

This situation continues in international cases, particularly in the foreign investment field. The increase of cross-border trade and development of science has become the new driving power of the world. The subsequent development in the world economy reached a point where the states, in order to secure their economic development, fought for investment of foreign capital in different fields of their economy.[5] Bilateral investment treaties (BITs) place foreign investors and states at the same level with the result that foreign investors feel secure and are encouraged to invest in other territories.

After the proliferation of BITs, arbitration emerged as the popular method to resolve disputes arising from foreign investment treaties.[6] Its popularity can be attributed to the fact that disputing parties are free to choose arbitrators, governing law, and also the seat of arbitration with 'efficiency, simplicity and manageable costs.'[7] However, the mechanism cannot be expected to be entirely independent from domestic jurisdictions[8] because in many cases arbitration awards are not enforced voluntarily by host states. Thus, when a losing party refuses to pay, the winning party then attempts to enforce the award through

1 Freya Baetens, 'Enforcement of Arbitral Awards: "To ICSID or Not to ICSID" is Not the Question' (2011) 5 Investment Treaty Arbitration and International Law, Juris Arbitration Series 211–28.

2 ibid 211.

3 ibid.

4 ibid.

5 Vasily Shubin, 'Enforcement of ICSID Arbitral Awards, Practice and Problems' (2012) 12 Korea University Law Review 11.

6 ibid.

7 Vincent O Nmehielle, 'Enforcing Arbitration Awards under the International Convention for the Settlement of Investment Disputes (ICSID Convention)' (2001) 7 Ann Surv Intl & Comp L 21.

8 ibid.

DOI: 10.4324/9781003216919-2

a local court within whose jurisdiction the losing party has assets.[9] This demonstrates that there is no guarantee that the losing party will comply with the terms of the award rendered by the arbitral tribunal.[10]

In such circumstances, enforcement obstacles in third-party states crop up. In order to facilitate and provide identical (uniform) standards for enforcement of international arbitration awards, the ICSID Convention[11] and the New York Convention,[12] have been brought into force. The New York Convention moderately overlaps with the ICSID Convention (the scope of application of the New York Convention also covers state–investor arbitral awards), and the relationship between the two conventions on the topic of enforcement is significant.[13] The point of similarity between these two conventions is that both conventions have provided the winning party with a facility whereby the said party is not required to procure an order of enforcement in two countries. In other words, one is where the decision is reached and the other is the enforcing country.[14] Under the provisions of the ICSID Convention, only a certified copy of the award is requested by the enforcing court.[15] In addition, both conventions include provisions about restricting the grounds upon which domestic courts can reject enforcement of such arbitral awards.[16] The conventions have successfully laid down uniform standards for national courts and have limited their discretion in rejecting enforcement of international arbitral awards.[17]

The ICSID Convention regulates only investment disputes and enforcement of ICSID awards between a member state and a foreign investor who is another member state's national. Their enforcement is hindered by sovereign immunity (ICSID awards are not reviewed by other courts or tribunals). The importance of the state sovereignty principle is that a sovereign state cannot be forced to obey the jurisdiction of another state.[18] This plea of sovereign defence is reproduced within national legislation (which varies from jurisdiction to jurisdiction)—this creates a clear sense of unpredictability and unreliability in international investment arbitration.[19] The fundamental problem arises from a difference in interpretation: some scholars assert that states accept an absolute waiver of immunity

9 Edward Baldwin, Mark Kantor, and Michael Nolan, 'Limits to Enforcement of ICSID Awards' (2006) 23 J Intl Arb.1.

10 Ifeuko Uwaifo, 'What is the Effect of the Defence of State Immunity on the Enforcement of Arbitral Awards? ("The Argentine Perspective")', (2009) 9 CAR 14. Also available at <http://www.dundee.ac.uk/cepmlp/gateway/?news=31250> accessed 7 June 2015.

11 Susan Choi, 'Judicial Enforcement of Arbitration Awards under the ICSID and New York Conventions' (1995–96) 28 NYU J Intl Law & Pol 175.

12 Flávio Spaccaquerche Barbosa, 'The Enforcement of International Investment Arbitral Awards: Is There a Better Way?" (2009) 6 Revista Brasileira de Arbitragem 7–34.

13 Giuliana Cane, 'The Enforcement of ICSID Awards: Revolutionary or Ineffective?' (2004) 15 Am Rev Intl Arb 439.

14 ibid 3.

15 Convention on the Settlement of Investment Disputes Between States and Nationals of Other States (1965) <https://icsid.worldbank.org/ICSID/StaticFiles/basicdoc/CRR_English-final.pdf> accessed 8 September 2021 Art. 54/2.

16 Convention on the Recognition and Enforcement of Foreign Arbitral Awards (New York Convention) (1958) <http://www.uncitral.org/pdf/english/texts/arbitration/NYconv/XXII_1_e.pdf> accessed 8 September 2021. Art. 5/2 and ICSID Convention (n 15) Art. 54.

17 Nmehielle (n 7) 22–24.

18 Uwaifo (n 10) 1.

19 ibid. See also Leonardo S. Borlini and Stefano Siligardi, 'Enforcement of Investment Arbitration Awards' (2020) Bocconi Legal Studies Research Paper 3730569 <https://papers.ssrn.com/sol3/papers.cfm?abstract_id=3730569> accessed 9 July 2021.

by entering into an arbitration agreement, while others claim that state immunity only applies to the jurisdiction in question. Although the principle applies to execution, it can be restricted to the commercial assets of the state, being set apart from diplomatic property, the state bank, or the central bank account.[20] An additional complication is introduced by the question of whether the state's commercial assets are mixed with public assets. This in turn leads into the question of whether they are attached or unattached. On the other hand, all of these enforcement obstacles pertain to unfavourable host states. If the losing party is a foreign investor, the result of enforcement changes is brought into question.[21]

In light of these circumstances, it is undeniable that international awards run the risk of being refused enforcement. This is attributable to public policy provisions and sovereign immunity obstacles (particularly within the foreign investment field). By virtue of the fact that there is no hierarchy among states, they cannot waive their immunity from jurisdiction and execution. If the award is rendered by other national courts, the enforcing state is justified in reviewing whether or not the award is against its own rules. The enforcement of non-national awards is complicated in instances where the enforcing state has not reviewed them. In order to obey a rule, the state should waive its immunity, indicating its will by signing conventions or agreements. However, if the conventions or agreements are insufficiently clear as to whether signatory states can waive their immunity by signing these conventions or agreements, the plea of immunity applies. The situation is further complicated by the fact that even if the waiver of immunity is a core component of agreements, third-party states may apply the principle of state immunity in accordance with their sovereignty act.[22]

The enforcement system under the ICSID Convention is presumed to be simpler and easier by practitioners and legal scholars. This is because there is no public policy obstacle; in addition, it also seems to be independent of domestic and international rules that are concerned with the enforcement of the awards.[23] However, states have expressed doubts about the ICSID system, sometimes even withdrawing from the ICSID Convention. This reiterates that going through ICSID does not automatically guarantee enforcement success.[24]

This chapter aims to analyse the origin of enforcement obstacles within the field of investment arbitration, with specific reference to the ICSID Convention. In the course of its engagement with this question, this chapter will also critically evaluate the extent to which host states might conceivably exert their sovereign power on foreign investors at the enforcement stage. While doing this, it will be found out the reasons for host states' bias on ICSID awards forces. In concluding, this chapter will, taking practice as its key point of reference, evaluate the state sovereignty reflection to the cases in enforcement of investment arbitral awards.

---

20 Uwaifo (n 10) 1.

21 Anna Joubin-Bret and Cabinet Joubin-Bret, 'The Effectiveness of the ICSID Mechanism Regarding the Enforcement of Arbitral Awards' in Julien Fouret (ed) *Enforcement of Investment Treaty Arbitration Awards* (Globe Business Publishing Ltd. 2015) 1.

22 ibid 99–113.

23 Cane (n 13) 4. Borlini and Siligardi (n 19).

24 Baetens (n 1) 3. See also David A Collins, 'Towards a Grand Unified Theory of International Economic Law' (2015) 12 MJIEL 140–66. Ecuador again signed the Convention on 21 June 2021. See <https://icsid.worldbank.org/en/Pages/News.aspx?CID=267> accessed 6 September 2021.

1.2 The enforceability of ICSID awards

The International Centre for Settlement of Investment Disputes (ICSID) is an autonomous international institution that was established by the Washington Convention, and which is mandated to concern itself with the settlement of investment disputes between states and nationals of other states. The ICSID currently includes 164 signatory member states, of which 156 are contracting states.[25] At the current time, ICSID is the only institution in the world that was specifically established to settle foreign investment disputes. The key features of ICSID awards, which are protected under the convention, are set out in more detail in the following.

1.2.1 Characteristics of ICSID awards

In the legal literature, 'award' is defined as 'the decision or determination rendered by arbitrators or commissioners, or other private or extrajudicial decision makers upon a controversy submitted to them.'[26] The term 'ICSID award' only refers to the ICSID tribunal's final decision. Both interim relief (refer to Article 47 of the ICSID Convention) and procedural orders made in the course of the proceedings do not fall within the parameters of this definition. Actions undertaken upon either basis cannot benefit from the advantages of ICSID final awards. To the same extent, initial preliminary decisions on jurisdiction cannot be considered as an award;[27] however, if these decisions are reproduced within the final ruling, then they can be considered to be binding as well. It should also be recognised that the pecuniary obligations imposed by the awards can only be enforced if they are final.[28] If the award is fully annulled, previous reference points disappear;[29] however, when the award is partially annulled, the annulled component is still binding. The provisions guiding annulment stipulate that the measure should be indicated in writing and be upheld by a majority vote within the tribunal. The stipulations for awards establish that they should engage with every question, while providing supporting reasons for any decision that is made. Provision should also be made for the incorporation of dissenting opinions.[30] Additionally, ICSID awards should possess the following attributes.

1.2.1.1 Final and binding

Article 53 establishes that an ICSID award is binding. This means that the losing party is legally obliged to comply with the award and the winning party is entitled to expect compliance. In the event that this is not forthcoming, the losing party can be said to have breached the legal obligation.[31] If an ICSID tribunal renders an award, other parties cannot initiate another dispute resolution mechanism before another ICSID tribunal, tribunal, or

---

25 Baetens (n 1) 17. The National Assembly of Angola approved Resolution No. 63/21, of September 1 2021. See <https://icsid.worldbank.org/about/member-states/database-of-member-states> accessed 5 September 2021.

26 Henry Campbell Black, *Black's Law Dictionary* (2 edn, West Publishing 1910) 1.

27 Lucy Reed, Jan Paulsson, and Nigel Blackaby, *Guide to ICSID Arbitration* (KIL 2004) 1.

28 John Collier and Vaughan Lowe, *The Settlement of Disputes in International Law; Institutions and Procedures* (OUP 1999) 73.

29 Reed, Paulsson, and Blackaby (n 27) 99.

30 ICSID Convention (n 15) Article 48.

31 UNCTAD, International Centre for Settlement of Investment Disputes; Binding Force and Enforcement (New York, Geneva 2003).

national court. The principle of *res judicata* applies.[32] In instances where a partial annulment under Article 52(3) is in force, the finality effect applies to the award's unannulled component. The ICSID ad hoc tribunals only allow for review under specific circumstances.[33] These are supplementation and rectification (Article 49(2)), interpretation (Article 50), revision (Article 51), and annulment (Article 52).[34]

1.2.1.2 Additional Facility

It should be acknowledged that awards rendered under Additional Facility Arbitration Rules are not subject to ICSID's recognition and enforcement procedures.[35] Awards made under the Additional Facility are subject to the national law of the place of arbitration and any applicable treaties. In other words, an award rendered under the Additional Facility can be subject to any review or appeal provided by the law of the place of arbitration.[36] These rules state that the arbitration must be held within a member state of the New York Convention. For this reason, awards cannot benefit from ICSID Convention advantages.

The institution's knowledge of key rules and its practical working experience makes it an attractive proposition. However, it is its ability to facilitate enforcement of the arbitral awards in contracting states that is most important in this respect. As Article 54 of the convention establishes, ICSID awards shall be recognised as 'an award rendered pursuant to this Convention as binding and enforce the pecuniary obligations imposed by that award within its territories as if it were a final judgment of a court in that State.'[37] In this manner, the enforcement term sets out the process through which a domestic court will recognise an arbitral decision as a binding court judgment.[38]

This benefit is a distinguishing feature, which helps to set the convention apart from its counterparts. It overcomes defects that arise through predominantly state immunity and public policy (it should be acknowledged that the former is, by virtue of the fact that public policy is not a restriction tool, a more prominent obstacle to ICSID awards), which make it difficult to enforce international decisions within member states.

Upon the face of it, ICSID seems to provide a sound basis for the full satisfaction of investment arbitral awards, an impression which is further compounded by the fact that foreign investors are clearly predisposed to settle their disputes within the institution. However, it should be acknowledged—even if only briefly—that the reality is somewhat at odds with this general impression. At the current point, this book will not focus upon these drawbacks, but will instead predominantly focus upon issues of enforcement.

It will begin with the general observation that states tend, by virtue of state immunity, to be reluctant to enforce international decisions rendered by other tribunals or courts in their territories.[39]

32 ibid 5.

33 Abby Cohen Smutny, 'Arbitration before the International Centre for Settlement of Investment Disputes' 2002 Business Law International 367. See also Ross P Buckley, 'Now We Have Come to the ICSID Party: Are Its Awards Final and Enforceable' (1992) 14 Syd LR 358.

34 UNCTAD, Binding Force and Enforcement (n 31) 5.

35 ibid.

36 ibid.

37 ICSID Convention (n 15) Article 54.

38 Smutny (n 33) 379.

39 J Martin Hunter and Javier Garcia Olmedo, 'Enforcement/Execution of ICSID Awards against Reluctant States' (2011) 12 JWIT 307. See also Choi, 'Judicial Enforcement of Arbitration Awards' (n 11).

By virtue of the formal equality of states, there is a clear tendency for state actors to resolve 'national' disputes within their own courts. In the contemporary environment, states have become members of several conventions and international treaties that oblige them to obey key provisions and apply relevant rules within their domestic legal systems. However, states have endeavoured to find reasons to resist these obligations. Public policy has been foremost in this respect, frequently being cited as the basis for refusing to implement an international award. In large part, its prominence in this respect is attributable to the fact that 'public policy' is a broad term, an attribute which makes it difficult to entrap within a precise definition and which largely accounts for its variation across different contexts. Fortunately, ICSID has taken steps to resolve this conspicuous ambiguity, providing a much-needed clarification in the process.

It is still open to debate whether the ICSID Convention satisfies the needs of the respective parties with regard to enforcement; to the same extent, it is also debatable whether the ICSID enforcement mechanism is more effective and attractive than non-ICSID systems within the investment arbitral award enforcement regime.[40] Closer attention suggests that ICSID awards are not, setting aside clear advantages that they enjoy in comparison to other conventions and systems, sufficiently effective at the enforcement stage. It can also be observed that ICSID does not voluntarily enforce international investment awards. Key actors are obviously aware of gaps and loopholes, a point further reiterated by the fact that they try to manipulate them in their favour.

1.2.1.3 No precedent

ICSID tribunals have no mandatory rule to follow previous decisions, a feature which further enhances their appeal to potential applicants.[41] Parties that previously received a negative decision therefore have an opportunity to benefit from a positive outcome in similar cases. In addition to the other advantages associated with ICSID awards, it is also clear that they are trustworthy and stable. This in turn raises the question of why disputing parties prefer to bring their respective cases before other institutions or national courts. With a view to answering this question, the positive and negative attributes of awards will be now considered, with specific reference to well-known cases. This, it is anticipated, will help us to address this perplexing question.

1.2.1.4 Post-award remedies

It may be asserted that disputing parties may not find annulment proceedings to be satisfactory. This is because, in legal practice, they can only be activated on restricted grounds which are listed in the convention,[42] thus causing disputing parties to suspect their effectiveness.[43] Many legal researchers have therefore suggested the establishment of an appellate body, as will be discussed, with a view to reinforcing the legitimacy and enforceability of the awards in member states.[44] The reasoning is that if the award is appealed by another

40 Baetens (n 1) 19.

41 UNCTAD, Binding Force and Enforcement (n 31) 7.

42 Gautami S Tondapu, 'International Institutions and Dispute Settlement: The Case of ICSID' (2010) 22 Bond L Rev 81–95.

43 Ibid. For example, India might have considered absence of chance to challenge the awards apart from some certain situations as a reason for not being a contracting state to ICSID Convention.

44 Nicolette Butler, 'The State of International Investment Arbitration: The Possibility of Establishing an Appeal Mechanism,' (PhD thesis, University of Leeds, School of Law, September 2012) 18. See Chapter 4.

tribunal or court, the disputing parties will be satisfied by the verifying merits of the award.[45] However, over the course of the following discussion we will instead explore the opposing proposition, namely that neither annulment nor the establishment of an appellate body can provide a sufficiently strong grounding for the enforcement of ICSID awards.

Unsurprisingly, the ICSID caseload statistics for 2021 clearly illustrate why it does not make sense to initiate annulment proceedings in ICSID. The report demonstrates that the ad hoc tribunal rejected most annulment applications. Some of the applications were also discontinued for a variety of reasons. However, the statistics illustrate that there was a dramatic increase in applications for annulment proceedings during 2011–21. Also, states are more likely to seek the annual ICSID awards so only 63 were initiated by the claimant/investor, and 88 were initiated by the host state/respondent (in ICSID arbitration).[46] Possible explanations include non-compliance with awards or dissatisfaction with the original tribunal's award. In 2021, 15 annulment proceedings were concluded.[47] While the ad hoc committee rejected the application for annulment of the award in three cases, two annulment proceedings were discontinued. In one case the award was partially annulled. In parallel, the average duration of annulment proceedings continued to decrease in 2021. This represents, when annulment proceedings concluded in the past are considered, a decrease of about 50 per cent.[48] Therefore, it is obvious that annulment proceedings under the ICSID Convention are open to delay, complying with the arbitral award in practice and even the duration of the proceedings has decreased in time.

1.3 Enforcement obstacles

It has been observed that '[r]eceiving an award is merely winning a battle, whereas receiving payment is winning the war.'[49] As this contribution affirms, the main concern is to receive the outcome of the award. In ICSID, this can often be as difficult to achieve as the enforcement of non-ICSID awards.[50] Under normal circumstances it should be voluntarily enforced by states; this is quite clearly established by Article 55 of the ICSID Convention.[51] If this is not the case, then a number of problems enter the equation. It has already been noted that recognition is, in the granting of international awards, a preliminary step to

45 ibid. However, Butler states that 'this finality has to be balanced against another legitimate goal; that of correctness of the decision.' In reply to this, Dolzer asserts that 'the principle of finality is typically given more weight than the principle of correctness.' Rudolf Dolzer and Christoph Schreuer, *Principles of International Investment Law* (OUP 2008) 4.

46 Yarik Kryvoi, Johannas Koepp, and Jack Biggs, 'Empirical Study: Annulment in ICSID Arbitration,' (2021) BIICL & Baker Botts <https://papers.ssrn.com/sol3/papers.cfm?abstract_id=3888110> accessed 1 September 2021. The ICSID Caseload—Statistics Issue 2021–2. See <https://icsid.worldbank.org/sites/default/files/Caseload%20Statistics%20Charts/The%20ICSID%20Caseload%20Statistics%202021-2%20Edition%20ENG.pdf> accessed 6 August 2021.

47 ibid.

48 ibid. See also Kryvoi, Koepp, and Biggs (n 46) 17.

49 Joseph M Cardosi, 'Precluding the Treasure Hunt: How the World Bank Group Can Help Investors Circumnavigate Sovereign Immunity Obstacles to ICSID Award Execution' Pepperdine Law Review 41 (2014) 3.

50 Piero Bernardini 'ICSID versus non-ICSID Investment Treaty Arbitration' in M A F Ballesteros et al (eds), *Liber Amicorum Bernardo Cremades* (La Ley 2010) 186 <media012970223709030bernardini_icsid-vs-non-icsid-investent.pdf> accessed 25 April 2016.

51 See <https://icsid.worldbank.org/apps/ICSIDWEB/process/Pages/Recognition-and-Enforcement-Convention-Arbitration.aspx> accessed 17 June 2015.

achieving the compliance of international awards in national courts. National courts, in the granting of international awards, once recognition has been acquired, enforcement or/ and execution proceedings can be introduced and initiated.[52] In the case of the ICSID, this recognition is already in place, being provided by contracting states who have signed the convention. This means that the awards assume the status of a national court decision in the state where enforcement is scheduled. Although the ICSID awards do not encounter the public policy hurdle, they are considerably more likely to come up against the serious obstacle of state immunity with regard to state assets, whether commercial or public. The likelihood that this will present a serious obstacle is further enhanced by the fact that enforcing states generally rely on state immunity as a defence against the seizure of their assets.[53] This suggests that the main achievement of the convention has been to change the name of the issue. This adjustment notwithstanding, enforcement issues still remain alive within this field. This situation can be traced back to the 'self-enforcing' feature of ICSID awards.[54]

Although self-governing systems are well established in the ICSID mechanism for the recognition and enforcement of awards, comparable systems for the execution of awards are not put in place by the ICSID Convention.[55] A number of domestic courts do not accept that the terms of enforcement and execution are identical. As such, it is appropriate to consider whether there are practical problems that pertain to the enforcement of ICSID awards.[56] The significance of this difference is also alluded to by the observation that 'the distinction between the two terms is also of practical importance since enforcement is governed and decreed by the Convention and its implementation by execution is governed by domestic law.'[57] In the first instance, it might be instructive to consider whether there is a difference between enforcement and execution, with a view to discerning their consequences. *Black's Law Dictionary* does not significantly aid the understanding by defining 'enforce' as 'put into execution';[58] however, closer examination reveals that 'execute' means 'proper steps in proper time,'[59] a definition which appears to suggest that enforcement is one step in advance of execution.

In confronting the state immunity defence at the enforcement stage, the winning investor anticipates a struggle to seize the losing state's assets at the execution stage. Closer engagement reveals that the convention interprets the two words to be identical

---

52 ibid.

53 Andrea K Bjorklund, 'State Immunity and the Enforcement of Investor-State Arbitral Awards' (2008) Practice 858.

54 Susan D Franck, 'The ICSID Effect? Considering Potential Variations in Arbitration Awards' (2010) 51 Va J Intl L 825. Vernon Cassin, 'ITA Workshop on Modern Enforcement of Arbitral Awards—Keynote Address' (2014) <http://kluwerarbitrationblog.com/2014/06/23/ita-workshop-on-modern-enforcement-of-arbitral-awards-keynote-address/> accessed 14 March 2017.

55 Fenghua Li, 'The Divergence and Convergence of ICSID and Non-ICSID Arbitration' (PhD thesis, Glasgow University 2015). 'Though the interpretation which best reconciles the equally authentic English, French and Spanish text of the ICSID Convention would be that "enforcement" and "execution" are identical in meaning' in Christoph H.Schreuer, *The ICSID Convention: a commentary* (CUP 2009) 1.

56 ibid 174. The first one is the defence based on domestic enforcement approach, which has typically been adopted by Argentina.

57 Aron Broches, 'Awards Rendered Pursuant to the ICSID Convention: Binding Force, Finality, Recognition, Enforcement, Execution' (1987) ICSID Review 318.

58 Black (n 26).

59 ibid.

in meaning; it also uses them interchangeably, thus creating further confusion.[60] The 1969 Vienna Convention on the Law of Treaties (VCLT) potentially offers a more sustainable basis of interpretation. According to the VCLT, 'enforcement' and 'execution' are identical in the convention. In the case of the ICSID Convention, a distinction was initially made between enforceability and execution, but this was removed during the first draft of the convention.[61] It was demonstrated that execution against a state would depend 'on the force of a final judgement in the country in which enforcement was sought.'[62] Hence, if a final judgment could not be enforced in a contracting state because of its sovereign act from execution, the award would meet the same fate.[63] Under the ICSID Convention there are two enforcing obstacles that impede awards in contracting states' territories. These are the stay of enforcement and the more prominent state immunity.

1.3.1 Stay of enforcement

A stay of enforcement may be requested by either party during the annulment proceeding, including all or part of the tribunal award.[64] The post-award remedy could deal with 'an award of damages, award of costs or some other form of relief' ordered by the first tribunal.[65] The interim/provisional stay continues until the ad hoc committee, subsequent to the receipt of observations from both parties, makes a clear determination.[66] If a stay is decided, the committee can, at the request of either party, terminate or change it. In addition, if the party requesting the stay cannot fulfil a condition for the stay ordered by the committee, then the stay may also be terminated.[67] After the rendering of a decision on annulment, the stay also automatically finishes.[68] At first glance, this may be dismissed as insignificant, however, it is important to remember that it may be used to manipulate or delay the enforcement procedure. In this circumstance, there is always the risk that the unfavourable party would not obey the award if it is not favourably annulled by the ad hoc committee.[69] There are two possible outcomes of a stay of enforcement: firstly, the final and binding of an award (this, it should be recognised, is exceptional). In this circumstance, the favoured party must wait to enforce the award until it is *pro tanto* postponed

60 Hunter and Olmedo (n 39) 311.

61 ibid 310–1.

62 ICSID Convention (n 15) Article 54.

63 Ruqiya B H Musa, Martina Polasek, and ICSID, 'The Origins and Specificities of the ICSID Enforcement Mechanism,' in Fouret (n 21) 13–33.

64 ICSID, Background Paper on Annulment for the Administrative Council of ICSID, 10 August 2012. See <https://icsid.worldbank.org/en/Documents/Background%20Paper%20on%20Annulment%202012_English.pdf#search=statistics%20on%20legal%20fees> accessed 10 August 2017. ICSID Convention Article 52(5); Arbitration Rule 54(1).

65 ibid 20.

66 ibid. The paper highlights Arbitration Rule 54(1) and (4): 'An expedited ruling may be requested, requiring the ad hoc Committee to decide within 30 days whether to continue the stay. The stay is automatically terminated if either party has requested an expedited ruling and the Committee does not continue the stay within 30 days of the request. See Arbitration Rule 54(2) and its explanatory note in ICSID Regulations and Rules, 1968, Doc. ICSID/4/Rev. 1.

67 ibid 20. Arbitration Rule 54(3).

68 ibid. 'ICSID Convention Article 52(6): If a Tribunal is reconstituted following a partial annulment, a party may request the stay of enforcement of the unannulled portion of the award until the date of the new tribunal's award. See Arbitration Rule 55(3). Although there have been several partial annulments with resubmissions, this situation has not yet occurred.'

69 Smutny (n 33) 379.

by the annulment process.[70] Secondly, is the circumstance in which Article 54 of the ICSID does not involve the stay of enforcement for the award. In this instance, Article 54's enforcement scheme is dependent upon any stay of enforcement.[71] This issue can be resolved by requesting financial guarantees or reasonable assurances from the losing party. Fortunately, this trend has emerged in the aftermath of 2006, providing plausible assurances to the committee.[72]

According to the ICSID reports, in the registered annulments, there have been several requests for the provisional stay.[73] These cases were conditional upon some type of security or written undertaking.[74] Although there is no reference to rules, with this feature apparently being absent from the ICSID Convention, the ad hoc committees have considerable judicial discretion, being enabled to determine whether a stay demand is subject to conditions upon a case-by-case basis.[75]

While looking after 2017, ad hoc committees have become slower to decide the stay of enforcement. They have decided on 38 applications, of which 32 were published. Fifteen applications were rejected, 7 cases received conditional stays and the remaining 10 cases received unconditional stays.[76] The approach of the ad hoc committees may be explained that some states use the annulment application to have stay enforcement and impeded enforcement of the award in practice. Therefore, the ad hoc committees try to hinder the delays in compliance with arbitral awards. Spain can be a good example in that a stay should be granted because of the legal quagmire it finds itself in as a result of arguably conflicting EU law and international law obligations have been rejected in all cases.[77]

70 *MINE v. Guinea,* ICSID Case No ARB/84/4, Interim Order No 1 on Guinea's Application for Stay of Enforcement of the Award, 12 August 1988, 4 ICSID Rep 111, 112. Arts 50(2), 51(4), 52(5) of the ICSID Convention. See Li (n 55) 170.

71 ibid.

72 ibid.

73 ICSID Background Paper on Annulment for the Administrative Council of ICSID (n 64) 20.

74 These cases are respectively: (i) *Amco Asia Corporation and others v. Republic of Indonesia,* ICSID Case No ARB/81/1, Interim Order No 1 Concerning the Stay of Enforcement of the Award of 2 March 1991; (ii) *Wena Hotels Limited v. Arab Republic of Egypt,* Case No ARB/98/4, Procedural Order No 1 of the ad hoc Committee concerning the continuation of the stay of enforcement of the award, 5 April 2001; (iii) *CDC Group Plc v. Republic of the Seychelles,* ICSID Case No ARB/02/14, Decision on Whether or Not To Continue Stay and Order in CDC Group plc v. Republic of the Seychelles of 14 July 2004; (iv) *Repsol YPF Ecuador S.A. v. Empresa Estatal Petroleos del Ecuador,* ICSID Case No ARB/01/10, Procedural Order No 1 concerning the Stay of Enforcement of the Award of Dec. 22, 2005; Procedural Order No 4 concerning the Stay of Enforcement of the Award of 22 February 2006; (v) *Ioannis Kardassopoulos v. The Republic of Georgia,* ICSID Case No ARB/05/18, Decision on Applicant's Request for a Continued Stay of Enforcement of the Award, 12 November 2010; Decision of the ad hoc Committee to terminate the Stay of Enforcement of the Award, 19 Jan. 19, 2011; (vi) *Ron Fuchs v. The Republic of Georgia,* ICSID Case No ARB/07/15, Decision of the ad hoc Committee on the Stay of Enforcement of the Award of Nov. 12, 2010; Decision of the ad hoc Committee to terminate the Stay of Enforcement of the Award, 19 January 2011; (vii) *Sempra Energy International v. The Argentine Republic,* ICSID Case No ARB/02/16, Decision on the Argentine Republic's Request for a Continued Stay of Enforcement of the Award of Mar. 05, 2009; Decision on Sempra Energy International's Request for the Termination of the Stay of Enforcement of the Award of 7 August 2009; (viii) *Elsamex, S.A. v. Republic of Honduras,* ICSID Case No ARB/09/4, Decision on the Continuation of the Stay of Enforcement of the Award, 7 January 2014; (ix) *Joseph C. Lemire v. Ukraine,* ICSID Case No ARB/06/18, Decision on Ukraine's Request for a Continued Stay of Enforcement of the Award, 14 February 2012.

75 Li (n 55) 171.

76 Kryvoi, Koepp, and Biggs (n 46) 17.

77 ibid.

A new trend, which has emerged from 2006, has suggested that reasonable assurances should be provided to the committee.[78] Therefore, in the annulment proceedings that grant to stays conditionally, financial security accounted for 37.5 per cent and letter of assurance on the applicant for 21 per cent. In only one case did the failing party agree to post a bank guarantee in exchange for a waiver of the right by the winning party; this was undertaken with a view to initiating enforcement proceedings pending the outcome of the annulment proceedings.[79] The absence of explicit rules in the ICSID Convention and the ad hoc tribunals discretionary power on conditions for a stay demonstrate that ad hoc committees undertake a new role with a view to ensuring better compliance in post-award enforcement, that is, in 'inducing compliance.'[80]

It should however be recognised that several practical problems may arise in instances where a stay of enforcement is subject to conditions.[81] For example, conditioning a stay request upon a posting of financial security might have a deterrent effect on annulment applications.[82] The *Patrick Mitchell v. Democratic Republic of the Congo* case exemplified this problem.[83] The ad hoc committee accepted Congo's argument. The state claimed the deterrent effect of posting financial security on a developing country's annulment submission, which had been made in good faith. The ad hoc committee emphasised that although requested conditions had a certain value, it was always a burden and would violate the right to seek post-award relief through invoking an annulment application.[84] In addition, financial security has the potential to cause economic hardship and conditionality, especially so in instances where the investor requests a stay of enforcement.[85]

Although these provisions appear to be preventive, there is still a risk, at a practical level analysis, that the failing party may choose not to commence annulment proceedings, meaning that the defence of sovereign immunity may come into play.[86] This can be attributed to the fact that the application of annulment is generally used as a tactic not to comply with the awards. This is a minor risk that derives from non-compliance with ICSID awards. In this situation, the fundamental problem of sovereign immunity arises under the ICSID Convention.

1.3.2 Sovereign immunity

To put it slightly differently, state immunity can be defined as a plea that can be claimed by one state against another state's national court adjudication and enforcement jurisdiction, being invoked upon the basis that the given grievance would damage the state's sovereignty.[87] This doctrine originated within the formal independence and equality of

78 Li (n 55) 171.

79 ibid 172.

80 Tsai-Yu Lin, 'Systemic Reflections on Argentina's Non-Compliance with ICSID Arbitral Awards: A New Role of the Annulment Committee at Enforcement?' (2012) 5(1) Contemp Asia Arb J 1, in Li (n 55) 173.

81 Li (n 55) 173.

82 ibid.

83 *Patrick Mitchell v. Democratic Republic of the Congo*, ICSID Case No ARB/99/7, Decision on the Stay of Enforcement of the Award of 30 November 2004, para 40.

84 ibid 173.

85 ibid.

86 ibid.

87 Hazel Fox and Phillipia Webb, *The Law of State Immunity* (3rd edn, OUP 2013).

states.[88] The initiation of a legal action against a state which defends state immunity is ultimately contingent upon the prior question of whether the state gave consent.[89] As a doctrine, state immunity was first used in the US, being applied in the *Schooner Exchange v. MacFadden*[90] case which addressed itself to an incident in which an American citizen's vessel was seized by the French government in 1812.[91] In the aftermath of its seizure, the vessel was remodelled as a military ship. Ultimately, the court decided to dismiss the action that had been initiated, citing state immunity as its justification.[92] In the aftermath of this decision, the doctrine of state immunity was described as an 'undisputed principle of customary international law.'[93] As Hesshas observed: 'It is the special feature of State immunity that it is at the point of intersection of international law and national procedural law.'[94] As a mixture of international and national law, state immunity is characterised by a high degree of complexity.[95]

Although state immunity in the 18th and 19th centuries was a strict right upholding each state against another, this changed in the 20th century, with participation in international trade originating a new approach to state immunity.[96] In the aftermath of this development, theories were evolved with a view to differentiating the acts of a sovereign government from commercial activities.[97] The defence of state immunity is a confusing area of law because, while states are willing to participate in international commercial fields, they tend to resist the narrowing scope of state immunity. Under these circumstances, it appears appropriate to work towards the balancing of international law and the municipal law of states. If this is not the case, then states will encounter a number of legal issues, ultimately resulting in the avoidance of trade relations.

The UN Convention on Jurisdictional Immunities of States and Their Property is based upon international sources that originate the principle of state immunity.[98] This convention was signed in 2004, clearly establishing that signatory states can argue against decisions taken by other states' courts, citing state immunity as a justification.[99] While the convention permits states to cite immunity in relation to certain matters (such as diplomatic properties and military assets), commercial assets are quite clearly not included.[100] Taking this consideration into account, the question necessarily arises of what will occur

88 Julian D M Lew, Loukas A Mistelis, and Stefan Kröll, *Comparative International Commercial Arbitration* (KIL 2003) 1.

89 Rowland Alaba Akande, 'Enforcement and Practicability of Sovereign Immunity Doctrine in International Commercial Arbitration' (2014) 7 J L & Pol 1.

90 *The Exchange v. McFaddon*, 11 U.S. 7 Cranch 116 116 (1812).

91 ibid.

92 Abdulrahman Mamdoh Saleem, 'To What Extent Do States Have the Right to Use its Sovereign Immunity Defence against ICSID Awards?' (2013) (University of Dundee–Centre for Energy, Petroleum and Mineral Law & Policy).

93 ibid 3.

94 Burkhard Hess, 'The International Law Commission's Draft Convention on the Jurisdictional Immunities of States and Their Property' (1993) 4 EJIL 269.

95 Fox and Webb (n 87) 1.

96 Lee M Caplan, 'State Immunity, Human Rights, and Jus Cogens: A Critique of the Normative Hierarchy Theory' (2003) 97 AJIL 741–81.

97 Saleem (n 92) 3. See also Caplan (n 96) 743.

98 United Nations Convention on Jurisdictional Immunities of States and Their Property, New York 2 December 2004. See <https://treaties.un.org/Pages/ViewDetails.aspx?src=IND&mtdsg_no=III-13&chapter=3& accessed> 25 May 2016.

99 Jasper Finke, 'Sovereign Immunity: Rule, Comity or Something Else?' 4 (2010) 21 EJIL 853–81.

100 The UN Convention 2004 (n 114) Article 10.

when commercial and diplomatic assets coalesce. How will the commercial assets be recognised and which criteria will be requested by national courts?

It will recognise that state immunity exists at two different stages, specifically jurisdiction and execution.[101] In addition to this, it would be necessary to establish whether the state's acts can be traced back to state capacity or its commercial capacity (*jure imperii* or *jure gestionis*).[102] However, this distinction is much more difficult to make in practice than in theory.[103] However, it is essential to make this distinction because some states claim absolute immunity even while acting in a commercial capacity.[104] In the subsequent discussion, general information about the doctrine of state immunity will be provided before the analysis proceeds to consider how the principle of state immunity creates problems in the enforcement of ICSID awards. At all points, attention will be specifically addressed to the two stages at which these problems arise.

1.3.2.1 Jurisdictional immunity

If an award is to be recognised and enforced, it is necessary for it to be rendered by an authority whose authority is comparable to domestic courts.[105] However, this may not be sufficient to enforce the award; as a respondent, the state must be immune from the jurisdiction of national courts.[106] The court which has applied to recognise and enforce the award is obliged to follow its national state's immunity laws.[107] Precisely because states are formally equal, they do not tend to readily enforce an award that has been rendered by another state's domestic court. The proliferation of foreign investment that has occurred as a consequence of BITs has restricted the scope of the doctrine of state immunity. This development notwithstanding, favourable investors still continue to encounter problems.

It has already been noted that most BITs include arbitration provision, with a view to settling disputes that have arisen from the interpretation of the treaties. Signatory states have therefore already agreed to waive their jurisdictional immunity by voluntarily signing treaties.[108] This development served to reiterate the restricted immunity theory which has been adopted in some national laws and international conventions.[109] The United Nations Convention on Jurisdictional Immunities of States and Their Property (UNCSI), in citing a particularly remarkable example, refers to instances in which states have implicitly waived their jurisdictional immunity by signing the treaties.[110]

The ICSID tribunals have jurisdiction to see cases. This means that national courts cannot, claiming jurisdiction, cite state immunity as a defence at a later stage. Taking the ICSID arbitration as a reference point, there are three conditions that must be met if the ICSID tribunal is to have jurisdiction over a dispute.[111] Articles 25 and 26 clearly establish

---

101 Akande (n 89) 145.
102 ibid.
103 ibid.
104 ibid. As stated by earlier European courts, it was considered that when a state enters into the market place the same as private individuals, they must be treated at the same level; indeed sovereign immunity of the state should be restricted.
105 Collier and Lowe (n 28) 270–2.
106 ibid.
107 ibid.
108 Akande (n 89) 145.
109 ibid.
110 Saleem (n 92) 4.
111 ibid 5.

that both states must be contracting to the convention.[112] In addition, the dispute must be subject to investment and parties must negotiate ICSID jurisdiction in writing. However, the waiver of immunity rights has been a controversial issue. This is primarily because there are still questions about what this means in practice. Simply waiving jurisdictional immunity is not sufficient to overcome the enforcement obstacles that pertain to ICSID awards. It has previously been asserted that a waiver 'must give a clear, complete, unambiguous and unmistakable manifestation of the sovereign's intent to waive immunity'[113] if it is to be valid. In the *Liberia Eastern Timber Corp v. Liberia* case,[114] Liberia challenged the award, arguing against the court's refusal of jurisdictional immunity. The court observed that 'since member states have agreed to enforce ICSID awards, then Liberia has contemplated the role of courts of all contracting states including the US to enforce against Liberian assets.'[115]

Taking the example into account, it is obvious that states waive their complete jurisdictional immunity plea when they become signatories to the reservation right, even when the ICSID Convention provides them with a chance not to accept jurisdictional immunity. This conduct clearly conveys the states' purpose and real intention. If they unconditionally signed the convention, it is unsustainable to argue that they are entitled to bring their jurisdictional immunity plea before the courts. Otherwise, it is a breach of the convention, meaning that the convention's sanctions must be enforced upon the state. The innate instinct of international investment arbitration is to safeguard the weaker side, such as foreign investors, from the sovereign power of host states. This explains why some conventions were arranged in a manner that would enable investors to resolve disputes with reference to objective criteria. This pattern has been cited in support of the claim that the convention's member states have the right to enter a plea of jurisdictional immunity. However, this proposition may not extend to the execution immunity plea (refer to the following section).

1.3.2.2 Immunity against execution

Immunity from execution is the core preoccupation for debates that pertain to the execution issue. It is the cornerstone of this book called immunity against execution. State immunity is not in itself an obstacle to arbitration; however, difficulties inevitably arise when the terms of discussion extend to the question of whether immunity extends from the establishment of jurisdiction to execution.[116] Enforcement obstacles are most likely to arise when a winning party attempts to enforce and execute its award against the host state. In addition, they are also likely to arise when a state entity in a third state which is member of the ICSID Convention attains the host state's assets.[117] Unless the state is

112 Although a disputing state is not member of the convention, it can agree to resolve the dispute under ICSID Additional Facility Rules.

113 Saleem (n 92) 5–6.

114 *Liberian Eastern Timber Corporation v. Republic of Liberia* (ICSID Case No. ARB/83/2).

115 Saleem (n 92) 7. For instance, the French courts still confuse the recognition of ICSID awards. The courts discuss whether the ICSID awards are against public policy in *Benvenuti & Bonfant v. Congo* and *SOABI v. Senegal*. As Schreuer notes with respect to these cases, 'the French courts do not seem to be fully aware of their lack of power to review ICSID awards.'

116 Collier and Lowe (n 28) 271–2.

117 ibid.

reluctant to evade its obligations, it may seek immunity from execution.[118] This strategy is generally more effective if the losing party is a state; this is because sovereign immunity places state assets under state protection.[119]

In this case, it is necessary to engage the overarching question from three different angles which are the enforcement, execution, and compliance.[120] Execution is specifically about the division of state assets and the distinction of commercial or public capacity, and the satisfaction of an international award by either party. In each of these instances, with a view to examining the key issues, it may be necessary to first establish whether the losing party is a host state or foreign investor.

In each of these instances, with a view to examining the key issues, it may be necessary to first establish whether the losing party is a host state or foreign investor.

It should be noted that key phrases (in particular 'enforcement' and 'execution') frequently give rise to confusion in practice.[121] As has already been acknowledged,[122] recognition is a basic precondition, particularly for ICSID awards, for the other steps. Article 54 of the convention clearly establishes that all member states must accept the ICSID awards as the basis of their local courts' decision. This is necessary if *res judicata* is to be applied and legal uncertainty is to be overcome. In addition, when the discussion turns to the distinction between enforcement, execution, and compliance, immunity obstacles again appear.[123]

Enforcement is an intermediate stage of compliance of an international award; it is less precise than the other two stages.[124] The meaning of the word 'enforcement' differs in accordance with the legal systems. In some instances it means 'exequatur' or 'declaration in an order that an arbitration award is in fact enforceable.' In other legal systems it relates 'an award creditor's legal right to execute its award such [as] receiving the monetary damages or collect the other remedies.' The key details of ICSID arbitration can be ascertained from the convention articles; in this document, 'recognition' and 'enforcement' are used like a single phrase which refers to all steps in order to fulfil an award but which 'stop[s] short of actual execution of an award.'[125]

As in the practice, enforcement tends to be defined as the forensic success of receiving a judgment from a national court; this enables an award creditor to enforce an arbitration award in that jurisdiction.[126] These proceedings, however, invariably come at a price, and entail considerable expenditures of time and money.[127] The disputing parties are usually aware that even achieving the enforcement application may not be sufficient to turn the

118 Akande (n 89) 145.

119 Graham Coop, Alvaro Nistal, Robert G Volterra, and Volterra Fietta, 'Sovereign Immunities and Investor-State Awards: Specificities of Enforcing Awards Based On Investment Treaties' in Fouret (n 21) 67–83.

120 Hunter and Olmedo (n 39) 308.

121 ibid 311.

122 See Section 1.3 'Enforcement obstacles.'

123 Collier and Lowe (n 28) 270–2.

124 ibid.

125 ibid.

126 Quentin Tannock, 'Judging the Effectiveness of Arbitration through the Assessment of Compliance with and Enforcement of International Arbitration Awards' 1(2005) 21 Arb Intl 71–90.

127 ibid. See also George K Foster, 'Collecting from Sovereigns: The Current Legal Framework for Enforcing Arbitral Awards and Court Judgments against States and Their Instrumentalities, and Some Proposals for Its Reform' (2008) 25 Ariz J Intl & Comp L 3 665–732.

award into money.[128] This is particularly true in instances where the award debtor is insolvent or does not possess significant assets.[129]

Execution is the last pedestal at which the collection of the outcome of the award is rendered. It needs to be assisted by local courts, whose intervention is the essential underpinning of execution.[130] Article 53 of the ICSID Convention allows states to enter an immunity plea to the execution platform.[131] In the aftermath of the convention's creation, the distinction has been a crucial component of the text, in large part due to the fact that there is, despite the best efforts of legal scholars, no clear framework of reference. One of the most perceptive observers of the convention has suggested, with reference to Article 54(1) that 'shall be enforceable' should have been replaced by 'enforce.'[132]

Once the definitions of these two main notions are taken into account, it becomes easier to understand the distinction between compliance and enforcement, and execution. When it is applied in international treaties, compliance is a concept that is synonymous with the good faith performance of treaty obligations.[133] However, the enforcement of arbitral awards has largely included challenges that respondent states have issued in response to adverse investment award decisions in national courts.[134] To put it differently, the link between them establishes that when the losing state does not voluntarily pay the arbitral award, the investor is permitted, prior to enforcement, to apply further judicial review of arbitral awards (this also applies to challenges that contest the enforcement of awards).[135] Indeed, it should be noted that enforcement does not mean automatically entail compliance with the award; rather, compliance is totally dependent upon the success of the enforcement proceedings.

'Enforcement' is a restrictive term that refers to measures jointly or unilaterally adopted by a competent authority that is undertaken to ensure respect for such international awards if they are not voluntarily complied with in practice. In contrast, 'compliance,' whether voluntary or enforced, formally occurs when the legal requirements of international agreements are met by respondent states.[136] In cases where ICSID awards are made, they are binding on the parties under Article 53; this establishes that the parties have a legal obligation to comply with awards.[137] Non-compliance with an award would be a breach of a legal obligation. This means that voluntary compliance is the norm for the convention.[138] If it is not deferred, a victorious party has a right to demand compliance due to the provision that the convention makes for enforcement. The only limit to enforcement is state immunity.[139] An award against a host state is obviously not enforced if this violates the rules on state immunity that are applied in the enforcing state.

---

128 ibid.

129 ibid.

130 Hunter and Olmedo (n 39) 312.

131 ibid 311.

132 Broches, 'Awards Rendered Pursuant to the ICSID Convention' (n 57) 318.

133 Alan S Alexandroff and Ian A Laird, 'Compliance and Enforcement,' Oxford Handbook of International Investment Law (2008) 1171–87.

134 ibid.

135 ibid 1173. See also Ian A Laird and Rebecca Askew, 'Finality Versus Consistency: Does Investor-State Arbitration Need an Appellate System' 7 (2005) J App Prac & Process 285.

136 Alexandroff and Laird (n 133).

137 UNCTAD, Binding Force and Enforcement (n 31).

138 Tannock (n 126) 89.

139 Baldwin, Kantor, and Nolanmake (n 9).

However, this does not entail that state immunity affects the award debtor's obligation under Article 53; this is because state immunity is merely a procedural obstacle to measures of execution. It is clear that successful reliance on state immunity may still violate the convention and therefore may lead to the usual outcome of state responsibility involving diplomatic protection under Article 27(1). In the ad hoc committee in *MINE v. Guinea*, this consequence was expounded in the following terms:

> It should be clearly understood, … that State immunity may well afford a legal defense to forcible execution, but it provides neither argument nor excuse for failing to comply with an award. In fact, the issue of State immunity from forcible execution of an award will typically arise if the State party refuses to comply with its treaty obligations. Non-compliance by a State constitutes a violation by that State of its international obligations and will attract its own sanctions. The Committee refers in this connection among other things to Article 27 and 64 of the Convention, and to the consequences which such a violation would have for such a State's reputation with private and public sources of international finance.[140]

It should also be acknowledged that a stay of enforcement suspends the obligation of compliance.[141] The expectation is that there will be timely voluntary (spontaneous) compliance and that, under Article 53, this will not incur long and costly enforcement proceedings.[142] However, the real situation may sometimes be the exact opposite; this is evidenced in instances which relate to (involuntary) compliance after the enforcement proceedings in different jurisdictions.

It should therefore be noted that non-compliance with the awards leads to enforcement procedures in domestic courts. In other words, enforcement is a technical set of procedures that parties use in order to obtain compliance. At this point it can be observed that execution also extends to involuntary compliance. The main distinction appears to be between (voluntary) compliance and (involuntary) enforcement. Although enforcement and formal compliance are meant to achieve the 'effectiveness' of the substantive obligations provided in treaties, they do not automatically imply this effectiveness.[143] Recent cases[144] have underlined that substantial difficulties in achieving complete claimant satisfaction at the enforcement and execution (of investment arbitration awards) still remain.[145] This situation arises because voluntary compliance is more satisfactory than involuntary compliance.

An additional point of interest arises within the fact that when the convention is translated to other languages (such as French and Spanish), 'enforcement' and 'execution' appear in identical forms.[146] Further comparison of the three texts reveals that the same convention appears to present different meanings.[147] This explains why it became necessary to adapt the 1969 VCLT to interpret the article.[148] The Vienna Convention establishes that these terms have the same meaning, thus permitting observers to use

140 Interim Order No. 1 on Guinea's Application for Stay of Enforcement of the Award (n 84).

141 UNCTAD, Binding Force and Enforcement (n 31) 10.

142 Tannock (n 126) 81.

143 Ibrahim F I Shihata, 'Implementation, Enforcement, and Compliance with International Environmental Agreements—Practical Suggestions in the Light of the World Bank's Experience' (1996) 9 Geo Intl Envtl L Rev 37.

144 ibid.

145 ibid.

146 Hunter and Olmedo (n 39) 311.

147 ibid.

148 ibid.

them interchangeably. However, this does little to resolve the question of whether the terms are identical in practice (a question that arises as a consequence of the fact that the precise interpretation of the two terms is dependent upon the rulings of national courts). Furthermore, Article 54(3) of the ICSID Convention provides contracting states with the ability to review ICSID awards at the last stage of execution. The convention provides member states with wide-ranging discretion to take national laws into account when they decide whether the arbitral award can be executed against certain assets. Article 55 also stressed this attribute by establishing that laws regulating state immunity in any member state shall not be derogated from the application of Article 54.[149]

It therefore appears that the execution of the ICSID awards is dependent upon the immunity law that is in force in the state where execution is sought. At this stage, foreign investors may encounter execution difficulties, something in large part attributable to the fact that ICSID does not provide 'self-governing' systems or the special protection of ICSID ends in the attachment of assets.[150] In this situation, it is imperative to establish whether the state's assets are being used for commercial or public purposes. It cannot be denied that, to a certain extent, the two are closely attached. However, ultimately the two must, taking the definition of commercial and public assets within the states' rules into account, be distinguished. Even at this point, states may still attempt to evade the award. It should also be acknowledged that states put in place different definitions; this increases the incentive for foreign investors to seek the most favourable third state that preserves the host states' assets. English law, for instance, establishes that any property of a foreign state 'for the time being in use or intended for use for commercial purposes' may be attached. However, if the relevant ambassador argues that it is not intended to be used for commercial purposes, it may not be seized until the applicant proves that this is not the case.[151] This is also the case for bank accounts; they may not be attached until the applicant can provide sufficient evidence that the accounts for the settlement contain commercial liabilities.[152] Upon closer reflection, it is clear that the UK has a particularly narrow approach to the definition of commercial property.[153] In comparison, French courts have instead sought to identify two co-existent conditions—specifically that the assets must be a commercial property and they must be used for commercial activities at the same time.[154] In order to disassemble some of the key issues, three well-known cases will now be analysed.

1.3.2.2.1 *LETCO v. Liberia* (in the USA)

As in most cases, the *LETCO v. Republic of Liberia*[155] proceedings encountered considerable execution problems. To briefly summarise the core features of the proceedings, the

149 ibid.

150 Smutny (n 33) 368.

151 Collier and Lowe (n 28) 270–2.

152 ibid.

153 Anirudh Krishnan, 'Obstacles to the Enforcement of Arbitral Awards against States—An International Perspective,' Critical Twenties (2011) <http://www.criticaltwenties.in/lawthejudiciary/obstacles-to-the-enforcement-of-arbitral-awards-against-states-an-international-perspective> accessed 4 June 2015. See also Saleem (n 92) 5.

154 Saleem (n 92) 5.

155 *Liberian E. Timber Corp. v. Gov't of the Republic of Liberia* (LETCO I), 650 F. Supp. 73 (S.D.N.Y. 1986), aff'd 854 F.2d 1314 (2d Cir. 1987); *Liberian E. Timber Corp. v. Gov't of the Republic of Liberia*, 659 F. Supp. 606 (D.D.C. 1987).

Liberian Eastern Timber Corporation (LETCO), a Liberian corporation controlled by a French national, had a concession to harvest more than 400,000 acres of Liberian timber. Liberia reduced the concession field by 279,000 acres, claiming contract infringements by LETCO before terminating the concession altogether in 1980. As a direct consequence, LETCO commenced arbitration proceedings under the ICSID Convention, citing the concession agreement as its basis. Although Liberia refused to attend the case, the tribunal still heard the matter. The tribunal ultimately established that $8,739,280 plus interest should be paid to LETCO. With a view to enforcing the award, LETCO applied to the US District Court, citing the ICSID Convention in the process. Judge Keenan, of the Southern District of New York, determined an *ex parte* order which would direct the enforcement of the arbitral award. Liberia subsequently objected to the *ex parte* order while seeking to override the execution of the judgment on its US-based property. District Court Judge Weinfeld rejected Liberia's move to vacate the judgment, observing that Liberia had, in accordance with the Foreign Sovereign Immunities Act (hereafter FSIA) waived its sovereign immunity from US jurisdiction by signing a consensual agreement with LETCO, thus establishing the basis for ICSID arbitration. However, it should be noted that the ICSID had previously established that state immunity should only be considered at the execution stage. This case clearly reiterates that even though ICSID awards do not encounter recognition obstacles, they do encounter execution issues (this was also reiterated in *Benvenuti & Bonfant v. Congo*[156]) and are therefore unable, as a result of US national laws, to be paid out. FSIA section 1610(a) established that the only exception is when a sovereign property is used for commercial purposes. It defines 'commercial activity as either a regular course of commercial conduct or a particular commercial transaction or act' and also establishes that 'the commercial character of an activity shall be determined by reference to the nature of the course of the conduct or particular transaction or act, rather than by reference to its purpose.'[157] In the LETCO case, the court used 'the rule of thumb' to decide whether it is a commercial or public activity. Cardosi observes that 'the nature of the conduct, as opposed to the purpose, places the focus on the means and not the ends.'[158] The most well-known examples include a state military purchasing clothing, an activity which is not defined as commercial. In addition, it should be noted that the state does not have to possess the item; it is sufficient for it to be the owner, even though control is retained by a third party (as in the Russian case).[159]

The court recognised that the ship owners' tonnage and registration fees were taxes designed to increase income for Liberia. The court determined that they were not included in the commercial exception, and therefore asserted that the investor was free to investigate another property that had been used for commercial purposes.[160] The US Court of Appeals for the Second Circuit confirmed this by showing no opinion. LETCO subsequently applied to the US District Court for the District of Columbia, with a view to

156 In that ICSID case, a foreign investor collected a exequatur by Paris to investigate the People's Republic of the Congo's assets in France but involving a restriction: 'no measure of execution, or even a conservatory measure shall be taken pursuant to the said award, on any assets located in France, without prior authorization of this court.' Assets were found but a problem arose with the purpose of usage whether commercial or public.

157 FSIA Article 1603(d) 2012.

158 Cardosi (n 49) 133.

159 ibid.

160 ibid.

freezing the bank accounts held by the Liberian embassy.[161] However, the court rejected this application upon the basis that it might be in breach of the Vienna Convention on Diplomatic Relations—this was despite the fact that some of the funds were used for commercial activities.[162] LETCO was therefore unable to receive any payment despite being the winner of the ICSID case.

1.3.2.2.2 *AIG Capital Partners, Inc. v. Republic of Kazakhstan* (in the UK)

This case clearly exemplifies how national sovereign immunity acts can be obstacles to execution. In *AIG Capital Partners, Inc. v. Republic of Kazakhstan*,[163] England's High Court of Justice refused to execute AIG's ICSID award of nearly $10 million, thereby refusing to funnel seized cash and securities (held in London by the National Bank of Kazakhstan; hereafter NBK) through a private third party.

In this case, the parties disputed whether securities provided by the third party were the property of the NBK [this would, in turn, render the assets immune under section 14 of the State Immunity Act 1978 (SIA)[164]]. The parties also intended to resolve the issue of whether assets invested in actively commercial assets were 'in use or intended for use for commercial purposes.'[165]

The English court directed its attention to the meaning of 'property,' seeking to clarify this word with reference to the SIA. For this reason, it understood the term to have a broad scope, clearly stating that any asset in which a state's central bank has a legal or contractual interest has, by extended implication, a plea of execution chance.[166] In its verdict, the court observed that the obstacle of categorisation, which pertains to the execution of the assets, not only sustains good relationships between states but also prevents companies from attempting to define funds as commercial.[167]

Finally, the court established that the property of the central bank could not, under SIA section 13(4), be used for commercial purposes. It therefore refused the claimants' objections that the financial transactions were undertaken for the purpose of making profit, thus meaning that it fell under the SIA definition of commercial purposes.[168] The court sought to justify its decision by presenting a 'clear and unambiguous' certificate which clearly stated that the ambassador did not intend to use the assets for commercial activities.[169]

It is particularly instructive to note that Turkey, which is categorised as a developing country, does not enjoy immunity in disputes pertaining to private relations law.[170] The Turkish

161 Saleem (n 92) 8.

162 Choi, 'Judicial Enforcement of Arbitration Awards' (n 11) 187.

163 *AIG Capital Partners, Inc. v. Republic of Kazakhstan*, [2005] EWHC (Comm) 2239, [1], [2006] 1 W.L.R. 1420 (Eng.).

164 As SIA Section 14(4) states: 'Property of a State's central bank or other monetary authority shall not be regarded for the purposes of subsection (4) of section 13 above as in use or intended for use for commercial purposes; and where any such bank or authority is a separate entity subsections (1) to (3) of that section shall apply to it as if references to a State were references to the bank or authority.' State Immunity Act, 1978, c. 33, 14 (U.K.).

165 *AIG Capital Partners, Inc. v. Republic of Kazakhstan* (n 163).

166 Cardosi (n 49) 141.

167 ibid.

168 State Immunity Act 1978, c. 33, 13(4) (n 164).

169 ibid.

170 Utku Cosar, 'Arbitration Guide IBA Arbitration Committee Turkey' International Bar Association 2013.

supreme court recently rendered a serious decision[171] on the attachment of council assets. In doing so, it asserted that the winning party can attach the council assets even if the council does not indicate them in the numerous clauses assets which can be attached in the official papers. It previously prevented the principle of legal security and was also open to manipulation. The supreme court determined that council property and assets of commercial capacity can be attached even if either item is not counted or attached to the list. In adding a further point of clarification, the court stated that it is crucial to show the property or assets that are directed towards the public benefit, clearly specifying that both should be indicated in the rules. Transparency is essential if the public interest is to be protected and trust is to be built within the state. To conclude, foreign investors should seek the member states whose sovereign immunity law facilitates the attachment of the host state's assets; by implication, lawyers representing investors will have to assume the burden in the investigation of said properties.

Taking each of these factors into account, it appears to be the host state that is most favourably disposed; by virtue of this feature, the focus may shift, by default, to investors who are not contracting to the convention. However, it should be noted that there is no direct sanction for investors' failure to comply with awards issued under the ICSID Convention.[172] Article 54 clearly establishes that there is an imbalance between the failure of investors and states parties. Unfortunately, this scenario is seldom evidenced in ICSID because there is a strong belief that the institution provides better support to foreign investors than the host states (in particular developing host states).[173] This claim results from the institutional bias against developing states. This belief has been increased by the fact that some Latin American countries have withdrawn from the convention, for example Bolivia's statement, in which it indicated that it would not comply with any ICSID award that favoured a foreign investor, was particularly problematic in this respect.[174] Nicaragua has removed the ICSID option from its international investment agreements (IIAs), with strong implications for its operation as a dispute settlement mechanism.[175] However, the accusation does not only relate to the institutional bias in arbitration outcomes; it also relates to the institution's status as an autonomous organisation.[176] It is well known that the ICSID has a close relationship with the World Bank, and this has called ICSID's integrity into question.[177]

171 Number of records 2014/194, decision number 2015/55, date of the verdict 17 June 2015. See <http://www.resmigazete.gov.tr/eskiler/2015/06/20150626-24.pdf> accessed 8 July 2015.

172 Collier and Lowe (n 28) 550.

173 Franck, 'The ICSID Effect? Considering Potential Variations in Arbitration Awards' (n 54). See also C Tietje et al, 'Once and Forever? The Legal Effects of a Denunciation of ICSID' (2008) <http://www.wirtschaftsrecht.unihalle.de/sites/default/files/altbestand/Heft74.pdf> accessed 29 March 2017. (Suggesting Bolivia's withdrawal from ICSID was due to 'ICSID's alleged bias.'). Sandra L. Caruba, 'Resolving International Investment Disputes in a Globalised World' (2007) 13 NZ Bus L Q 128, 150. Foster (n 127): 'In recent years, ICSID and the ICSID Convention have increasingly become targets of criticism by countries facing liability under ICSID awards, who have accused ICSID of being biased in favour of investors, and have described the Convention as a threat to their sovereignty.' William W Park, 'Arbitrator Integrity: The Transitory and the Permanent' (2009) 46 San Diego L Rev 629, 658.

174 Sebastian Perry, 'Bolivia Ramps up Anti-ICSID Rhetoric' (2010) Global Arb Rev <http://tinyurl.com/6hf5cja> accessed 22 November 2017.

175 Fernando Cabrera Diaz, 'South American Alternative to ICSID in the Works as Governments Create an Energy Treaty, Investment Treaty News' (2008) Intl Inst for Sustainable Dev, Winnipeg, Man 7.

176 Franck, 'The ICSID Effect? Considering Potential Variations in Arbitration Awards' (n 54) 845.

177 Amanda L Norris and Katina E Metzidakis, 'Public Protests, Private Contracts: Confidentiality in ICSID Arbitration and the Cochabamba Water War' (2010) 15 Harv Negot L Rev 31, 63–64.

While Franck's empirical research for pre-2007 ICSID cases clearly helps to clarify the accusations, it does not indicate a clear institutional tendency. In addition, it is obviously difficult to measure this kind of bias. However, it might be said that the institution tends to protect investors against developing countries. This is, it should be noted, consistent with the purpose of the ICSID. However, from the perspective of developing states, this is particularly disappointing, as they tend to have higher expectations of the institution.[178]

It should also be recognised that this research only includes pre-2007 arbitration awards, as opposed to the life cycle of all ICSID disputes—this perhaps provides a greater degree of optimism for the institution.[179] Perhaps it is not warranted to advocate the wholesale abandonment, or radical rejection, of ICSID arbitration.

The most obvious reference point in this instance is the well-known case of Turkey and the Uzan Group. The Uzan Group has not paid the ICSID award related to the legal costs, with the convention remaining silent on this point. The Vienna Convention clearly establishes that, when interpreting international treaties, relevant rules of international law should be applied to the relations between the parties.[180] Upon this basis, domestic courts may take into consideration some 'abuse of right,' 'denial of justice,' 'unfair and inequitable treatment,' or 'good faith,' conceiving of them as the foundation upon which state obligations, such as those set out within Article 54, can be interpreted, establishing a narrow foundation for execution obligations in the process.[181] If this is the case, states cannot conceal their assets behind a diplomatic facade (e.g. by the establishment of the Turkey council or the underreporting of assets).

A closer analysis of the New York Convention's conception of execution immunity enables us to establish that investors theoretically have a defence of implied waiver of immunity from execution. This is because the convention has no express reservation of immunity from execution, an attribute which clearly distinguishes it from Article 55 of the ICSID Convention. Some jurisdictions have also put this understanding into practice, as the *Creighton v. Qatar* case[182] clearly illustrates.[183] In this case, municipal law provided the basis on which this was achieved. However, ultimately the case did not resolve the state immunity issue—domestic sovereign immunity acts facilitate enforcement of the awards or make them difficult to enforce. This in turn encourages foreign investors to investigate which member states would be more predisposed to a restrictive sovereign immunity approach.

1.3.2.2.3 *Sedelmayer v. Russian Federation*

Franz Sedelmayer v. Russia was another successful non-ICSID case.[184] In this instance, a German businessman, operating under the Germany–Russia BIT, brought his expropriation investment claim before the Stockholm Chamber of Commerce (SCC). The SCC ultimately ruled in favour of the investor, who sought to attach the commercial assets

---

178 Franck, 'The ICSID Effect? Considering Potential Variations in Arbitration Awards' (n 54).

179 ibid 914.

180 ibid.

181 Li (n 55) 178.

182 *Creighton v. Ministre des Finances de l'État du Qatar*, Cass 1 e civ 6, 6 July 2000.

183 ibid.

184 Nytt Juridiskt Arkiv [NJA] [Supreme Court] 2011-07-01 Ö 170-10 (Swed.) (*Sedelmayer v. Russian Federation*) (unofficial translation), available at <http://www.arbitration.sccinstitute.com/Views/Pages/GetFile.ashx?portalId=89&cat=95788&docId=1081823&propId=1578> accessed 13 July 2015.

of Russia in Sweden, rendering an award of $2.3 million in 1998. The supreme court of Sweden approved the decision of the Svea Court of Appeal, ruling that a property in Sweden, owned by the Russian Federation but used mainly for commercial purposes, should be allowed to waiver its immunity from attachment. The supreme court cited the 2004 UN Convention, whose adoption the Swedish government had publicly supported in 2009, but which had not yet entered into force. The UN Convention establishes that sovereign property may be executed if the property is 'specifically in use or intended for use by the State for other than government diplomatic purposes.'[185]

The court interpreted this provision to mean that state property 'which is to a substantial extent … used as a premise for the state's officials (or for a different official use …) should be covered by immunity from enforcement measures.'[186] The key question that needed to be resolved was whether the property was used for commercial and diplomatic purposes. The court rendered a ruling that significantly diverged from previous decisions, holding that state property used for non-commercial activities may not be immune from attachment.[187] The investor succeeded in demonstrating that, of the 48 apartments, just 17 had been used for diplomatic purposes, thus establishing that the apartments 'were of non-commercial, but also non-official nature.'[188] The investor subsequently obtained a writ of attachment of Russia's assets in Sweden. To date, the investor has recuperated approximately €1.2 million, requiring an additional total of €4.5 million to settle remaining Russian debts.[189]

Under these circumstances, it may be questioned if the enforcement of an award would be easier if the investor attached the losing state's entity or state-owned company assets. Closer attention suggests that this may be, if not impossible, difficult. An instructive example is provided by *TMR Energy Ltd. v. State Property Fund of Ukraine (SPF)*,[190] in which TMR had received an award from the SCC against the SPF of Ukraine, which was held to be an organ of the state. TMR initiated the enforcement process against the state's cargo aircraft. However, the Ukrainian government rejected this, claiming the award is against the SPF, meaning that the cargo's aircraft cannot be attached. The court investigated whether the SPF should be considered as an organ of the state that operates under its own rules and which is controlled by the state. This was particularly important because, if it was established that the state had used the state-owned company or state entity as a shield, it would be easier to satisfy the award.[191]

Arbitration awards against a state entity are enforced under Article 54 of the ICSID Convention and Article III of the New York Convention. Contracting with the state or a company/entity under its control has always been difficult, particularly when a dispute

185 ibid para 15.

186 Cardosi (n 49) 141.

187 ibid 142–3.

188 *Sedelmayer v. Russian Federation* (n 209) para 22.

189 Robert Amsterdam, 'How to Make Russia Pay Its Debts: An Interview with Franz Sedelmayer' (1 Feb 2012) <http://www.eurasiareview.com/01022012-how-to-make-russia-pay-its-debts-an-interview-with-franz-sedelmayer/> accessed 13 July 2015.

190 *TMR Energy Ltd. v. State Property Fund of Ukraine and State Property Fund of Ukraine* (ANTK Antonov), [2004] NLSCTD 244.

191 Sylvia T Tonova, Baiju S Vasani, and Jones Day, 'Enforcement of Investment Treaty Awards Against Assets of States, State Entities and State-Owned Companies' in Fouret (n 21) 83–97.

arises with the investor.[192] Enforcement is further complicated when a plea of sovereign immunity is issued against a state or its entities.

State immunity is a considerable obstacle to the enforcement of awards even when the state waives its immunity from jurisdiction and execution—the case of Noga against the Soviet Union was particularly instructive in this respect.[193] In this case, the state waived 'all right to immunity relative to execution of the arbitral award,' while the Soviet government clearly established that it would not rely on 'any immunity from suit, from enforcement, [or] seizure.' The Paris Court of Appeal later rescinded the attachment of diplomatic property and assets by emphasising that the earlier ruling and waiver were not valid. The French courts did not abandon this restrictive approach in 2021.[194] In terms of the *Commissions Import Export SA v. Democratic Republic of Congo* case, the French Supreme Court declared that central bank accounts are not attachable assets according to Article L.153-1 of the Monetary and Financial Code (CMF). Thus, debate on waiver of state immunity was unnecessary. It is crucial to remark that the attachment pursued the Democratic Republic of Congo's account with the Bank of Central African States (BEAC), and not those of the Central Bank of Congo (CBC). The BEAC operates as the central bank of six African states covering the CBC. The extensive terms of Article L.153-1, which uses the notions 'central bank' and 'monetary authority,' provide protection of not only the CBC, but also any other entity like the BEAC. However, there is a fundamental difference between these two banks, and the BEAC actually benefits from the privileges and immunities of international organisations under Article 6.1 of its charter. In the court decision, Article 6.6 of the BEAC's charter was not addressed and 'only the net credit balances of accounts opened in the books of the Central Bank may be subject to seizure, in execution of a final judicial decision.' It is also interesting why the option was ruled out.[195] On the other hand, the court did not include UNCSI Articles 18–19, which allows attachment of central banks accounts if there is an express waiver.[196] These French decisions are controversial in the field of international law, because it is widely accepted that states should have the power to waive their rights—any encroachment on this principle could be perceived as a limitation of a state's self-governance.[197] However, French courts are very striking to apply state immunity if there are no certain commercial assets of the state.

1.4 Conclusion

ICSID awards frequently encounter enforcement obstacles—this applies even though the convention prevents the review of national courts and other tribunals, clearly distinguishing non-ICSID awards. In academia, the ICSID is frequently presented as the most

192 ibid.

193 *Federation of Russia v. Noga*, 128 JDI 116, 121–2 (2001).

194 Cour de cassation, civile, Chambre civile 1, 12 mai 2021, 19-13.853, Publié au bulletin.

195 Sally El Sawah, '"Waiver of State Immunity over Central Bank Accounts! Say No More!", French Supreme Court Rules' (EAPIL, 5 August 2021) <https://eapil.org/2021/08/05/waiver-of-state-immunity-over-central-bank-accounts-say-no-more-french-supreme-court-rules/> accessed 11 August 2021.

196 ibid. According to Sally El Sawah, 'Any kind of State property which is not evidently and ostensibly commercial, will be protected by State immunity from execution, and when the conditions for an exception thereto can be met, French courts could avoid the discussion by inventing a new layer of protection that it may call un-attachability' (n 195).

197 Saleem (n 92) 8.

powerful and effective means through which disputes can be resolved. The preceding discussion has drawn this broad representation into question by reiterating the point that ICSID protection ends after a decision has been rendered. The initial representation should therefore be qualified by a recognition that while the ICSID has significant power to satisfy the interests of foreign investors' in practice, it is also associated with a range of execution problems. There is a clear danger that this pronounced shortcoming could ultimately contribute to forum shopping. The preceding cases have clearly reiterated that ICSID awards encounter the state immunity issue at the execution stage, being distinguished in this respect from non-ICSID awards. To put it slightly differently, while the reasons for non-enforceability may be different for ICSID awards and non-ICSID awards, the outcomes are ultimately very similar. The preceding discussion has clearly established that losing states may not leave their commercial assets in other signatory countries. Furthermore, these same states may not establish purely commercial activities in other ICSID-contracting states. However, it should also be recognised that cordial diplomatic relations between states may militate against efforts—upon the part of investors—to attach each other's assets. This situation also prevails under the New York Convention. In an ad hoc arbitration, it would be advisable, taking enforcement purposes into account (in addition to investigating where the assets of the losing party are held), for the respective parties to arbitrate in a New York Convention signatory state.[198]

A number of researchers have suggested that an appellate body should be established, with a view to resolving pronounced enforcement problems. These assertions rest upon a prior premise that annulment is not sufficient to fulfil the requirements of state parties with regard to legality. However, it should be recognised that the issue is not so much the quality of the decision; rather, it is the reluctance of host states to comply with ICSID awards. In light of these considerations, the ICSID enables sovereign immunity to be used against execution, functioning as a plea in practice. This empowers states to make rules that favour them. Ultimately, the losing party is most frequently the foreign investor—this applies in most cases because 'winning *a case is just a battle but not the actual war!*'

If a stronger enforcement system in international investment awards is to be established, the New York Convention's enforcement stage must be examined in more detail. In the final chapter, the convention will be examined in more depth before a range of solutions are outlined and suggested. It must first be acknowledged that there is always an element of risk in international investment, something which is in large part attributable to the fact that one of the parties is a state. Although it can be safely assumed that arbitration has provided a degree of equality, this feature is frequently insufficient to satisfy investors and also host states, thus meaning that investment arbitration loses significance.[199] Over time, international investment arbitration seems to have gradually lost its reliability, confidence, and practicability.

---

198 ibid.

199 Nmehielle (n 7) 29. Van den Berg stresses that effectiveness totally depends on whether the award can be enforced or not. Albert Jan van den Berg, 'Some Recent Problems in the Practice of Enforcement under the New York and ICSID Conventions,' (1987) 2 ICSID Review Foreign Investment Law Journal 439.

Bibliography

Akande R A, 'Enforcement and Practicability of Sovereign Immunity Doctrine in International Commercial Arbitration' (2014) 7 *J.L.& Pol.* 1.

Alexandroff A S and Laird I A, 'Compliance and Enforcement' *The Oxford Handbook of International Investment Law* (2008) 1171–1187.

Amsterdam R, 'How to Make Russia Pay its Debts: An Interview with Franz Sedelmayer' (Feb. 1, 2012) <http://www.eurasiareview.com/01022012-how-to-make-russia-pay-its-debts-an-interview-with-franz-sedelmayer/> accessed 13 July 2015.

Baetens F, 'Enforcement of Arbitral Awards: 'To ICSID or Not to ICSID' is Not the Question' in Todd J. Weiler and Ian A. Laird (ed), *Investment Treaty Arbitration and International Law* (Juris Legal 2011) <http://ssrn.com/abstract=2130694> accessed 22 June 2016.

Baldwin E, Kantor M, and Nolanmake M, 'Limits to Enforcement of ICSID Awards' (2006) 23 *J. Int'l Arb.* 1.

Barbosa I S, 'The Enforcement of International Investment Arbitral Awards: is there a Better Way?' (2009) 6 *Revista Brasileira de Arbitragem* 7–34.

Berg A J., 'Some Recent Problems in the Practice of Enforcement under the New York and ICSID Conventions' (1987) 2 *ICSID Review* 439.

Bernardini P, 'ICSID versus non-ICSID Investment Treaty Arbitration' in Ballesteros M A F, et al (eds), *Liber Amicorum Bernardo Cremades* (La Ley 2010) 186. <media012970223709030bernardini_icsid-vs-non-icsidinvestent.pdf> accessed 25 April 2016.

Bjorklund A K, 'State Immunity and the Enforcement of Investor-state Arbitral Awards' (2008) *Practice* 858.

Black H C, *Black's Law Dictionary* (2nd edn, West Publishing 1910) 1.

Borlini L S and Siligardi S, 'Enforcement of Investment Arbitration Awards' (2020) Bocconi Legal Studies Research Paper, 1. <https://papers.ssrn.com/sol3/papers.cfm?abstract_id=3730569> accessed 9 July 2021.

Broches A, 'Awards Rendered Pursuant to the ICSID Convention: Binding Force, Finality, Recognition, Enforcement, Execution' (1987) *ICSID Review* 318.

Buckley R P, 'Now We Have Come to the ICSID Party: Are Its Awards Final and Enforceable' (1992) 14 *Syd LR* 358.

Butler N, 'The State of International Investment Arbitration: The Possibility of Establishing an Appeal Mechanism' (The University of Leeds, School of Law, September 2012 18).

Cane G, 'The Enforcement of ICSID Awards: Revolutionary or Ineffective?' (2004) 15 *Am Rev Intl Arb* 439.

Caplan L M, 'State Immunity, Human Rights, and Jus Cogens: A Critique of The Normative Hierarchy Theory' (2003) 97 *AJIL* 741–781.

Cardosi J M, 'Precluding the Treasure Hunt: How the World Bank Group Can Help Investors Circumnavigate Sovereign Immunity Obstacles to ICSID Award Execution' (2014) 41 *Pepperdine Law Review* 3.

Caruba S L, 'Resolving International Investment Disputes in a Globalised World' 13 *N.Z. Bus. L.Q.* 128, 150 (2007).

Cassin V, 'ITA Workshop on Modern Enforcement of Arbitral Awards—Keynote Address' (2014) http://kluwerarbitrationblog.com/2014/06/23/ita-workshop-on-modern-enforcement-of-arbitral-awards-keynote-address/ accessed 14 March 2017.

Choi S, 'Judicial Enforcement of arbitration Awards under the ICSID and New York Conventions' (1995–1996) 28 *N.Y.U.J.Int'l Law & Pol.* 175.

Collier J and Lowe V, *The Settlement of Disputes in International Law; Institutions and Procedures* (OUP 1999) 73.

Collins D A, 'Towards a Grand Unified Theory of International Economic Law' (2015) 12(2) Manchester J. Int'l Econ. L. 140–166.

Coop G, Nistal A, Volterra R G, and Fietta V, 'Sovereign Immunities and Investor-State Awards: Specificities of Enforcing Awards Based On Investment Treaties' in Julien Fouret (ed), *Enforcement of Investment Treaty Arbitration Awards* (Globe Business Publishing Ltd. 2015) 67–83.

Cosar U, 'Arbitration Guide IBA Arbitration Committee TURKEY' International Bar Association 2013.

Diaz F C, 'South American Alternative to ICSID in the Works as Governments Create an Energy Treaty, Investment Treaty News' (2008) *Int'l Inst. for Sustainable Dev., Winnipeg, Man.* 7

Dolzer R and Schreuer C, *Principles of International Investment Law* (OUP 2008) 4.

Finke J, 'Sovereign Immunity: Rule, Comity or Something Else?' (2010) 21(4) *EJIL* (2010) 853–881.

Foster G K, 'Collecting from Sovereigns: The Current Legal Framework for Arbitral Awards and Court Judgments Against States and Their Instrumentalities, and Some Proposals for its Reform' (2008) 25 *Ariz. J. Int'l & Comp. L.* 665, 705.

Fox H and Webb P, *The Law of State Immunity* (3rd edn, OUP 2013).

Franck S D, 'ICSID Effect-Considering Potential Variations in Arbitration Awards' (2010) 51 *Virginia Journal of International Law* 825.

Hess B, 'The International Law Commission's Draft Convention on the Jurisdictional Immunities of States and Their Property' (1993) 4 *EJIL* 269.

Hunter J M and Olmedo J G, 'Enforcement/Execution of ICSID Awards against Reluctant States' (2011) 12 *JWIT* 307.

ICSID, 2012 Background Paper on Annulment for the Administrative Council of ICSID, 10 August 2012. <https://icsid.worldbank.org/en/Documents/Background%20Paper%20on %20Annulment%202012_English.pdf#search=statistics%20on%20legal %20fees> accessed 10 August 2017.

ICSID, 2013 Annual Report. <http://documents.worldbank.org/curated/en/608571468336018162/pdf/81 8060WBAR0ENG00Box379835B00PUBLIC0.pdf> accessed 10 August 2017.

Joubin-Bret A and Joubin-Bret C, 'The Effectiveness of The ICSID Mechanism Regarding the Enforcement of Arbitral Awards' in Julien Fouret (ed) *Enforcement of Investment Treaty Arbitration Awards* (Globe Law and Business Publishing 2015) 99–113.

Krishnan A, 'Obstacles to the Enforcement of Arbitral Awards Against States- an International Perspective, Critical Twenties' (2011) <http://www.criticaltwenties.in/lawthejudiciary/obstacles -to-the enforcement-of-arbitral-awards-against-states-an-internationalperspective> accessed 04 June 2015.

Kryvoi Y, Koepp J, and Biggs J, Empirical Study: Annulment in ICSID Arbitration (2021) BIICL & Baker Botts. <https://papers.ssrn.com/sol3/papers.cfm?abstract_id=3888110> accessed 1 September 2021

Laird I and Askew R, 'Finality Versus Consistency: Does Investor-State Arbitration Need an Appellate System' (2005) 7 *J. App. Prac. & Process* 285.

Lew J D M, Mistelis L A, and Kröll S, 'Comparative International Commercial Arbitration' *Kluwer International Law* (2003) 1.

Li F, 'The Divergence and Convergence of ICSID and non-ICSID Arbitration' (PhD thesis, Glasgow University 2015).

Lin T Y, 'Systemic Reflections on Argentina's Non-Compliance with ICSID Arbitral Awards: A New Role of the Annulment Committee at Enforcement?' (2012) 5(1) *Contemp Asia Arb J* 1.

Nmehielle V O, 'Enforcing Arbitration Awards under the International Convention for the Settlement of Investment Disputes (ICSID Convention)' (2001) 7 *Ann. Surv. Int'l & Comp. L.* 21.

Musa R B H, Polasek M, and ICSID, 'The Origins and Specificities of the 315 ICSID Enforcement Mechanism' in Julien Fouret (ed) *Enforcement of Investment Treaty Arbitration Awards* (Globe Business Publishing Ltd. 2015) 13–33.

Norris A L and Metzidakis K E, 'Public Protests, Private Contracts: Confidentiality in ICSID Arbitration and the Cochabamba Water War' (2010) 15 *Harv. Negot. L. Rev.* 31, 63–64.

Park W W, 'Arbitrator Integrity: The Transitory and the Permanent' (2009) 46 *San Diego L. Rev.* 629, 658.

Perry S, 'Bolivia Ramps up Anti-ICSID Rhetoric' (2010) *Global Arb. Rev.* <http://tinyurl.com/6hf5cja last> accessed 22 November 2017 in Franck S D, 'The ICSID Effect? Considering Potential Variations in Arbitration Awards' (2010) 51 Va J Intl L 825.

Reed L, Paulsson J, and Blackaby N, *Guide to ICSID Arbitration* (KIL 2004) 1.

Saleem A M, 'To What Extent Do States Have the Right to Use its Sovereign Immunity Defence against ICSID Awards?' (2013) (University of Dundee - Centre for Energy, Petroleum and Mineral Law & Policy).

Sawah S E, '"Waiver of State Immunity over Central Bank Accounts! Say No More!", French Supreme Court Rules' (EAPIL, 5 August 2021) https://eapil.org/2021/08/05/waiver-of-state-immunity-over-central-bank-accounts-say-no-more-french-supreme-court-rules/ accessed 11 August 2021

Shihata I F I, 'Implementation, Enforcement, and Compliance with International Environmental Agreements- Practical Suggestions in the Light of the World Bank's Experience' (1996) 9 *Geo. Int'l Envtl.L.Rev.* 37.

Shubin V, 'Enforcement of ICSID Arbitral Awards, Practice and Problems' (2012) 12 Kor. UL Rev. 11.

Smutny A C, 'Arbitration before the International Centre for Settlement of Investment Disputes' (2002) *Business Law International* 367.

Tannock Q, 'Judging the Effectiveness of Arbitration through the Assessment of Compliance with and Enforcement of International Arbitration Awards' (2005) 21(1) *Arb Intl* 71–90.

Tietje C et al., 'Once and Forever? The Legal Effects of a Denunciation of ICSID' 6(1) *Transnat'l Disp. Mgmt.* 5 (Mar. 2008).

Tondapu G S, 'International Institutions and Dispute Settlement: The Case of ICSID' (2010) 22 *Bond L.Rev.* 81–95.

Tonova S T, Vasani B S, and Day J, 'Enforcement of Investment Treaty Awards 319 Against Assets of States, State Entities and State-Owned Companies' in J Fouret (ed), *Enforcement of Investment Treaty Arbitration Awards* (Globe Business Publishing Ltd. 2015) 83–97.

UNCTAD, 'Investor-State Disputes: Prevention and Alternatives to Arbitration' (2010) 16–17.

UNCTAD, International Centre for Settlement of Investment Disputes, *Binding Force and Enforcement* (New York, Geneva 2003).

Uwaifo I, 'What is the Effect of the Defence of State Immunity on the Enforcement of Arbitral Awards? ('The Argentine Perspective')' (2009) 9 *CAR* 14. <http://www.dundee.ac.uk/cepmlp/gateway/?news=31250> accessed 7 June 2015.

The ICSID Caseload Statistics Issue 2021-2. <https://icsid.worldbank.org/sites/default/files/Caseload%20Statistics%20Charts/The%20ICSID%20Caseload%20Statistics%202021-2%20Edition%20ENG.pdf> accessed 06 August 2021.

CHAPTER 2

Obstacles in enforcement of non-ICSID awards

2.1 Introduction: Enforceability of non-ICSID awards (the New York Convention)

The New York Convention is a successor to the Convention on the Execution of Foreign Arbitral Awards and the Geneva Convention (which concerned the execution of foreign awards, having been drafted by the International Chamber of Commerce in 1927).[1]

The Geneva Convention and specifically the arbitration clauses of the Geneva Protocol establish the basis for the arranged enforcement of arbitral awards.[2] In instances where the enforcement of the contract to arbitrate has proven to be problematic, the protocol has been of considerable benefit.[3] However, it should be acknowledged that the Geneva Convention has made a much less significant contribution to the enforcement of arbitral awards. In large part, this is attributable to the difficulties that winning parties have encountered in the enforcement of arbitral awards, having been required to prove the conditions requested[4] and the validity of the arbitral award. Article V of the New York Convention has made a particularly significant contribution in eliminating these burdens by establishing that the burden of proving the conditions falls upon the party opposed to the enforcement of arbitral awards.[5] The convention entered into force on 10 June 1958.[6]

While the New York Convention predominantly focused upon the recognition and enforcement of foreign arbitral awards, it did not directly address the clear need for a uniform law that would govern the process of commercial arbitration at the international level. In the absence of a standard law for arbitration, the New York Convention encountered a number of obstacles. The UNCITRAL Model Law establishes the basis for the essential harmonisation and improvement of national laws. It engages all stages of the arbitral process, extending from the arbitration agreement to the recognition and enforcement of the arbitral award. Equally importantly, it also reflects and reproduces a worldwide consensus on the principles and central problems of international arbitration practice. It applies across different regions, jurisdictions, and economic systems. However, there are still points of complication and potential uncertainty. Local law is foremost in this respect,

1 Samuel Pisar, 'The United Nations Convention on Foreign Arbitral Awards' (1959) 33 S Cal L Rev 14.

2 ibid 15.

3 ibid.

4 Leonard V. Quigley, 'Accession by the United States to the United Nations Convention on the Recognition and Enforcement of Foreign Arbitral Awards' (1960) 70 Yale L J 1049.

5 United States courts have uniformly held that the burden of proof is now on the party resisting enforcement. *The Bremen v. Zapata Off-Shore Co.* 407 U.S. 1 (1972).

6 Convention on the Settlement of Investment Disputes Between States and Nationals of Other States (1965) <https://icsid.worldbank.org/ICSID/StaticFiles/basicdoc/CRR_English-final.pdf> accessed 18 December 2015. Convention on the Recognition and Enforcement of Foreign Arbitral Awards (New York Convention) (1958) <http://www.uncitral.org/pdf/english/texts/arbitration/NYconv/XXII_1_e.pdf> accessed 10 December 2015.

DOI: 10.4324/9781003216919-3

potentially being countereffective to the arbitral process and the selection of the place of arbitration. In instances where this uncertainty is pronounced, a party may hesitate or refuse to agree to a seat of arbitration, objecting to something that would, under different circumstances, be deemed to be appropriate.

The range of acceptable places of arbitration clearly broadens in instances where the UNCITRAL Model Law is in place, with this innovation helping to establish an international standard which is grounded within solutions acceptable to parties from different legal systems.[7] While meeting desired principles of predictability and accuracy,[8] these benefits help to explain why the United Nations Commission on International Trade Law (UNCITRAL) adopted the model law in 1985. The law was drafted with a view to directly address concerns pertaining to national laws on arbitration, with a view to initiating improvements and the harmonisation of domestic laws, thus overcoming diversification and legal standards that were insufficiently aligned with international needs and requirements.[9] Legislation based on the UNCITRAL Model Law has been enacted in 72 jurisdictions, meaning that it has not been enacted in 30 jurisdictions (in a total of 102 jurisdictions in total).[10] Upon this basis, it appears safe to assume that the adoption of the UNCITRAL Model Law will continue to expand in the near and distant future.[11]

The New York Convention has been adopted in over 82 nations, providing an international foundation for the reciprocal recognition of arbitral awards. Taking this broad percolation into account, it seems appropriate to observe that the convention is 'the most important Convention in the field of arbitration and … [t]he cornerstone of current international commercial arbitration.'[12] It has four articles relating to the enforcement of awards, however, only one of them will be discussed in this section. The following discussion will be closely focused upon Article V, which establishes the grounds for refusing international arbitral awards by national courts. The discussion will also focus upon Article V(2)(b), which permits a domestic court to refuse enforcement of arbitral an award if the award is against its public policy.

The main goal of the New York Convention is to restrict national courts' discretion with regard to arbitral awards. This is particularly important because international arbitration has close relations to domestic courts. In addition, national courts are frequently unwilling

7 UNCITRAL Model Law on International Commercial Arbitration 1985 with amendments as adopted in 2006 <https://www.uncitral.org/pdf/english/texts/arbitration/ml-arb/0786998_Ebook.pdf> accessed 26 April 2016.

8 Habrielle Kaufmann-Kohler, 'Globalization of Arbitral Procedure' (2003) 36 Vand J Transnatl L 1313.

9 Anil Changaroth, 'International Arbitration–A Consensus on Public Policy Defences?' (2008) 4 AIAJ 143.

10 See <http://www.uncitral.org/uncitral/en/uncitral_texts/arbitration/1985Model_arbitration_status.html> accessed 10 February 2016. However, England did not adopt it of course, because England took the view that it was for counties which have underdeveloped arbitration systems. Also, Chapter 12 of the Swiss Private International Law Act of 1987 applies 'if the seat of the arbitration is in Switzerland.' Wording of similar effect is found in the Dutch, Italian, and Swedish acts.

11 Hon. Mr. Justice James Farley (Canada), Lord Peter Millett (England), Hon. Mr. Adolfo Rouillon (Argentina), and ed. Fourth Multinational Judicial Colloquium UNCITRAL—INSOL International 16–17 July 2001, London Hilton Metropole, London Evaluation Session. <http://www.uncitral.org/pdf/english/news/FourthJC.pdf> accessed 15 February 2016. See also UNCITRAL 2012 Digest of Case Law on the Model Law on International Commercial Arbitration 1.

12 Michael H Strub Jr, 'Resisting Enforcement of Foreign Arbitral Awards under Article V (1) (e) and Article VI of the New York Convention: A Proposal for Effective Guidelines' (1989) 68 Tex L Rev 1031.

to enforce awards. For this reason, the New York Convention outlines a number of rules which limit the basis upon which the enforcement of arbitral awards can be refused.

The historical record clearly demonstrates that enforcement is the most significant bar to arbitration. If an international arbitral award is to be enforced in a national court, it must pass through the two steps of recognition and enforcement. Recognition is a first step, meaning that the dispute requires no further litigation; enforcement entails that, subsequent to recognition, domestic courts will assume the main role. In contrast with ICSID awards, non-ICSID awards may encounter enforcement obstacles at the recognition stage. This is attributable to the fact that the New York Convention upholds public policy objections as the basis upon which the enforcement of the awards can be declined. For this reason, the winning party must initially overcome public policy issues. If it is successful in this respect, it then addresses itself to the second enforcement obstacle (state sovereignty) at the execution stage of the New York Convention.[13]

In this chapter, first the advantages and disadvantages of the New York Convention will be debated, and the public policy obstacle will be analysed in terms of national and international perspectives. Then the chapter concludes with non-compliance awards to compare the significance of both the conventions in practice.

2.2 Benefits of the New York Convention

Closer inspection makes it clear that the New York Convention (NYC) possesses a variety of advantages with regard to the recognition and enforcement of arbitral awards. The main advantage is that the convention narrows the basis upon which the enforcement of awards can be refused in member states. This means that the *numerus clausus* clearly outlines the circumstances under which an enforcement application can be rejected. It should also be noted that arbitral awards are the final determination.[14] To this extent, an arbitral award must be binding—the convention effectively substitutes for the notion of 'final' that is articulated within the 1927 Geneva Convention. Article V(1)(e) of the NYC establishes that the courts of a contracting state may refuse to enforce an arbitral award if it has not yet become binding on the parties. This course of action can also be undertaken in instances where an application has been made to the domestic court for a review of the award.[15] There are, however, some exceptions. For example, in England, if the case has not been pleaded, it is not sufficient that there has been an application to the domestic court for a review of the award under Article 103(5) of the Arbitration Act 1996.[16] This provision is in place to prevent the phenomenon of forum shopping. This establishes that after a decision has been rendered by an arbitral tribunal, further consideration should not be given to the merits of the award. Also, winning parties have the opportunity to request enforcement in all convention member states. This applies because, within the field of investment arbitration, it is clearly difficult to enforce the award if the host state possesses assets in other member states. As such, it is reasonable to initiate the enforcement process at this point.

13 ibid 1033.

14 Pelagia Ivanova, '*Forum Non Conveniens* and Personal Jurisdiction: Procedural Limitations on the Enforcement of Foreign Arbitral Awards under the New York Convention' (2003) 83 BUL Rev 899.

15 Robert Merkin and Louis Flannery, *Arbitration Act 1996* (5th edn Routledge 2014) 1.

16 ibid 409.

In most commercial disputes, the respective parties will voluntarily honour arbitral awards. Investment disputes differ in this respect, in large part because of the fact that it is more difficult to comply with the arbitrator's judgment.[17] It should also be remembered that applications to enforce an award in the defendant's state of domicile frequently encounter difficulties. If the award is not rendered under the ICSID Convention, it may instead be enforced under the NYC. Questions of applicability are not likely to arise, because it can be assumed that ICSID awards are easier to enforce than non-ICSID awards. This makes it more likely that the winning party will proceed through the ICSID's enforcement regime—this applies even in instances where the enforcing state is a contracting party to the NYC. However, it should be remembered that in exceptional circumstances (e.g. if the enforcing state is not a member of the ICSID Convention but is instead a member of the New York Convention, or if the disputing parties choose the ICSID Additional Rules to settle their disputes even if they are members of the ICSID Convention), the victorious party will, under the NYC, have the opportunity to enforce the award.[18] Although Turkey is a member of the ICSID Convention, the bilateral investment treaty (BIT) between Turkey and Iran does not provide this option, as the latter has not contracted to the convention. Iran is however a member of the NYC; if an award is not complied with voluntarily, Turkey or Iran will enforce the award under the NYC. This helps to explain why the NYC is necessary, even though the ICSID has its own enforcement mechanism for investment disputes. If the investment dispute has not been resolved by the ICSID arbitration rules, it is preferable to seek enforcement in other member states of the NYC.[19] It has already been noted that arbitral awards are not self-executing. Unless there is voluntary compliance, the arbitrators have no power to enforce the award; this means that the award must enter into judgment, and is ultimately executed through the state's enforcement mechanism. Under these circumstances, the relative benefits of arbitration, in comparison to litigation, are less of a preponderant consideration.

Although it comprises the ICSID Convention, the NYC often presents clear disadvantages. This is because non-ICSID awards encounter public policy challenges at the first stage of recognition. However, the ICSID awards also present a clear obstacle—the only benefit of the convention is that it cuts out the recognition stage. While public policy does not present itself as an obstacle, it is conceivable that these awards may encounter the sovereign immunity from execution obstacle at the last stage of execution. In addition to this, the NYC also has a review option for non-ICSID awards by the national courts. In other words, the decision can be viewed from another perspective. The NYC is also crucial because if the state wishes to review whether foreign arbitral awards conflict with its public policy (this does not apply to members of the ICSID Convention), it can

17 Ibrahim FI Shihata, 'Towards a Greater Depoliticization of Investment Disputes: The Roles of ICSID and MIGA' (1986) 1 ICSID Rev—FILJ 1. O Thomas Johnson Jr and Jonathan Gimblett, 'From Gunboats to BITs: The Evolution of Modern International Investment Law' in Karl P Sauvant (ed), *Yearbook on International Investment Law & Policy 2010–2011* (OUP 2012) 692.

18 *Yugraneft Corp v. Rexx Management Corp*, 2010 SCC 19 [2010] 1 SCR 649, para 18. See also Ank Santens and Damien Nyer, 'Difficulties Enforcing New York Convention Awards in the U.S. against Non-U.S. Defendants: Is the Culprit Jurisprudence on Jurisdiction, the Three-Year Time Bar in the Federal Arbitration Act, or Both?' (23 December 2009), in Inna Uchkunova and Oleg Temnikov, 'Enforcement of Awards under the ICSID Convention—What Solutions to the Problem of State Immunity?' (2014) 29 ICSID Review 187–211.

19 Ivanova (n 14). See also Rowland Alaba Akande, 'Enforcement and Practicability of Sovereign Immunity Doctrine in International Commercial Arbitration' (2014) 7 J L & Pol 1.

conceivably benefit from the NYC. In practice, non-signatory countries of the ICSID still remain members of the NYC.[20] These countries or their nationals can therefore use the NYC to enforce their arbitral awards.

2.3 Drawbacks of the New York Convention

The New York Convention has clear drawbacks, a number of which are evidenced in practice. These are attributable to the fact that states do not tend to enforce arbitral awards easily, their membership of the New York Convention (which pertains to issues of pre-enforcement) notwithstanding. The New York Convention establishes some exceptions of enforceability, which are clearly drafted in Article V, being identical in form to those listed in Article 36 of the UNCITRAL Model Law.[21] Article V(1) of the New York Convention broadly establishes that enforcement may be refused if:

(a) The arbitration agreement was invalid;
(b) The award-debtor was unable to present his case;
(c) The dispute was not within the scope of the arbitration agreement;
(d) The composition of the arbitral tribunal or the arbitral procedure was not in accordance with the parties' agreement or, in the absence of agreement, with the law of the seat; or
(e) The award has been set aside by the courts of the seat.[22]

Although this view is supported by a literal reading of Article V of the New York Convention, it should be noted that this inference is potentially misleading.[23] The article indicates the outline of exceptions to the pro-enforcement provisions of the New York Convention.[24] It aims to promote uniformity in the interpretation and treatment of international arbitral awards. Article V(2)(b) allows national courts broad discretion in the determination of whether an arbitral award is consistent with public policy. With a view to bringing out this point in fuller perspective, it may be beneficial to directly reference Article V(2):[25]

> Recognition and enforcement of an arbitral award *may also be refused* if the competent authority in the country where recognition and enforcement is sought finds that:
>
> (a) The subject matter of the differences is not capable of settlement by arbitration under the law of that country; or
> (b) The recognition or enforcement of the award would be contrary *to the public policy of that country.*

At present, public policy (*ordre public*) is one of the serious issues pertaining to the enforcement of arbitral awards under the New York Convention. Article 36 of the UNCITRAL

20 See <http://www.newyorkconvention.org/countries> accessed 12 October 2017.
21 UNCITRAL, 2012 Digest of Case Law on the Model Law (n 11) 1.
22 New York Convention (n 6) Article V(2).
23 Jonathan Hill, 'The Exercise of Judicial Discretion in Relation to Applications to Enforce Arbitral Awards under the New York Convention 1958' (2015) Oxford J Legal Stud 1.
24 Ivanova (n 14) 906.
25 New York Convention (n 6) Article V(2). Emphasis added.

Model Law also attends to this issue in more detail.[26] With regard to the grounds upon which an award may be set aside, there is a close resemblance between Article 36(1) of the UNCITRAL Model Law and Article V of the New York Convention.[27] An additional difficulty arises from the fact that the terms of the New York Convention are not clearly defined (particularly public policy). Because there is no broadly accepted definition of the practice, domestic courts are predisposed to interpret it with reference to their own notion of public welfare. At times, this treatment sometimes negatively impacts the interests of the winning party.

In 1955, the Economic and Social Council of the United Nations founded an ad hoc committee, with a view to establishing a draft convention.[28] The committee initially suggested an article which would refer to awards 'clearly incompatible with public policy or with fundamental principles of law (*ordre public*) of the country in which the award is sought to be depended upon' (it should also be based upon the wording of the Geneva Convention).[29] Although this sentence was not adopted in its literal wording, the drafting committee implicitly invoked it, including the words 'clearly' and 'fundamental' in its report. Their intention was to narrow the application of the rule to cases in which recognition and enforcement would be 'distinctly contrary to the basic principles of the legal system of the country where the award is invoked.'[30] This point is further reiterated by Article V(2)(b), which clearly addresses itself to 'the public policy of that country.'[31] Upon this basis, it can be inferred that the drafters of the New York Convention did not struggle to harmonise public policy or to create a common international standard.[32]

Finally, it is difficult to understand judicial practice in the enforcement of arbitral awards with reference to the use of judicial discretion by enforcing courts. Ultimately, the enforcement of a foreign award within a country is dependent on 'the application of an established framework of rules and principles.'[33] This suggests that the central challenge is to establish how the provisions of the New York Convention should be interpreted; to the same extent, it is also essential to establish, with reference to Article V of the New

26 UNCITRAL Model Law Article 36(b): 'If the court finds that: (i) the subject-matter of the dispute is not capable of settlement by arbitration under the law of this State; or (ii) the recognition or enforcement of the award would be contrary to the public policy of this State.' The wording of the UNCITRAL Model Law on grounds for overturning an award is of course the same as the New York Convention. See UNCITRAL Model Law on International Commercial Arbitration 1985 with amendments as adopted in 2006 <https://www.uncitral.org/pdf/english/texts/arbitration/mlarb/0786998_Ebook.pdf> accessed 26 April 2016.

27 UNCITRAL 2012 Digest of Case Law on the Model Law (n 11) 134.

28 Professor Pierre Mayer (France), Chairman Mr Audley Sheppard (UK), Co-Rapporteur Dr Nagla Nassar (Egypt), 'International Law Association–London Conference (2000) Committee on International Commercial Arbitration "Keeping the Unruly Horse in Control" or Public Policy as a Bar to Enforcement of (Foreign) Arbitral Awards' (2000) <https://www.juridice.ro/wp-content/uploads/2016/03/Raport-2000.pdf> accessed 22 June 2015.

29 ibid 8.

30 Report of the Committee on the Enforcement of International Arbitral Awards, 28 March 1955, UN Doc. E/2704 and E/AC.42/4/Rev.1.

31 New York Convention (n 6) Article V(2).

32 Professor Pierre Mayer (France), Chairman Mr Audley Sheppard (UK), Co-Rapporteur Dr Nagla Nassar (Egypt): Co-Rapporteur, 'International Law Association–London Conference (2000) Committee on International Commercial Arbitration "Keeping the Unruly Horse in Control" or Public Policy as a Bar to Enforcement of (Foreign) Arbitral Awards' (2000) <https://www.juridice.ro/wp-content/uploads/2016/03/Raport-2000.pdf> accessed 22 June 2015.

33 Hill (n 23) 304.

York Convention, the level of uncertainty that is associated with judicial discretion.[34] It could be objected, for instance, that domestic courts are expanding the list of exceptions to dangerous proportions. Upon this reading, the list has a precedential value which potentially puts in place a slippery slope of judicial discretionary escape hatches.

This may contribute to a turn back to ex-dispute resolution mechanisms, a development which could be attributable to procedural or public policy concerns. This will also further reinforce the phenomenon of forum shopping. With a view to precluding this outcome, courts should play an active role in enforcing foreign awards, taking the text and spirit of the New York Convention as their reference point.[35] When the New York Convention's enforcement procedures are compared to the ICSID Convention's counterpart provisions, it appears, at first glance, that the disadvantages of the former outweigh those of the latter. With a view to establishing which convention is better placed to enforce investment arbitral awards in practice, the issue of public policy will now be analysed in detail.

2.3.1 Public policy

'A very unruly horse, and when once you get astride it you never know where it will carry you. It may lead you from the sound law. It is never argued at all but when other points fail.'[36]

In most countries, a foreign award must be acknowledged by domestic courts at the recognition stage. This process, which is focused exclusively upon formal aspects, culminates in an acknowledgement of foreign awards by local courts. The courts must establish whether a local resident had an opportunity to defend him- or herself in accordance with a due process of law within the foreign jurisdiction (*loci arbitrii*). The merits of the case can only be judged again within the enforcing under very limited circumstances. This establishes that national courts do not have the opportunity to undertake duplicate investigations. There are a number of grounds (in particular public policy) upon which disputes can be pursued.[37]

Public policy is one among a number of exceptional reasons pertaining to the enforcement of arbitral awards. In this respect, it is a uniquely 'fluid' concept that permits of a number of different interpretations.[38] It should be noted that contracting state parties to the New York Convention and UNCITRAL Model Law generally acquiesce to the enforcement of arbitral awards if the relevant conditions of recognition and enforcement have met under the relevant legal provisions (Article V of the New York Convention and Article 36 of the UNCITRAL Model Law). Under these circumstances, provisions of the New

---

34 ibid.

35 Ivanova (n 14) 920.

36 J Burrough in *Richardson v. Mellish*, 2 Bing. 229, 252, 130 Eng. Rep. 294, 303 (1824).

37 Gianmaria Ajani, Wanderley Fernandes, Daniel Levy et al, 'Protection of Direct Foreign Investment: Public Policy Exception Impact on Foreign Direct Investments: "Court (Non) Enforcement of Arbitration Decisions Based on Public Policy Exception"' (2014) LSGL Research Paper 1.

38 'Public policy concerns may be raised by the parties or by the court ex officio. "Public policy" is not defined in the New York Convention, but the underlying rationale is "the right of the State and its courts to exercise ultimate control over the arbitral process." Public policy is a fluid concept, changing to suit the needs of society. Although leading arbitrators believe that public policy "plays a much greater role in the theory of arbitration than in practice," the argument does arise on occasion, albeit typically only when other objections fail.' In Stacie I Strong, 'Enforcing Class Arbitration in the International Sphere: Due Process and Public Policy Concerns' (2008) 30 U Pa J Intl Bus L 1.

York Convention will be applied, supplanting national codes (such as the Turkish Private International Law Code, Spanish Law on Arbitration, and the US Federal Arbitration Act) in the process. Article VII of the New York Convention does however establish that any interested party can benefit from the enforcing state's national provisions. In addition, the arbitral award can also be enforced under the national codes.

It has already been noted that arbitration cannot completely detach itself from national courts and rules. This also applied to the New York Convention. The convention does not set out procedural provisions that pertain to enforcement. Article III of the convention establishes that this is to be left to the law of the enforcing state—under these circumstances, recognition and enforcement are sought within national courts. The national court does not have, apart from the very limited grounds set out in Article V, the power to review the convention. In other words, the judge's discretion to refuse recognition and enforcement is delimited by the terms set out in Article V. The party claiming for refusal of enforcement has the burden of proof. However, if the judge recognises a public policy or non-arbitrability issue, he or she may consider *ex officio and refuse enforcement of the award.*[39]

Both the New York Convention and Article 36 of the UNCITRAL Model Law ascribe considerable importance to the concept of 'public policy.' Similarly, International Chamber of Commerce (ICC) rules go to great lengths to ensure that they do not contravene public policy.[40] However, it should be recognised that none of the international conventions on the enforcement of arbitral awards, in addition to the UNCITRAL Mode Law, touch upon international public policy.[41] It is striking to reflect that Article 26 of the Organisation for the Harmonisation of Business Law in Africa (OHADA) Uniform Act[42] represents the only attempt to achieve a harmonised concept of 'international public policy' that operates across different contexts.[43] It might be assumed that this objective would be easier to achieve within conventions that have few members (such as the OHADA, which has 18 members) and regional groupings in which member states share cultural, economic, or political affinities. Taking this as the starting point, it might be suggested that the New York Convention, which has a total of 168 members, presents a particularly formidable challenge.[44] This fact notwithstanding, there have been attempts to harmonise public policy exceptions, with a view to establishing meaningful guidelines that will assist the interpretations of the courts. The International Law Association's Report on Public Policy as a Bar to Enforcement of International Awards (which was issued in July 2000) and the Final Report on Public Policy as a Bar to Enforcement of

39 Ajani, Fernandes, Levy et al (n 37) 9.

40 See from Bennar Balkaya, 'IBA Recognition and Enforcement of Arbitral Awards—Study on Public Policy' (2015) <http://www.ibanet.org/LPD/Dispute_Resolution_Section/Arbitration/Recogntn_Enfrcemnt_Arbitl_Awrd/publicpolicy15.aspx> Turkey part, accessed 17 February 2016.

41 ibid 7.

42 OHADA is the Organisation for the Harmonisation of Business Law in Africa (l'Organisation pours l'Harmonisation en Afrique du Droit des Affaires). It was set up to harmonise commercial law in the Franc zone and came into being with the signing of the OHADA Treaty on 17 October 1993, subsequently modified by another treaty signed on 17 October 2008 in Quebec, which is not yet enforceable. <http://www.nortonrosefulbright.com/files/ohada-25764.pdf> accessed 17 February 2016.

43 See OHADA Uniform Act <http://www.ohadalegis.com/anglais/AUArbitrage_gb.pdf> accessed 12 February 2016.

44 See <https://uncitral.un.org/en/texts/arbitration/conventions/foreign_arbitral_awards/status2> accessed 20 June 2021.

International Arbitral Awards (which was issued in 2002) were particularly significant developments in this respect.[45] Both reports 'attempt to define public policy by reference to "violations of basic notions of morality and justice"'; as a significant prelude to this objective, they also seek to establish how public policy is to be treated in international instruments and national legislation.[46]

This suggests a certain tension, with national courts being obliged to find a balance between domestic rules and values and the arbitral awards themselves.[47] An additional point of discussion arises in relation to the articulation of international and national public policy within the New York Convention.[48] This is particularly important because the question of whether the convention conceives public policy at the national or international level has given rise to sustained debate and discussion. It has extremely important implications for the interpretation of the cases.[49] In a number of jurisdictions, the two concepts are clearly distinguished, with the international concept being defined in narrower terms.[50]

If these tensions are to be resolved, it will first be necessary to clarify precisely how 'public policy' is defined by the New York Convention. It is clear that the absence of a generally recognised definition has made the issue more complicated than it needs to be.[51] Closer reflection reveals that it is an undeniable fact that the ambiguity, subjectivity, and unpredictability associated with the concept of public policy have significantly reduced the effectiveness and efficiency of international arbitration.[52] With a view to overcoming this defect, international and national definitions will be revisited, with a view to resolving this enigma. It should be recognised that this endeavour will, if successfully realised, substantially reduce time constraints and the various demands associated with international trade, commerce, and foreign investment.[53]

2.3.1.1 International public policy

International public policy tends to be defined in terms that are narrower than its national counterpart. As Frank Sanders has observed: 'International public policy, according to a generally accepted doctrine is confined to violation of really fundamental conceptions

---

45 Strong (n 38) 66.

46 ibid.

47 Audley Sheppard, 'Interim ILA Report on Public Policy as a Bar to Enforcement of International Arbitral Awards' (2003) 19 Arb Intl 217–48.

48 Ibid. 'Dr van den Berg has commented that the public policy defence rarely leads to a refusal of enforcement: one of the reasons being a distinction drawn between domestic and international public policy.'

49 Mayer, Sheppard, and Nassar (n 32) 13. 'The Supreme Court, in *Scherk -v- Alberto-Culver Co.* recognised the difference between international and domestic public policy. It enforced an agreement to arbitrate a claim arising in international trade, although arbitration of a similar claim would have been barred had it arisen from a domestic transaction.'

50 UNCITRAL 2012 Digest of Case Law on the Model Law (n 11) 160. See the Indian case, *Oil & Natural Gas Corporation Ltd. v. Saw Pipes Ltd.*, Supreme Court, India, 17 April 2003, [2003] INSC 236. The broad concept was also extended to the recognition of foreign awards in *Phulchand Exports Ltd. v. OOO Patriot*, Supreme Court, India, 12 October 2011, [2011] INSC 1038. The supreme court held in an action to set aside an award that 'unlike for the proceedings to enforce foreign awards, in setting aside proceedings it is not necessary to adopt a narrow interpretation of the concept. As has been stated by a German court, the difference between the two concepts is one of degree and not of category.'

51 Wasiq Abass Dar, 'Understanding Public Policy as an Exception to the Enforcement of Foreign Arbitral Awards' (2015) 1 EJCL 316–50.

52 ibid 316.

53 ibid .

of legal order in the country concerned.'[54] Some countries have already incorporated the concept of an international public policy into their legislation—France and Portugal are two relevant examples in this respect. A Singapore court has already established, with reference to Article 34 of the UNCITRAL Model Law, that the terms under which domestic and international awards are set aside and enforced are similar.[55] This is why the court specifically stated that there is no need to distinguish between the two observing that all awards that fall within the framework of legislation on international arbitration are regarded to have an 'international focus.'[56]

It should be acknowledged that these countries define international public policy as the 'international public policy to which Article 1502.5 refers can only mean the French conception of international public policy or, in other words, the set of values a breach of which could not be tolerated by the French legal order, even in international cases.'[57] Portuguese legislation, meanwhile, refers to the 'principles of Portuguese international public policy.'[58]

These examples suffice to demonstrate that some countries offer subjective definitions of the term. However, in cases of confusion, reference is made to national legislations and courts.[59] A Spanish court has therefore defined 'public policy' as '[p]ublic, private, political, moral and economic legal principles that are absolutely mandatory for the preservation of a societal model for a nation and at a given time'; by virtue of these features it provides protection against 'arbitrary, patently unreasonable or unreasonable decisions' that would breach the right to strong judicial protection.[60]

Other countries define public policy with reference to the enforcement of arbitral awards, presenting it as a body of universal principles that are shared by nations of similar civilisation, which aspires to the protection of fundamental human rights and which is often embodied in international declarations or conventions.[61] The Swiss Federal Tribunal in *W. v. F. and V* (1994)[62] invoked a 'universal conception of public policy, maintaining that an award will be incompatible with public policy if it is contrary to the fundamental moral or legal principles recognised in all civilised countries.'[63] Cases undertaken in the aftermath of this definition have worked upon the assumption that certain activities (such as corruption, drug trafficking, smuggling and terrorism) are illegal across virtually the whole world.[64]

---

54 Sheppard (n 47) 220.

55 UNCITRAL 2012 Digest of Case Law on the Model Law (n 11) 161.

56 *AJT v. AJU, Court of Appeal,* Singapore, 22 August 2011, [2011] SGCA 41, para 37. See also *Phulchand Exports Ltd. v. OOO Patriot,* Supreme Court, India 12 October 2011, [2011] INSC 1038, in the context of enforcement proceedings.

57 Philippe Fouchard, Emmanuel Gaillard, and Berthold Goldman, *Fouchard, Gaillard and Goldman on International Commercial Arbitration* (Gaillard and Savage (ed.), Kluwer, 1999), paras. 1645-1. In Sheppard (n 47) 220. .

58 ibid.

59 ibid 218.

60 *Uniprex S.A. v. Grupo Radio Blanca,* Madrid Court of Appeal, Spain, 22 March 2006, case No. 178/2006-4/2004.

61 Sheppard (n 47) 220. 'The Milan Court of Appeal (referred to above) may have had in mind a more transnational concept when it described international public policy.'

62 Decision dated 30 December 1994, (1995) Bull. ASA 217.

63 ibid 221.

64 Ibid. For instance, *European Gas Turbines SA v. Westman International Ltd,* 30 September 1993.

2.3.1.2 National public policy

A literal interpretation of the New York Convention establishes that 'national public policy' pertains to the country in which enforcement is sought. It should however be acknowledged that the fundamental aim of the New York Convention is to facilitate enforcement of foreign arbitral awards—thus, if convention rules are only interpreted with reference to the national concept, then a substantial violation will have been inflicted upon the convention's purpose. This is attributable to the fact that, while the main aim of the convention is to ensure the successful enforcement of foreign awards, there are a number of jurisdictions, each of which is liable to interpret the obstacle differently. In working towards a common view, it is necessary to limit the reasons and also leave sufficient gaps so as to modify the obstacle in accordance with the time and situation. This adjustment is made easier by the fact that, as has already been noted, public policy is a fluid concept that cannot be restricted to a precise or strict framework. In a national context, it is beneficial to begin from the assumption that, if the award is contrary to the enforcing countries' public policy, it may instead be enforced in another member country that is party to the convention. One case which is particularly instructive in this regard is *Karaha Bodas Co LC v. Perusahaan Pertambangan Minyak Dan Gas Bumi Negara*.[65] The Hong Kong court ruled that if an award was rejected because of allegations of impropriety in the US, it could not again be raised in enforcement proceedings in Hong Kong. However, the English court in this instance did not accept the respondent's public policy defence under the English law.[66] Upon this basis, it is reasonable to infer that, if a court uses the national concept as an obstacle, it should not, upon the basis that it had been ruled to be contrary to public policy in an earlier jurisdiction, reject the award.

One of the most well-known cases is *Yukos Capital SARL v. OJSC Rosneft Oil Co.*,[67] in which the situation approximated to the preceding description. The English Court of Appeal stated that even though a Netherlands court had ruled that the Russian judgment infringed Dutch public policy (upon the basis that it was tainted by bias and political interference), this judgment only pertained to domestic public policy—this meant that the English court ultimately had the discretion to decide whether the Russian crucial court decision was recognised or not.[68]

The general tenor of the preceding discussion demonstrates that there is a tendency for national courts to interpret public policy at the international level. However, in terms of the notion of public policy in the New York Convention it cannot be said to be comprehensive or specific. Upon this basis, it can be inferred that the precise definition of public policy is contingent upon time, place, and other factors. However, this does not mean that national courts are possessed of a broad right to shape public policy in accordance with the case. As a starting point, it should be recognised that every state has its own traditions, public values, and goods, and that these may change over time. For this reason, it may be difficult to draft a generally applicable definition of public policy. In the last analysis, the notion of public policy is embodied within jurisprudence and the

65 *Karaha Bodas Co LLC v. Perusahaan Pertambangan Minyak Dan Gas Bumi Negara,* [2003] 380 HKCU 1.

66 ibid.

67 *Yukos Capital SARL v. OJSC Rosneft Oil Company* [2014] EWHC 2188 (Comm).

68 Merkin and Flannery (n 15) 386–412.

court's decision. With regard to articulations of public policy that have been made with reference to the New York Convention, there are a number of useful doctrines that may help to more clearly articulate international or national public policy. They are set out in more detail next.

Firstly, the term 'national public policy' also encompasses 'international public policy.' By virtue of this feature, the former assumes a number of 'international' features and attributes. Secondly, it should be recognised that the New York Convention only references international public policy—this is despite the fact that it is literally inscribed within the enforcing state's national public policy.[69] It is upon this basis that states become signatories to the convention.

Thirdly, it should be recognised that the New York Convention's notion of public policy relates to both national and international reference points.[70] If an attempt is made to differentiate the two elements, then the end result will be superficial and insubstantial. Member states must protect their publics, being careful to balance public interest and comity to foreign arbitral awards. This is often extremely difficult to achieve; however, the obstacles are not insurmountable and judges should use logic to establish if there is a discernible impact upon public policy. In all likelihood, any dangers should be foreseeable and possible to anticipate in advance. If this was not the case, then the term could be manipulated and adapted to a number of purposes. With *W.R. Grace* courts established that public policy must be 'well-defined and dominant,' being ascertained with 'reference to laws and legal precedents and not in relation to general considerations of supposed public interests.'[71]

Any attempt to resolve the overarching issue should begin by noting that member states have drawn upon a range of doctrines to interpret awards with reference to international notions of public policy—this is despite the fact that the New York Convention directly refers to national public policy,[72] although it should be acknowledged that it has created a common international understanding and harmonisation of public policy defences in the process. Despite these positive developments, some observers have argued in favour of the establishment of a new international court, with a view to restricting the impact of discretion upon arbitral awards.[73] However, these measures are in themselves insufficient and the next chapter will accordingly work towards a different solution.

---

69 In discussing the term 'public policy,' 'it was understood that it was not equivalent to the political stance or international policies of a State but comprised the fundamental notions and principles of justice … It was understood that the term "public policy," which was used in the 1958 New York Convention and many other treaties, covered fundamental principles of law and justice in substantive as well as procedural respects. Thus, instances such as corruption, bribery or fraud and similar serious cases would constitute a ground for setting aside.' Merkin and Flannery (n 15) 394

70 ibid.

71 James P. Moran, 'Public Policy Exception in Judicial Review of Arbitration Awards [*Iowa Electric Light and Power Company v. Local Union* 204, *International Brotherhood of Electrical Workers*, 834 F.2d 1424 (8th Cir. 1987)],' (1989) 15 Wm Mitchell Law Review 767.

72 Inci Ataman-Figanmeşe, 'Milletlerarasi Ticarî Hakem Kararlarinin Iptal ve Tenfiz Davalari Yoluyla Mahkemelerce Mükerrer Kontrole Tâbi Tutulmalari Sorunu ve Bu Sorunun Giderilmesine Yönelik Iki Öneri' (2011) 2 *Milletlerarası Hukuk ve Milletlerarası Özel Hukuk Bülteni* 35–81.

73 Ph. Fouchard, 'La portée internationale de l'annulation de la sentence arbitrale dans son pays d'origine' (1997) Review Arbitration 351–2, in Ataman-Figanmeşe (n 72) 72.

2.4 ICSID and non-ICSID awards: Enforceability in different jurisdictions

In order to understand the significance of the NYC and ICSID Convention for enforcing states, it is useful to focus on concrete cases. No formal statistic or record will demonstrate which convention has been more successful in ensuring enforcement, and so it may be useful to consider the recent research of Emmanuel Gaillard and Ilija Mitrev Penushliski, which focuses on compliance with investment awards. The empirical and theoretical study of compliance has a valuable contribution to make to the understanding of international law, and a more sustained investigation of compliance will make it possible to measure the gap between authority and effectiveness.[74] This empirical work covers the investment arbitration experience of the 32 most sued states,[75] and it covers approximately 70 per cent of all cases initiated by the end of 2019. The report has significant research, but it also covers limited information, because it is hard to find out the exact numbers and results from the states and investors in the field.

It is essential to analyse non-compliance with ICSID and non-ICSID awards more deeply, as this will provide a clearer understanding of which one should be preferred in the field during future disputes. A clearer understanding of the approaches adopted by enforcing states may provide further insight into reasons for non-compliance, and this could help to resolve current investor–state dispute settlement (ISDS) problems. In this area, it has actually previously been stressed that there was no problem with paying the awards in the past. But within the lack of legitimacy, impartiality of the current ISDS and of course political reasons may lead host states to non-comply by claiming public policy and state sovereignty as a shield in practice. In terms of third states, they may not encounter with the host state in order to protect economic and political relations with the host state so they may tend to non-comply the awards as well. But this situation totally depends on the third state's power over the host state. If the third state is capital exporting, it does not consider the host state view in practice. States or investors can use their power to lobby or pressure international platforms. Using other means to seek enforcement in different jurisdictions is a hassle.

It might be appropriate to start with the famed state regarding non-compliance—Russia—which uses public policy and state sovereignty as a blanket. As mentioned in the previous chapter,, *Franz Sedelmayer v. Russian Federation* is a well-known case. Although Sedelmayer was successful in recovering a part of the amount, he endured countless proceedings and extraordinary efforts to receive the money. In parallel with this, Russia brought a case related to a US$65 million tax arrears claim against Sedelmayer before the Russian courts and won. However, the French courts refused to enforce the decision due to a breach of public policy. Until August 2017, Russia had not complied with the award.[76] Also, Russia has another unpaid award that is part of the Yukos awards. This

74 Stephen M Schwebel, 'The Compliance Process and the Future of International Law' (1981) 75 ASIL 178–9 in Emmanuel Gaillard and Ilija Mitrev Penusliski, 'State Compliance with Investment Awards' (2021) ICSID Review–Foreign Investment Law Journal.

75 The states are Argentina, Venezuela, Spain, Egypt, Czech Republic, Mexico, Poland, Canada, Ecuador, Ukraine, Peru, Russia, India, Libya, Kazakhstan, Kyrgyz Republic, Romania, Bolivia, Hungary, United States of America, Croatia, Georgia, Colombia, Moldova, Turkey, Slovakia, Turkmenistan, Serbia, Costa Rica, Italy, Bulgaria, and Algeria.

76 *Mr Franz Sedelmayer v. The Russian Federation* through the Procurement Department of the President of the Russian Federation, SCC, Arbitration Award (7 July 1998).

case also involved diplomatic pressure and lobbying during the recognition proceedings. Russia's diplomatic notes indicated any enforcement related to Russian assets would result in a reciprocal amendment of their legislation, meaning that court authorisation would be required for the attachment of a foreign state's property.[77]

Four out of the seven pending arbitrations against Ukraine have been brought before the arbitral tribunal on the basis of the Russia–Ukraine BIT or indirectly by Russian nationals. But there has been significant political tension between the two states since 2014, and so it is possible that Ukraine will not comply with any adverse awards that favour Russian nationals.[78]

Another unpaid award was in *Walter Bau AG v. Kingdom of Thailand.* In 2009, the UNCITRAL tribunal rendered an award of €29 million against the state, but it refused to comply, and so the investor sought enforcement in the United States and Germany. The proceedings in Germany included the successful seizure of the Thai crown prince's aircraft, and the Thai government responded by issuing a bank guarantee in exchange for the aircraft's release. But it is not clear if the award complied.[79]

The most well-known unpaid ICSID cases are CMS Gas, Azurix Corp, Vivendi Universal, Continental Casualty, and National Grid and those rendered by Argentina in the period 2000 to 2008. The rights in the CMS Gas, Vivendi Universal, Continental Casualty, and National Grid awards favoured US creditors. Argentina refused to comply with the awards and maintained investors could, in following Russia's example, only enforce the awards through proceedings in Argentina's courts. The US responded with lobbying. This included espousing creditors' claims, withdrawing trade benefits extended to Argentina by the US Generalized System of Preferences (GSP) regime and voting against the World Bank and Inter-American Development Bank providing loans to Argentina.[80] After that, US President Obama concurred that

> it is appropriate to suspend Argentina's designation as a GSP beneficiary developing country because it has not acted in good faith in enforcing arbitral awards in favor of United States citizens or a corporation, partnership, or association that is 50 percent or more beneficially owned by United States citizens.[81]

Argentina then agreed to settle the five awards in October 2013 by issuing sovereign bonds at a discount.[82]

In the case of Venezuela, Rusoro had an award of $1.2 billion in August 2016.[83] It accordingly began enforcement proceedings in Canada, the United Kingdom, and the United States against the assets of PDVSA, the Venezuelan state-owned gas and oil company, including its commercial ones. In 2018, rulings by US and Canadian courts recognised the award and paved the way for enforcement on terms that favoured Rusoro. After a year, Rusoro agreed to settle the dispute with the state paying the award, and Venezuela

77 Carl Schreck, 'Russia Warned France of Reprisals Months before Yukos Asset Freeze' (RFERL, 19 June 2015) accessed 23 June 2021.

78 Gaillard and Penusliski (n 74).

79 *Walter Bau Ag (In Liquidation) v. The Kingdom of Thailand,* UNCITRAL case.

80 See Chapter 4, Section 4.3.2. 'Activating the World Bank.'

81 See 'Obama Tells Argentina to Pay Up' (Global Arbitration Review, 16 November 2011) accessed 11 June 2020, in Gaillard and Penusliski (n 74) 14.

82 Gaillard and Penusliski (n 74) 14.

83 *Rusoro Mining Ltd v. Bolivarian Republic of Venezuela,* ICSID Case No ARB(AF)/12/5, Award (22 August 2016).

then instituted set-aside proceedings in France and the Paris Cour d'Appel by annulling the award in 2019. Rusoro announced its intention to quash the French Cour de Cassation and indicated it would seek to obtain appropriate compensation for its expropriated assets by pursuing necessary remedies.[84]

The *Crystallex v. Venezuela* case also did not comply with the award. Crystallex received an award of $1.38 billion in April 2016, which was recognised by both the Canadian and US courts.[85] Although the Venezuelan government agreed to a settlement worth more than $1 billion in 2017, it then failed to make the scheduled payment. Crystallex then resumed its enforcement actions in the US with the aim of attaching PDVSA assets. The US District Court of Delaware granted Crystallex's request in August 2018. In a rare holding that pierced the 'veil' of a company, the court closely examined the extent to which Venezuela controlled the day-to-day activities of PDVSA, and found the latter was Venezuela's alter ego. Rusoro and Crystallex also allege that Venezuela is shielding its assets from enforcement by transferring them out of the territories where enforcement actions are initiated, and they accordingly filed petitions to US courts. However, the Third Circuit denied Crystallex's petition in 2018 because of insufficient evidence and observed that the 'intent behind this series of transactions was to hinder creditors.'[86]

Spain's experience as a host state is also relevant. Although it honoured its international obligations under BITs and defended the ISDS system, it has been a respondent in arbitrations about renewable energy industry regulatory amendments that it applied. It has not complied with the awards voluntarily, and so investors initiated petitions (mostly in the US) with the aim of achieving enforcement. In defence, Spain claimed the tribunals lacked jurisdiction and that European Union law would consider payment of the awards to be a form of state aid, and therefore unlawful. But, in any case, there is no information on compliance with the awards.[87] Also Spain uses annulment proceedings to delay the enforcement of the awards in practice as underlined before.[88]

In most cases, Ecuador agreed to a settlement several years after both the award and the seeking of annulment. However, in the Chevron cases, it initiated recognition and enforcement proceedings in the US. Alongside the recognition of Chevron's award in the US, the Chevron (I) award was paid five years after an unsuccessful setting-aside attempt. A month after the US Supreme Court dismissed Ecuador's appeal, it paid $112 million to Chevron. In the second and larger Chevron dispute against Ecuador about the Lago Agrio, as of 31 December 2019, Chevron lobbied the US government to withdraw trade benefits provided to Ecuador at a time when arbitration proceedings were still ongoing. Ecuador withdrew from the ICSID Convention in 2009 and denounced its BITs. However, just 11 years later, it signed the ICSID Convention again.[89]

Kazakhstan provides another example of an unpaid arbitral award that has several enforcement proceedings against it. In 2013, the tribunal rendered nearly $500 million in favour of the Stati family, although Kazakhstan's government alleged fraud had

84 See CA Paris, 29 janvier 2019, n16/20822 [Paris Court of Appeal, 29 January 2019, n16/20822].

85 *Crystallex International Corporation v. Bolivarian Republic of Venezuela*, 2016 ONSC 4693. Order, *Crystallex International Corporation v. Bolivarian Republic of Venezuela*, No 1:16-cv-00661 (DDC Mar 25 2017).

86 *Crystallex Intl Corp v. Petroleos de Venezuela*, SA, 879 F3d 79 (3d Cir 2018).

87 Gaillard and Penusliski (n 74) 22–23.

88 See Chapter 1, Section 1.3.1 'Stay of Enforcement.'

89 Gaillard and Penusliski (n 74) 29–30.

occurred. One year later, the Stati family initiated enforcement proceedings in Belgium, Italy, Luxembourg, the Netherlands, Sweden, the UK, and the US. In 2017, courts in the Netherlands and Belgium froze assets worth $22.6 billion that were held on behalf of the National Bank of Kazakhstan (NBK),[90] and also applied the same treatment to shares (worth $5.2 billion) that Samruk-Kazyna, a Kazakh sovereign wealth fund, held in a Dutch company. But the Belgian courts subsequently reduced the attachment order on the NBK assets to $530 million, the amount of the award. And in Luxembourg, the court ordered a decision against other assets that were estimated to be worth $450 million. In January 2018, the Swedish courts granted attachment shares worth US$100 million to various companies. And in 2019, the investor also obtained favourable decisions from the Italian and Belgian courts after the award was declared to be enforceable.[91]

As can be recognised in the aforementioned cases, both conventions can remain incapable to comply with the investment awards. Apart from these cases, there are probably many cases that have not been paid. However, the practice can teach us how to manage the enforcement proceedings for future. This is crucial because if a new enforcement mechanism for the ISDS is not established, there are only two options to receive the award payment in practice. Therefore, with a view to better understanding the options for international investment dispute resolution, the points at which the two conventions converge and diverge should be also identified. The ICSID and the New York Convention enforcement systems establish a series of control mechanisms that guard against the 'blind' enforcement of awards at different stages; these include the annulment procedure and the national review procedure. Even though both conventions possess safeguard mechanisms, some countries withdrew from the ICSID Convention, citing doubts about it. Nonetheless, they remained members of the New York Convention.[92] In addition, there are also several economically advanced states that are not contracted to the ICSID Convention.[93]

Just as with ICSID awards, non-ICSID awards are binding—in fact, the only point of variation is that ICSID awards closely resemble the final decisions of the enforcing state's national courts.[94] Baldwin, Kantor, and Nolanmake make an important contribution when they observe that even final decisions may be challenged under a number of jurisdictions.[95] However, it is undoubtedly the case that, some practitioners may underestimate non-ICSID awards if the award is given under UNCITRAL rules. For the disputing parties, the central concern usually arises when they encounter a refusal to enforce the arbitral award; it is this that enables it to be reviewed within the limited form of the New York Convention.

90 *Ascom Group SA, Anatolie Stati, Gabriel Stati and Terra Raf Trans Traiding Ltd. v. The Republic of Kazakhstan*, SCC Case No V 116/2010, Award (19 December 2013).

91 *National Bank of Kazakhstan, Republic of Kazakhstan v. Bank of New York Mellon SA/NV London Branch* [2017] EWHC (Comm) 3512 [24–25, 31]. See 'Dutch Court Lifts Multibillion Kazakh Asset Freeze' (Global Arbitration Review, 24 January 2018) <https://global arbitrationreview.com/article/1153060/dutch-court-lifts-multibillion-kazakh-asset-freeze> accessed 16 June 2020.

92 Ibid. Brazil, Venezuela, and Bolivia.

93 Iran, Brazil, Canada, India, Mexico, Russia, and South Africa.

94 ICSID Convention Article 53. See Convention on the Settlement of Investment Disputes Between States and Nationals of Other States (1965) <https://icsid.worldbank.org/ICSID/StaticFiles/basicdoc/CRR_English-final.pdf> accessed 18 December 2015.

95 Edward Baldwin, Mark Kantor, and Michael Nolan, 'Limits to Enforcement of ICSID Awards' (2006) 23 J Intl Arb 1.

In fact, sovereign immunity coupled with analysis of the public policy factor in relation to their functions to enforcement should be critically analysed. Firstly, it is necessary to see the value and effect of sovereign state immunity in the arbitration process, such as how sovereign power impinges on the rights of foreign investors.[96] As mentioned, an international principle establishes that a host state has the privilege of autonomy over what occurs and how it acts on its own territory. It therefore has considerably more power than a foreign investor in negotiations and subsequent disputes This superiority may be exercised in the claim of immunity from actual jurisdiction of an arbitral tribunal or from the execution of an arbitration award.[97] Sovereign immunity is a broad principle that encompasses all potential executive and legislative action on a host territory; the examination of its influence will therefore be limited to the context of investment arbitration with foreign businesses. This will enable an assessment of the extent to which states use immunity to deprive foreign investors of their rewards; by implication, this will enable a clearer understanding of the means through which the latter can avoid this course of action.[98] In practice, state immunity can be seen as a procedural bar that precludes the execution of arbitral awards against the host state's particular assets when ICSID Article 53(1) is breached.[99] It is therefore apparent that the issue of sovereign immunity only arises when the actual measure of execution is taken under Article 55, with a view to enforcing the award's pecuniary obligations.[100] Most international commercial arbitration instruments allow a national court to decline the enforcement of a final award. This is not limited to grounds that resemble Article 52(1), but can also extend to a lack of arbitrability on the subject matter of the dispute, along with an inconsistency with public policy concerns.[101] It is therefore apparent that the annulment procedure under Article 52(1) of the ICSID Convention prevents the lack of arbitrability and public policy defences.[102]

Although both the ICSID Convention and NYC were established to facilitate arbitral awards, they also establish a different basis that domestic courts may invoke when refusing to enforce an award.[103] While public policy provides one option in this respect, it is important to note that it does not have a clear or precise definition—as such, it is generally used as a 'safety valve' or 'escape clause' for a municipal court to refuse an arbitral award.[104] Public policy defence is predominantly brought before a national court for enforcement of an arbitral award under the NYC. This is because it is widely accepted that the award may be refused if it is opposed to the country's public policy at the recognition stage.[105]

96 Nasser Mehsin Al-Adba, *The Limitation of State Sovereignty in Hosting Foreign Investments and the Role of Investor–State Arbitration to Rebalance the Investment Relationship* (University of Manchester 2014) 181.

97 Martin Dixon, Robert McCorquodale, and Sarah Williams, *Cases and Materials on International Law* (OUP 2003) 331 in Al-Adba (n 96) 183.

98 ibid.

99 Alexis Blane, 'Sovereign Immunity as a Bar to the Execution of International Arbitral Awards' (2009) 41 NYU J Intl L & Pol 1.

100 Christoph H Schreuer, *The ICSID Convention: A Commentary* (CUP 2009) 1.

101 Kamal Huseynli, 'Enforcement of Investment Arbitration Awards: Problems and Solutions' (2017) 3 Baku State University Law Review 40–74.

102 ibid 46.

103 ibid.

104 ibid 61.

105 Vasily Shubin, 'Enforcement of ICSID Arbitral Awards, Practice and Problems' (2012) 12 Korea University Law Review 11.

In contrast, in the ICSID Convention, the losing state does not only lack any opportunity to challenge the merits of the arbitral award; it is also the case that this award cannot be refused upon any grounds, for example the law governing arbitral awards, public policy, or the non-arbitrability of the dispute.[106] However, even the ICSID has no express ground f public policy. Article 52 provides some grounds for an annulment which may fall within the scope of international public policy (including corruption in a member of the tribunal or serious departure from a fundamental rule of procedure).[107] At the level of principle, the public policy of the tribunal's seat and that of the enforcing state are irrelevant—they cannot intervene 'whenever public international law applies by reason of its priority.'[108]

Nevertheless, it can be presupposed that a state's international public policy could become an active consideration if awards are made or possibly enforced in a state which is not party to the tribunal's establishing treaty regime (e.g. the ICSID Convention).[109] By virtue of the fact that arbitral awards are final, international public policy would not be included; whether the award complies with international public policy is not reviewed by the enforcing state.[110] An ad hoc committee considers annulment of an award and a truly international public policy becomes an appropriate and necessary standard of review.[111] It must be noted that while annulment on the grounds of national public policy is not possible under the ICSID Convention, the awards that genuinely violate international public policy should be annulled upon the grounds that they could be viewed as falling within the scope of Article 52(1)(b) (the tribunal has manifestly exceeded its powers by failing to apply the international law that the parties have chosen as part of the applicable law).[112] Furthermore, the annulment grounds set out in Article 52(1)(c) and (d) clearly establish that corruption on the part of a member of the tribunal and serious departure from fundamental rules of procedure can also be presumed to be international public policy.[113] If the ICSID award is, under Annulment Article 52, held to violate international public policy, it can also be said to impede the enforcement of the award. Accordingly, a stay of enforcement may be requested by either party during the annulment proceeding.[114] It is therefore an enforcement obstacle for the award until the decision of the annulment ad hoc committee is issued.

It can be assumed that the worst-case scenario is one in which a domestic court refuses to enforce an award, citing grounds established by the New York Convention in the

---

106 Susan Choi, 'Judicial Enforcement of Arbitration Awards under the ICSID and New York Conventions' (1995–6) 28 NYU J Intl Law & Pol 175. Huseynli (n 101) 47.

107 Khanpoj Joemrith, 'Enforcing Arbitral Awards Against Sovereign States: The Validity of Sovereign Immunity Defence in Investor-State Arbitration' (PhD thesis University of London 2015). See <http://eprints.soas.ac.uk/22784> accessed 24 November 2017. See also Freya Baetens, 'Enforcement of Arbitral Awards: "To ICSID or Not to ICSID" is Not the Question' (2011) 5 Investment Treaty Arbitration and International Law, Juris Arbitration Series 211–28.

108 Nartnirun Junngam, 'Public Policy in International Investment Law: The Confluence of the Three Unruly Horses' (2016) 51 Tex Intl L J 45.

109 ibid 94.

110 ibid.

111 ibid 95.

112 ibid.

113 ibid.

114 ICSID, Background Paper on Annulment for the Administrative Council of ICSID, 10 August 2012. See <https://icsid.worldbank.org/en/Documents/Background%20Paper%20on%20Annulment%202012_English.pdf#search=statistics%20on%20legal%20fees> last accessed 10 August 2017. ICSID Convention Article 52(5); Arbitration Rule 54(1).

process. At this point, the claimant can conceivably apply to another member state of the New York Convention, with a view to ensuring the enforcement of the award. At least one member state should be in a position to enforce the award; if this is not the case, the status of the award is open to question in the first instance. An ICSID annulment creates an even more dramatic situation—after a refusal to enforce, the original award still exists in international order. However, when an annulment committee rejects the annulment of the award, serious doubts may arise in relation to the legal validity of the original award's reasoning. The ICSID awards cannot be reviewed—if there is an issue pertaining to the award, then it will remain. This serious problem does not present itself so easily under the New York Convention.

With regard to state immunity, both conventions leave the issue of immunity to municipal courts or applicable treaties—accordingly, courts or treaties take different routes.[115] Delaume suggests that this focus upon sovereign immunity from execution is confused and unresolved; as such, it might be required to seek prior approval by the executive branch of government.[116] Submission to arbitration is accepted as a waiver of immunity from jurisdiction; however, it should not be assumed that this extends to a waiver of immunity from execution. In addition, the foreign investor must prove the debtor state's assets are used for commercial purposes. This is crucial because this obligation (to prove the character of the assets held by the investor in the host state or third state) is a substantial burden. Indeed, this implies a substantial expenditure of labour upon the part of the lawyers who represent the investor. In addition, this arrangement is also dependent upon the debtor state's comity. Clear concerns have therefore been voiced with regard to the proposition that international conventions can overrule a defence of sovereign immunity from execution under an internal law.[117] Chamlongrasdr has highlighted this concern: 'international conventions can be said to have a prevailing effect over the forum State's laws when they appear to be in conflict.'[118]

At this point, the relationship between enforcing states' domestic law and international conventions is considered with a view to uncovering a waiver of sovereign immunity from execution.[119] It has already been noted that Van den Berg supports a single immunity rule.[120] To put it differently, a waiver of sovereign immunity from execution could be implied from a waiver of sovereign immunity from jurisdiction. This is consistent with the application of the *pacta sunt servanda* principle,[121] which clearly establishes that a state must comply with an arbitration award if it has consented to arbitration under the treaty obligations.[122]

However, the ICSID Convention also allows states to claim the right of state immunity if the award breaches their sovereignty.[123] They therefore state that their action of

115 Schreuer, *The ICSID Convention: A Commentary* (n 100) 1117–8.

116 Georges R Delaume, 'Foreign Sovereign Immunity: Impact on Arbitration,' 38(2) Arb J 34 (1983) 45.

117 Joemrith (n 107) 179.

118 Dhisadee Chamlongrasdr, *Foreign State Immunity and Arbitration* (Cameron May 2007) 1.

119 Joemrith (n 107) 180.

120 Albert Jan van den Berg, 'Some Recent Problems in the Practice of Enforcement under the New York and ICSID Conventions,' (1987) 2 ICSID–Review Foreign Investment Law Journal 439, in Joemrith (n 107) 182.

121 Vincent O Nmehielle, 'Enforcing Arbitration Awards under the International Convention for the Settlement of Investment Disputes (ICSID Convention)' (2001) 7 Ann Surv Intl & Comp L 21.

122 Joemrith (n 107) 182.

123 Schreuer, *The ICSID Convention: A Commentary* (n 100) 1117–8.

non-compliance with the award does not breach the convention.[124] Although the NYC does not explicitly mention the provision of state immunity, the victorious party may, under the NYC, face state immunity from execution in two ways.[125] The first pertains to the application of Article V(2)(b) of the NYC, which relates to the public policy concerns of enforcing states.[126] As Stephan Toope observes:

> 'Either for reasons of international comity or of internal constitutional structure, it is believed that the courts should not complicate potentially sensitive foreign policy issues by "interfering" to order execution against property vested in a foreign State.'[127]

The second way relates to the application of Article III of the NYC, which establishes that the arbitral award should be enforced in accordance with the laws of the territory where the enforcement of that arbitral award is sought.[128] Investors have claimed, with reference to the NYC, that states, in agreeing to arbitration,[129] waive their immunity from execution and jurisdiction. However, this view is generally disapproved of, in part because it is totally dependent upon the states' interpretation of the conventions.

In conclusion, it is undeniable that the absolute immunity doctrine in the execution of ICSID awards derives from both political and economic reasons.[130] Execution is usually seen as a severe interference with the rights of a state. Strict absolute immunity 'leaves a sour taste in the mouth of justice.'[131] However, restrictive state immunity is the most commonly accepted view. National courts should recognise that international law cannot develop in a vacuum; by virtue of this fact, it demands their active willingness and engagement.[132] In addition, domestic courts should recognise that it is, if their national economic benefits and interests are to be furthered, essential to enforce foreign arbitral awards.[133]

Both the ICSID and non-ICSID awards establish state immunity from the execution bar.[134] The ICSID Convention, the New York Convention, and regional treaties are all similar in this respect. Sovereign immunity clearly establishes that public assets and properties used for public purposes cannot be attached in many jurisdictions. With regard to state sovereignty, most countries have broadly comparable rules that pertain to public purposes and assets.

---

124 ibid.

125 Huseynli (n 101) 52.

126 ibid.

127 Stephen J. Toope, 'Mixed International Arbitration: Studies in Arbitration between States and Persons' 141 (1990) in Huseynli (n 101) 52.

128 Huseynli (n 101) 52.

129 ibid.

130 ibid.

131 Nmehielle (n 121) 35.

132 ibid.

133 Choi, 'Judicial Enforcement of arbitration Awards' (n 106) 175–216. See also J Gillis Wetter, 'Pleas of Sovereign Immunity and Act of Sovereignty before International Arbitral Tribunals' (1985) 2 J Intl Arb 1.

134 It should be showed that several regional treaties do provide for an explicit or implicit exception on state sovereignty, including the Inter-American Convention on Extra-Territorial Validity of Foreign Judgments and Arbitral Awards, the Riyadh Convention on Judicial Cooperation between States of the Arab League, and the Uniform Act on Arbitration Law of the Organisation for the Harmonization of Business Law in Africa. The 2004 UN Convention on Jurisdictional Immunities of States (not yet in force) exempts from immunity 'property [...] specifically in use or intended for use by the State for other than government non-commercial purposes.'

There are no official records of compliance of investor state awards that relate to ICSID and non-ICSID awards. However, according to a UNCITRAL Commission survey, which is tasked with monitoring the implementation of the New York Convention in national legislation, the procedural mechanisms appear to indicate that member states have enacted the convention rules within their national laws.[135] A further similarity originates within the fact that if the host state objects to the enforcement of the award in front of the courts of a third state, there is very little difference between ICSID and non-ICSID awards. Jurisprudence clearly demonstrates that the enforcement of non-ICSID awards is not more contested than ICSID awards.[136]

Within the literature, there is no statistical data that clearly demonstrates how many awards have not been paid in favour of investors or host states, with the exception of Emmanuel Gaillard and Ilija Mitrev Penushliski's empirical work.[137] However, this empirical work has also shortcomings because some of the disputing parties did not response whether they comply with the awards. There is considerable disagreement on this point, in large part due to the fact that it is difficult to predict the legally 'correct' result ex ante.[138] At this point, it is also important to note that institutions do not monitor the compliance of the awards rendered by their tribunals. In addition, confidentiality is also another hindrance that impedes attempts to ascertain an exact or precise number. Susan Frank, whose work has made an important ongoing contribution to work on non-compliance arbitral awards, has highlighted a number of important considerations. These include '(1) how much investors actually receive after an award, (2) which investors pay costs for awards rendered against them, and (3) the scope of governmental noncompliance with awards.'[139] Further empirical research which engages at each of these points could make it easier to identify the future of investment arbitration and also ICSID awards.

However, the proposition that non-compliance awards in favour of respondent states are deteriorating can be supported with reference to relevant examples, which clearly illustrate the astronomical costs of investment arbitrations.[140] In, costs and legal fees amounted to approximately $20 million;[141] UPS v. Canada *PSEG v. Turkey* took seven years to settle;[142] in *Plama v. Bulgaria*, the investor's costs were nearly US$4.7 million, the respondent's costs were US$7 million, and the tribunal's costs were about US$1 million.[143] In *Pey Casado v. Chile*, while the state's costs were US$4.3 million, the investor's reduced costs were US$2 million.[144]

135 'See <http://www.uncitral.org/uncitral/en/uncitral_texts/arbitration/NYConvention_implementation.html> accessed 8 August 2017.

136 August Reinisch, *Enforcement of Investment Awards, Arbitration under International Investment Agreements* (OUP 2010) 671–97. See also Baetens (n 107) 12.

137 Susan D Franck, 'Empirically Evaluating Claims about Investment Treaty Arbitration' (2007) 86 NC L Rev 1.

138 ibid 49.

139 ibid 64.

140 Susan D Franck, 'Rationalizing Costs in Investment Treaty Arbitration' (2011) 88 Wash U Global Stud L Rev 769, 777.

141 *PSEG Global Inc. et al. (U.S.) v. Turkey* (ICSID Case No ARB/02/05) Award (19 January 2007) 352.

142 *United Parcel Service of America v. Canada* (UNCITRAL) 2 Award (24 May 2007) para 29.

143 *Plama Consortium Limited v. Republic of Bulgaria* (ICSID Case No. ARB/03/24) Award (27 August 2008), paras 310, 312, 322–4.

144 *Pey Casado v. Chile* (n 323) paras 723–4, 730–1.

In *ADC v. Hungary*, the claimant's reduced costs were US$7.6 million.[145] In *Siag v. Egypt*, the investor's costs were US$6 million, the state's costs were US$3.5 million, and the tribunal's costs were US$600,000.[146] An average investment arbitration costs nearly US$9.7 million.[147] The high aggregate amounts of costs should be evaluated with reference to the question of whether investor–state arbitration is able to efficiently share and enforce liabilities for costs.[148] Respondents suffer from estimated average annual legal costs ranging from US$1 million to $2 million for each dispute.[149] The expected legal fees in the Czech Republic exceeded $13.8 million for one case which was conducted over a single year.[150] In *Jan Oostergetel and Theodora Laurentius v. Slovakia*, the state's costs were estimated to be $16 million.[151] In *Libananco*, Turkey's costs amounted to $35 million,[152] and in *EDF v. Romania*, the respondent's costs amounted to $18.5 million.[153] These highly complex and very often high-value investment disputes demonstrate that the risk of non-compliance in favour of the respondent states is a serious issue. This is clearly reiterated by the fact that, in instances where the respondent succeeds, costs amount to the entire financial outcome of the dispute.[154]

To sum up, as Freya Baetens has observed: '"To ICSID or not to ICSID" is not the (relevant) question.'[155] This is due to the fact that, in practice, ICSID and non-ICSID awards frequently encounter the same enforcement obstacles. In some instances, the ICSID awards can be significant; in other instances, this can apply to non-ICSID awards. There are sufficient grounds (although no formal evidence) to sustain the proposition that both conventions have positive and negative attributes. The essential point is that there need to be new ways to solve enforcement issues in investor–state disputes. These disputes clearly differ from others, primarily with regard to the features of the disputing parties. With a view to making arbitration stronger in the field, a more effective solution should be found and applied in member states, with a view to ensuring that arbitration sustains attention and engagement. This point will be broadly developed in Chapter 4.

2.5 Conclusion

It would be more accurate to observe that the ICSID Convention has its own enforcement system, thus removing ICSID awards from the scope of the New York Convention. The New York Convention has a bar which allows non-ICSID awards to be reviewed by the

---

145 *ADC v. Hungary* (ICSID Case No ARB/03/16) Award (2 October 2006) para 543.

146 *SIAG v. Arab Republic of Egypt* (ICSID Case No ARB/05/15) Award (1 June 2009) paras 604–5, 611–2, 631.

147 Matthew Hodgson, 'Counting the Costs of Investment Treaty Arbitration,' GAR 24 March 2014.

148 Franck, 'Empirically Evaluating Claims about Investment Treaty Arbitration' (n 137).

149 UNCTAD, Occasional Note: International Investment Disputes on the Rise, 1–7, U.N. Doc. UNCTAD/WEB/ITE/IT/2004/2 (29 November 2004) <http://www.unctad.org/sections/dite/iia/docs/webiteiit20042_en.pdf> last accessed 26 November 2017.

150 Franck, 'Empirically Evaluating Claims about Investment Treaty Arbitration' (n 137) 67.

151 Cecilia Olivet, 'A Test for European Solidarity, the Case of Intra-EU Bilateral Investment Treaties' (2013) Transnational Institute. See <https://www.tni.org/files/download/briefing_on_intra-eu_bits_0.pdf> last accessed 28 November 2017.

152 *Libananco Holdings Co. Limited v. Republic of Turkey* (ICSID Case No. ARB/06/8).

153 *EDF (Services) Limited v. Romania* (ICSID Case No. ARB/05/13).

154 Christine Sim, 'Security for Costs in Investor–State Arbitration' Arbitration International 33 (2017) 427–95.

155 Baetens (n 107) 19.

member states' national courts, thus enabling courts to exercise discretion on the arbitral awards. One of the main benefits of the local review is that it confirms the accuracy of the awards. However, this competent local authority has the power to refuse the awards on the grounds listed in the New York Convention, meaning that interpretation of public policy that it is out of the Convention grounds list. This is attributable to the fact that the New York Convention does not define the notion, providing domestic courts with broad discretion in the development of an interpretation.

The list of exceptions in the New York Convention appears to be exhaustive; however, there is disagreement as to whether a court can enforce an award even if one of the grounds is established. The English view is that there is no discretion; however, other countries have taken a different view.[156] Furthermore, non-ICSID awards may also come up against state sovereignty in the New York Convention, even if the obstacle is not explicitly enumerated in the convention.

ICSID or non-ICSID awards with regard to investment disputes are not effective in the enforcement stage, even though they each have their own advantages or disadvantages. In the past, the central issue had been enforcement in other states, meaning that it is difficult to accept enforcing an award without any review in the states where enforcement is sought. For this reason, efforts were made to establish a common system within the conventions for the states. However, as can be clearly witnessed, this innovation has not overcome enforcement obstacles. It should also be noted that these conventions do not completely ignore domestic law. It is also open to discussion whether domestic law should be included. However, the overlooked point is that investment arbitration has increasingly lost its adequacy and efficiency, in large part due to enforcement bars.

The preceding discussion has clearly demonstrated that it is difficult to establish which framework is better suited to the enforcement of arbitral awards. In this respect, the New York Convention does not appear to be inferior to enforcement under the ICSID system. This suggests that the best option can be selected with reference to the particularities of the individual case, such as the disputing parties' membership to the conventions and the losing state's assets. Practitioners should take these points into account before bringing the investment dispute before the ICSID tribunal. If enforcement problems are to be resolved, it will be necessary to find practical and easily applicable ways in which the ICSID mechanism's execution can be overcome, thus establishing the basis for increases within investment arbitration.

Bibliography

Ajani G, Fernandes W, Levy D et al. 'Protection of Direct Foreign Investment: Public Policy Exception Impact on Foreign Direct Investments:' Court (Non) Enforcement of Arbitration Decisions Based on Public Policy Exception' (2014) Law Schools Global League (LSGL) Research Paper 1.

Akande R A, 'Enforcement and Practicability of Sovereign Immunity Doctrine in International Commercial Arbitration' (2014) 7 *J.L. & Pol.* 1.

Al-Adba N M, *The Limitation of State Sovereignty in Hosting Foreign Investments and The Role of Investor-State Arbitration to Rebalance The Investment Relationship* (University of Manchester 2014) 181.

156 Merkin and Flannery (n 15).

Ataman-Figanmeşe I, 'Milletlerarasi Ticarî Hakem Kararlarinin Iptal ve Tenfiz Davalari Yoluyla Mahkemelerce Mükerrer Kontrole Tâbi Tutulmalari Sorunu ve Bu Sorunun Giderilmesine Yönelik Iki Öneri' (2011) 2 *Milletlerarası Hukuk ve Milletlerarası Özel Hukuk Bülteni* 35–81.

Baetens F, 'Enforcement of Arbitral Awards: 'To ICSID or Not to ICSID' is Not the Question' in Todd J. Weiler and Ian A. Laird (ed), *Investment Treaty Arbitration and International Law* (Juris Legal 2011) <http://ssrn.com/abstract=2130694> accessed 22 June 2016.

Baldwin E, Kantor M, and Nolanmake M, 'Limits to Enforcement of ICSID Awards' (2006) 23 *J. Intl Arb.* 1.

Balkaya B, 'IBA Recognition and Enforcement of Arbitral Awards- Study on Public Policy' (2015) Turkey part, accessed 17 February 2016.

Blane A, 'Sovereign Immunity as a Bar to the Execution of International Arbitral Awards' (2009) 41 *N.Y.U. J. Intl L. & Pol.* 1.

Chamlongrasdr D, *Foreign State Immunity and Arbitration* (Cameron May 2007) 1.

Changaroth A, 'International Arbitration -A Consensus on Public Policy Defences?' (2008) 4 *A.I.A.J.* 143.

Choi S, 'Judicial Enforcement of arbitration Awards under the ICSID and New York Conventions' (1995–1996) 28 *N.Y.U.J. Intl Law & Pol.* 175.

Dar W A, 'Understanding Public Policy as an Exception to the Enforcement of Foreign Arbitral Awards' (2015) 1 *EJCL* 316–350.

Delaume G R, 'Foreign Sovereign Immunity: Impact on Arbitration' 38(2) *Arb. J.* 34 (1983) 45.

Dixon M, Mc Corquodale R, and Williams S, *Cases and Materials on International Law* (OUP 2003) 331.

Franck S D, 'Empirically Evaluating Claims about Investment Treaty Arbitration' (2007) 86 *N.C. L. Rev.* 1.

Franck S D, 'Rationalising Costs in Investment Treaty Arbitration' (2011) 88 312 *Wash UL Rev* 777.

Gaillard E and Penusliski I M, 'State Compliance with Investment Awards' (2021) 35 *ICSID Review* 40–594 . .

Hill J, 'The Exercise of Judicial Discretion in Relation to Applications to Enforce 313 Arbitral Awards under the New York Convention 1958' (2016) 36 *Oxford J. Legal Stud.* 304–333.

Hodgson M, 'Counting the Costs of Investment Treaty Arbitration' *GAR* 24 March (2014) <http://trade.ec.europa.eu/doclib/press/index.cfm?id=1608> accessed 13 November 2017

Huseynli K, 'Enforcement of Investment Arbitration Awards: Problems and Solutions' (2017) 3 *Baku St. U.L. Rev.* 40–74.

Ivanova P, 'Forum Non Conveniens and Personal Jurisdiction: Procedural Limitations on the Enforcement of Foreign Arbitral Awards under the New York Convention' (2003) 83 *B.U.L. Rev.* 899.

Joemrith K, 'Enforcing Arbitral Awards Against Sovereign States: The Validity of Sovereign Immunity Defence In Investor -State Arbitration' (PhD Thesis, 2015 University of London). See from http://eprints.soas.ac.uk/22784 accessed 24 November 2017

Johnson O. T Jr and Gimblett J, 'From Gunboats to BITs: The Evolution of Modern International Investment Law' in Karl P Sauvant (ed), *Yearbook on International Investment Law & Policy 2010–2011* (OUP 2012) 692.

Junngam N, Public Policy in International Investment Law: The Confluence of the Three Unruly Horses, (2016) 51 *Tex. Intl L. J.* 45.

Kaufmann-Kohler H, 'Globalization of Arbitral Procedure' (2003) 36 *Vand. J. Transnatl L.* 1313.

Mayer P (France): Sheppard A (UK): Nassar N (Egypt): Co-Rapporteur, International Law Association-London Conference (2000) Committee on International Commercial Arbitration Keeping the Unruly Horse in Control or Public Policy as a Bar to Enforcement of (Foreign) Arbitral Awards, (2000). https://www.juridice.ro/wp-content/uploads/2016/03/Raport2000.pdf accessed 22 June 2015

Merkin R and Flannery L, *Arbitration Act 1996* (5th edn, Routledge 2014) 1.

Moran J P, 'Public Policy Exception in Judicial Review of Arbitration Awards' (1989) 15 *Wm. Mitchell Law Review* 767.

Pisar S, 'The United Nations Convention on Foreign Arbitral Awards' (1959) 33 *S. Cal. L. Rev.* 14.

Quigley L W, 'Accession by the United States to the United Nations Convention on the Recognition and Enforcement of Foreign Arbitral Awards' (1960) 70 *Yale L. J.* 1049.

Reinisch A, *Enforcement of Investment Awards, Arbitration under International Investment Agreements* (OUP 2010) 671–697.

Santens A and Nyer D, 'Difficulties Enforcing New York Convention Awards in the U.S. against Non-U.S. Defendants: Is the Culprit Jurisprudence on Jurisdiction, the Three-Year Time Bar in the Federal Arbitration Act, or Both?' 23 December 2009.

Schreck C, 'Russia Warned France of Reprisals Months before Yukos Asset Freeze' (RFERL, 19 June 2015) accessed 23 June 2021.

Schreuer C H, *The ICSID Convention: A Commentary* (CUP 2009) 1

Schwebel S M, 'The Compliance Process and the Future of International Law' (1981) 75 *ASIL* 178–179.

Sheppard A, 'Interim ILA Report on Public Policy as a Bar to Enforcement of International Arbitral Awards' (2003) 19 *Arb Intl* 217–248.

Shihata I F, 'Towards a Greater Depoliticization of Investment Disputes: The Roles of ICSID and MIGA' (1986) 1 *ICSID Rev—FILJ* 1.

Shubin V, 'Enforcement of ICSID Arbitral Awards, Practice and Problems' (2012) 12 Kor. UL Rev. 11.

Sim C, 'Security for Costs in Investor–State Arbitration' *Arbitration International* 33 (2017) 427–495.

Strong S I, 'Enforcing Class Arbitration in the International Sphere: Due Process and Public Policy Concerns' (2008) 30 *U. Pa. J. Intl Bus. L.* 1.

Strub M H J, 'Resisting Enforcement of Foreign Arbitral Awards under Article V (1) (e) and Article VI of the New York Convention: A Proposal for Effective Guidelines' (1989) 68 *Tex. L. Rev.* 1031.

Olivet C, 'A Test for European solidarity, the case of intra-EU Bilateral Investment Treaties' (2013) Transnational Institute. <https://www.tni.org/files/download/briefing_on_intra-eu_bits_0.pdf> accessed 28 November 2017.

Toope S J, Mixed International Arbitration: Studies in Arbitration between States and Persons 141 (1990) 1.

Uchkunova I and Temnikov O, 'Security for Costs in ICSID Arbitration' (2015) 326 *Kluwer Arbitration Blog.* <http://kluwerarbitrationblog.com/2015/02/10/security-for-costs-in-icsidarbitration/> accessed 07 March 2017

UNCITRAL, 2012 Digest of Case Law on the Model Law on International Commercial Arbitration 1.

UNCITRAL Model Law on International Commercial Arbitration 1985 with amendments as adopted in 2006 <https://www.uncitral.org/pdf/english/texts/arbitration/mlarb/0786998_Ebook.pdf> accessed 26 April 2016

Wetter J G, 'Pleas of Sovereign Immunity and Act of Sovereignty before International Arbitral Tribunals' (1985) 2 *J. Intl Arb.* 1.

CHAPTER 3

Potential enforcement obstacles in a future multilateral investment court (MIC)

3.1 Introduction

The establishment of a multilateral investment court (MIC) is a quite recent proposal that aims to replace the current investor–state dispute settlement (ISDS), because the most advanced economic states distrust its fairness and impartiality.[1] Investor-state disputes occur in most international legal-political domains. Despite the states provide fair and equitable treatment, and prompt, adaquate and effective compensation for expropriation of investments and MFN, in addition to other benefits, they have not understood the actual consequences and obligations that IIAs have created.[2]

The behaviour of host states caused hundreds of arbitration cases in the 1980s and 1990s, and this resulted in millions of dollars of compensation being ordered for the exercise of sovereignty against foreign investors.[3] Discontent with the system then grew as a result of pro-investor bias, inconsistent awards, and other factors. IIAs do not take into account the state's responsibility to provide public health, security, and environmental protection.[4] Aside from substantive issues, IIAs have a number of procedural issues that relate to the lack of an appeal mechanism to review a number of factors that include the tribunal award, third-party funding, the choice of arbitrators, transparency, and *amicus curiae.*[5]

In the last decade, policymakers have proposed several solutions to these issues. The Mauritius Convention, for example, sought to increase the transparency of ISDS proceedings by providing public access to dispute proceedings, papers, and other sources. Canada, the European Union, Norway, and the United States have also proposed national and regional solutions that include model bilateral investment treaties (BITs); some of these clarify their rules, whereas others focus on public interests.[6] But some states have

1 Thomas Dietz, Marius Dotzauer, and Edward S Cohen, 'The Legitimacy Crisis of Investor-State Arbitration and the New EU Investment Court System' (2019) 26 Review of International Political Economy 749–72.

2 Rhea Tamara Hoffmann, 'The Multilateral Investment Court: A Stumbling Block for Comprehensive and Sustainable Investment Law Reform' (2018) ESIL 1. See <https://papers.ssrn.com/sol3/papers.cfm?abstract_id=3363926> accessed 10 July 2021.

3 Lauge Poulsen, *Bounded Rationality and Economic Diplomacy: The Politics of Investment Treaties in Developing Countries* (CUP 2015).

4 Marc Bungenberg and Anna M Holzer, 'Potential Enforcement Mechanisms for Decisions of a Multilateral Investment Court' in Gunes Unuvar, Joanna Lam, and Shai Dothan (eds), *Permanent Investment Courts: The European Experiment* (Springer 2020) 75–117.

5 ibid.

6 Gunes Unuvar, 'Reforming Investor–State Dispute Settlement: Reflections on the UNCITRAL Working Group III and Beyond' (*Turkish Law Blog*, 9 May 2019) <https://turkishlawblog.com/read/article/120/reforming-investor-state-dispute-settlement-reflections-on-the-uncitral-working-group-iii-and-beyond> accessed 14 June 2021.

DOI: 10.4324/9781003216919-4

begun to terminate their BITs because they lack legitimacy and have indicated they do not wish to renegotiate IIAs.[7]

It has already been noted that the enforcement of an award is a significant step in the whole arbitration process, and the current ISDS has several problems that include enforcement issues. Until now, the framework of the proposed court has remained uncertain. However, the United Nations Commission on International Trade Law (UNCITRAL) has said it would establish a multilateral work by 7 July 2017. The UNCITRAL Working Group III held its 41st session in Vienna on 15–19 November 2021, and the appellate body and enforcement issue was on its agenda.[8]

Although this new investment court proposal sounds great in some respects, its relationship with European Union (EU) law and function in traditional ISDS are still unclear. When the 2009 Lisbon Treaty came into effect, foreign direct investment (FDI) powers were transferred from European Union member states to the European Union itself.[9] The European Commission, as the European Union's main external trade actor, then began to negotiate IIAs and investment chapters in enlarged free trade agreements (FTAs).[10] The EU proposed the new investment court system that already covers free trade agreements with Canada (CETA) and Vietnam,[11] and also agreed to an Investment Court System (ICS)-covering Transatlantic Trade and Investment Partnership (TTIP) with the US.

Both agreements include substantive protection standards and enforcement mechanisms that apply in disputes, which both relate to state–state and investor–state arbitration. But it was not clear if the European Commission would venture into investor–state agreements in investor–state arbitration.[12]

This chapter discusses the enforcement step by respectively referring to the establishment of an ICS/MIC and its enforcement mechanism, the creation of a new international convention for the investment court, and the benefits of existing conventions (specifically the NYC and ICSID). And it also considers the potential risks associated with the enforcement of MIC awards in contracting and third states. It concludes by evaluating the significance of the proposed court system, and asks if it is likely to be productive or ineffective in the future.

3.2 MIC enforcement mechanism

The main aim of a two-tier investment court system is to provide coherence and consistency in ISDS. In order to achieve this, guidance principles applicable to the court's

7 ibid. Gunes Unuvar observes that a number of states have begun to terminate their BITs, whether by cancelling them entirely or by renegotiating newer and more favourable IIAs. Ecuador, Indonesia, India, South Africa, and Venezuela are a few examples. Other significant global actors, such as Brazil, do not have IIAs that allow ISDS.

8 See <https://uncitral.un.org/en/working_groups/3/investor-state> accessed 10 August 2021.

9 August Reinisch, 'The European Union and Investor-State Dispute Settlement: From Investor-State Arbitration to a Permanent Investment Court' (2016) 2 CIGI 1. Wybe Douma, 'Investor-State Arbitration in the Light of EU Policy and Law after the Lisbon Treaty' (The Hague, The Netherlands) 16 April 2017.

10 ibid.

11 Hannes Lenk, 'An Investment Court System for the New Generation of EU Trade and Investment Agreements: A Discussion of the Free Trade Agreement with Vietnam and the Comprehensive Economic and Trade Agreement with Canada,' see <http://www.europeanpapers.eu/en/system/files/pdf_version/EP_EF_2016_I_033_Hannes_Lenk.pdf> accessed 14 November 2017.

12 Reinisch, 'The European Union and Investor-State Dispute Settlement' (n 9).

decisions should be outlined and then an effective enforcement mechanism should be put in place.[13] The UNCITRAL Working Group has often underlined the importance of enforcement for an effective justice system. A strong MIC enforcement mechanism and decisions by the permanent appellate body therefore depend on specific binding guidance, the *res judicata* effect, control of public policy, and state sovereignty.[14] The example of the New York Convention (NYC), where global access and the construction of a sufficiently (harmonised) enforcement regime that benefits 160 states have taken 60 years to emerge, suggests that it will take states a long time to fully accept membership of the MIC.[15] Here it is instructive to recall the example of the International Centre for Settlement of Investment Disputes (ICSID), which was not asked to address a single dispute in the seven years after the convention was signed.[16] It should also be remembered that any MIC enforcement regime can become a competitor to the NYC and ICSID Convention. This possibility of fragmentation in itself provides sufficient grounds for suggesting that the application of the MIC should be suspended until it can provide broad mass access.[17]

The EU hopes to emulate the World Trade Organization's (WTO) role in resolving international trade and investment disputes.[18] Lack of legitimacy is one of the enforcement obstacles, and it arises because host states are not satisfied with the one-tier system, and so they demand another eye to review the correctness of the awards in practice. If this is not there, they will not enforce these awards in their territories. The Comprehensive Economic and Trade Agreement (CETA) therefore covers the permanent appellate body. Its members have 'the qualifications required in their respective countries for appointment to judicial office' or are 'jurists of recognized competence' with 'demonstrated expertise in public international law.' They have expertise 'in international investment law, international trade law and the resolution of disputes arising under international investment or international trade agreements.' Independence is crucial, as the jurists of the court and the appellate body should not be affiliated with the government.[19] CETA also establishes ICS members should not be 'counsel or [p]arty-appointed expert or witness in any pending or new investment dispute.'[20] If there is a conflict of interest, the president of the International Court of Justice (ICJ) may be asked to make a decision.

13 Gloria Alvarez, Saadia Bhatty, Nikos Lavranos, and Alexander Leventhal, 'Ensuring The Effective Recognition and Enforcement of MIC Decisions to the UNCITRAL Working Group No. III on ISDS Reforms' (2020) EFILA <https://uncitral.un.org/sites/uncitral.un.org/files/mediadocuments/uncitral/en/efila_submission_to_uncitral_wg_iii.pdf> accessed 25 June 2021.

14 ibid.

15 ibid.

16 Norbert Horn and Stefan Kröll, *Arbitrating Foreign Investment Disputes* (KIL 2004) 1.

17 ibid. It might be suggested that if an MIC enforcement regime applies in certain pro-enforcement jurisdictions (e.g. Canada, EU member states, Hong Kong, Japan, and Singapore), this would be sufficient to ensure that the regime is 'effective.' But this underestimates the ability of respondent states to 'judgment proof' their assets in these states. Even though a 'critical mass' of states have ratified the convention, exceptions to its applications may prevail if there are any reciprocity reservations.

18 Maria Fanou, 'The Independence and Impartiality of the Hybrid CETA Investment Court System: Reflections in the aftermath of Opinion 1/17' (2020) (4) Europe and the World: A Law Review 1. <https://ucl.scienceopen.com/hosted-document?doi=10.14324/111.444.ewlj.2020.26> accessed 7 May 2021.

19 ibid. It is clarified that this does not amount to a general ineligibility of any person receiving remuneration from a government. The EU intentions seem to be revealed when looking at the text of other agreements which attempt to clarify the meaning of 'government affiliations' to exclude academics, persons receiving pensions, or having other family relationships with government officials, as well as persons who were previously government employees. CETA does not elaborate much on this general prohibition of government affiliation.

20 ibid.

But the MIC has a hybrid nature. The language of the CETA drafters employs a complex terminology, which does not clarify if the MIC is a kind of arbitral body or court. This has important implications for enforcement because CETA does not only provide recourse to the ICSID Secretariat but also incorporates the International Bar Association (IBA) Guidelines for conflicts of interest in international arbitration.[21] And the ICS also aspires to use legal instruments that include the New York Convention and ICSID Convention. It is essential to acknowledge how the type of ICS causes the various complexities associated with this reliance and to also address the thorny issue of how ICS awards are enforced.[22]

Although there has not been a certain arrangement of the enforcement system, the CETA, FTA, and TTIP cover similar obligations to the ICSID Convention and NYC. The agreement provisions generally clarify the MIC awards are final and binding, and also clarify the awards are enforced by the enforcing states in accordance with their domestic law, and that the disputing parties have a chance to appeal if they do not satisfy the first judgment. The key debate is if the MIC can be made stronger by referring to existing conventions or establishing a new one. If the MIC is considered within the framework of the court system and existing international instruments are used, the MIC would probably challenge the systematic problems in the recognition and enforcement stages.[23] After first considering the ICSID Convention and the NYC in order to assess their potential use for the enforcement of court awards, the chapter then examines a new MIC convention and asserts it as the most desirable option.

3.2.1 The ICSID Convention

Application of the Convention on the Settlement of Investment Disputes between States and Nationals of Other States (ICSID Convention) would efficiently guarantee the recognition and enforcement of MIC decisions,[24] and this applies because it has a self-contained enforcement system and applies to a large number of states in practice. It is obvious that applying an existing instrument is preferable to establishing a new ground for enforcement. This is due to the fact that the ICSID Convention's experience of enforcement is internationally accepted, as confirmed by the fact that contracting states mostly voluntarily comply with its awards.[25]

In the enforcement of MIC awards under the ICSID Convention, the first approach is to modify the ICSID Convention or allow modifications between some convention member states as a permissible *inter se*. This means that non-modifying states do not have to enforce MIC awards such as the ICSID awards, but they can be enforced under the NYC in the non-contracting states of TTIP and CETA.[26] Although the modification approach of the ICSID Convention seems appropriate, it may, in retrospect, have contributed to various problems.

21 ibid.

22 ibid.

23 Hongling Ning and Tong Qi, 'Multilateral Investment Court: The Gap Between the EU and China' (2018) 4 The Chinese Journal of Global Governance 154–75.

24 Hoffmann (n 2).

25 However, there are still non-complied ICSID awards. See Chapter 1 and Chapter 2.

26 European Parliamentary Research Service, 'From Arbitration to the Investment Court System (ICS): The Evolution of CETA Rules' (June 2017) <https://www.europarl.europa.eu/RegData/etudes/IDAN/2017/607251/EPRS_IDA(2017)607251_EN.pdf> accessed 25 June 2021.

The first question relates to the type of MIC decision and, more specifically, if it is an arbitral award or judicial decision. This is crucial because the answer may clarify the enforcement stage. Closer examination of the MIC hybrid system shows that the CETA and TTIP establish a court, but also use the term 'the award' to refer to enforcement. There were many examples of mixed claim commissions that conjoined investors and the host states, but perhaps the foremost example was the Iran–US Claims Tribunal (IUSCT)[27] that was established in 1981, which included judges appointed by two states who were tasked with determining a number of disputes between state nationals. The permanent arbitral body is still active. This semi-arbitral body's decisions were enforced under the NYC, although they cannot be enforced under the ICSID Convention. This applies because it is a strict instrument that does not refer to the disputing parties' interests in the enforcement stage. This can be ascertained from the language of the text, as 'unless otherwise' or 'except otherwise agreed' are not used.[28] Awards rendered by the semi-arbitral body cannot be assumed to be ICSID awards and as a natural consequence cannot be enforced accordingly.

The finality of the awards is a second problem. It is well-established that ICSID awards are final and binding, and this means that if the MIC awards are enforced under the ICSID Convention, they must be final. While the ICSID cannot further review the award rendered by the tribunal, MIC awards can be appealed to review correctness (errors of law). The appealed MIC awards are not final, and must go back to the first tribunal. If the appellate body rejects the appeal, the award is final and is ready to be enforced. The ICSID Convention only applies to the decisions of the MIC Appellate Body or first instance decisions that cannot be appealed anymore.[29] First instance decisions also cannot be annulled and revised under Articles 51 and 52 of the ICSID Convention, and may only be applicable to the MIC's second instance decisions.[30] One of the main advantages of the ICSID awards is that they cannot be appealed under Article 53(1), meaning that arbitration takes less time than would be required for appealing awards.[31]

After the MIC proposal, the ICSID began to be reformed, with particular emphasis on its appeal body factor. However, this may damage the feature of the institution and undermine its legitimacy, and so a final decision has not been made.[32] It is also not clear that, once modification is taken into account, the reasons given for annulling the ICSID will be the same as those for appealing the MIC appeal. It should also be considered which types of MIC decisions will be accepted as final and binding. It is crucial for the enforcing state to consider if interim decisions, pecuniary awards, or other burdens will be enforced in its territory. And this is because the ICSID Convention establishes that such decisions cannot be executed in third states. And if the decision is not pecuniary (e.g. fulfilment of treaty obligations), the question arises of how the enforcing state compels the losing party. Here it should be remembered that ICSID only facilitates the enforcement of monetary

27 Juan Pablo Charris-Benedetti, 'The Proposed Investment Court System: Does It Really Solve the Problems?' (2019) 42 Revista Derecho del Estado 83–115. The tribunal has finalised more than 3,900 cases.

28 Bungenberg and Holzer (n 4).

29 Ning and Qi (n 23).

30 ibid.

31 See Chapter 4, Section 4.3.4 'Proposal to reform the ICSID rules.'

32 ibid.

decisions,[33] and if the MIC seeks to force states to comply with treaty obligations by revising the ICSID Convention, it would clearly be very problematic.

Third, if the EU agreements refer to the ICSID Convention, then it may be incompatible. And an additional *ratione personae* issue may arise because the EU is not a contracting party to the ICSID Convention. When the EU has to answer to an ICSID tribunal, the tribunal would lack jurisdiction over the case, as Article 25 of the convention establishes. The commission therefore seeks to access the ICSID Convention. However, this may only be an option if Article 67 (which restricts membership of the convention) is amended.[34]

Articles 65 and 66 of the ICSID make it possible to amend the convention. But this may not be practical because some states are totally opposed to the MIC.[35] In order to bypass them *inter se*, it may be possible to resort to Article 41 of the 1969 Vienna Convention on the Law of Treaties (VCLT). Accordingly, the EU and its member states and contracting parties can enter into *inter se* agreements on the ICSID Convention when they issue demands within the parameters established by Article 41 of the VCLT.[36] This *inter se* agreement also does not affect rights of the non-contracting states established by the *res inter alios acta* principle.[37]

But there is still a question around the VCLT solution, as it allows *inter se* modification in certain circumstances.[38] In other words, this solution is possible if it is not prohibited by the respective treaty and also does not refer to a provision whose derogation is incompatible with convention is to facilitate the enforcement of ICSID awards in contracting states. But if the proposed modification is applied, it is only implied in the case of state consent. The purpose of the convention is not therefore realised, as it also provides

---

33 As requested, the ICSID Tribunal awarded a two-tier legal remedy: Burundi would only have to pay damages if it failed to fulfil its contractual obligation to perform within a fixed period of time. Although national law established an obligation to act and associated legal consequences, it could only be enforced voluntarily. This solution enables the state to autonomously decide if a change in the law applied to the performance of the contract or damages could better be implemented. *Ioan Micula and others v. Romania*, ICSID Case No. ARB/05/02, Decision on Jurisdiction and Admissibility, 24 September 2008, paras 166–8; *ATA Construction v. Jordan*, ICSID Case No. ARB/08/2, Award, 18.5.2010; *Franck Charles Arif v. Moldova*, ICSID Case No. ARB/11/23, Award, 8 April 2013.

34 August Reinisch, 'Will the EU's Proposal Concerning an Investment Court System for CETA and TTIP Lead to Enforceable Awards?—The Limits of Modifying the ICSID Convention and the Nature of Investment Arbitration' (2016) 19 Journal of International Economic Law 761.

35 Marc Bungenberg and August Reinisch, *From Bilateral Arbitral Tribunals and Investment Courts to a Multilateral Investment Court: Options Regarding the Institutionalization of Investor-State Dispute Settlement* (Springer Nature 2020).

36 Richard Happ and Sebastian Wuschka, 'From the Jay Treaty Commissions towards a Multilateral Investment Court: Addressing the Enforcement Dilemma' (2017) 6 Indian J Arb L 113.

37 Article 34 of the VCLT.

38 Article 41 of the VCLT: Agreements to modify multilateral treaties between certain of the parties only

1. Two or more of the parties to a multilateral treaty may conclude an agreement to modify the treaty as between themselves alone if:
   (a) the possibility of such a modification is provided for by the treaty; or
   (b) the modification in question is not prohibited by the treaty and:
      (i) does not affect the enjoyment by the other parties of their rights under the treaty or the performance of their obligations;
      (ii) does not relate to a provision, derogation from which is incompatible with the effective execution of the object and purpose of the treaty as a whole.
2. Unless in a case falling under paragraph 1(a) the treaty otherwise provides, the parties in question shall notify the other parties of their intention to conclude the agreement and of the modification to the treaty for which it provides.

enforcement in non-disputing parties as well. With regard to MIC *inter se* modification, enforcement is only available in the EU and contracting parties to the MIC. In the case of the appellate body, the main difference of the ICSID awards is that they are final and binding, and are not therefore subject to review by the national courts. If the modification creates an option to appeal, it may be assumed to be contrary to the convention purpose. But here it should be remembered that amendments to the ICSID Convention cannot be implied. A number of wide-ranging alternatives should therefore be considered, such as the shifting of the annulment procedure by the appellate. If this replacement provides more effective enforcement of ICSID awards, it will help to realise its purpose and objects.[39] And here it should be remembered the ICSID debated the appeal mechanism a few years ago.[40]

With regard to procedural issues, the rules of the Vienna Convention on the Law of Treaties (VCLT) apply to treaties entered into force after 27 January 1980, but the ICSID Convention entered into force almost 14 years before.[41] In the event that the issue of customary international law arises, the VCLT rules can be applied to the ICSID Convention because the latter only focuses on treaty interpretation[42] and does not refer to *inter se* modification.

In sum, it can be concluded that the proposed modification to the ICSID Convention is not appropriate in practice, and this applies because the ICSID is the most important institution to settle investment disputes and has its own enforcement method. The MIC is, however, a clear competitor. Linking the two conventions may therefore result in the loss of ICSID Convention members. And drafting an additional protocol to the ICSID Convention for the MIC may not be seen as an elegant approach.

The European Federation for Investment Law and Arbitration (EFILA) suggests that the ICSID Convention is the best option for the enforcement of MIC awards. However, if it does not work and the NYC is implied, the MIC should be considered as a public policy obstacle.

3.2.2 New York Convention

It is well known that non-ICSID awards need to be enforced under the NYC rules. It may not be appropriate to link the MIC to the ICSID Convention. Alternatively, awards made under a future standing mechanism are capable of being enforced under the NYC. But this still leaves a number of issues that include the term of the arbitral award under the convention, public policy issues, and the amendment of the NYC under the VCLT.

The first question is whether MIC awards can be enforced under the NYC. Richard Happ and Sebastian Wuschka refer to the CETA, TTIP proposal, and draft EU–Vietnam FTA, and state:

39 Reinisch (n 34) 765.

40 Yusuf Çalışkan and Ahmet Dülger, 'Time for the Appeal Tribunal in Investment Arbitration: Lessons from WTO' in Cigdem Nas and Mustafa Erkan (eds), *International Investment and Trade Agreements: Recent Developments and Problems* (Oniki levha 2021).

41 Reinisch (n 34) 765.

42 ibid.

> For the purposes of Article 1 of the New York Convention on the Recognition and Enforcement of Foreign Arbitral Awards, final awards issued pursuant to this Section shall be deemed to be arbitral awards and to relate to claims arising out of a commercial relationship or transaction.[43]

The NYC does not fall within the definition of an arbitral award.[44] However, it is important to note that this convention does give more consideration to the substance than the form, and this is important because its identification as a court judgment or arbitral award does not depend on its denomination.[45] The objective criterion for an arbitral award is if the arbitrators' final decision on (all or part of) a dispute that is submitted to them relates to a procedural or substantive issue.[46] Enforcement of awards rendered by 'permanent arbitral bodies' is also possible under NYC Article 1(2), which states '"arbitral awards" shall include not only awards made by arbitrators appointed for each case but also those made by permanent arbitral bodies to which the parties have submitted.'[47] This seems similar to the Permanent Court of International Justice (PCIJ) arbitral award definition. It is first crucial to establish what is meant by 'permanent arbitral bodies.' A well-known example is the US–Iran tribunal on this question. In this example, the US and Iran established a tribunal that would settle investment disputes between their nationals and the host state. The tribunal normally cannot be accepted as a permanent arbitral body, and this is because the Iran–US tribunal has historical importance that restores their relations. The US Ninth Circuit Court of Appeals also confirmed a California District Court's holding in *Iran v. Gould*, in which it stated that '[t]he Convention certainly is applicable to the claim here in that the Tribunal is a permanent arbitral body.'[48] And it did this by applying the NYC to enforce the tribunal. The Iran and US tribunal might be claimed to be a broad interpretation of 'permanent arbitral bodies.' Although permanent arbitral bodies should not be appointed in each dispute, it is not clear if the institution may appoint arbitrators.[49] Moreover, disputing parties should voluntarily consent to resolve the dispute before the MIC. While mutual consent is the fundamental feature of arbitration, it should be noted that its existence does not convert a court into a tribunal.[50]

Some scholars have, however, claimed that the MIC should be compared with the ICJ rather than the NYC because their forms are similar to each other.[51] But if the MIC is accepted as an ICJ form, the enforcement of its decisions is not effective and so the establishment of a court for investment does not make sense in practice. The purpose of the court proposal is to overcome the deficiencies of the current ISDS and so TTIPs use the

---

43 Happ and Wuschka (n 36).

44 In the history of the convention, the Australian delegate proposed that enforcing states should decide on the definition of the award. However, this would give states more power to manipulate decisions related to enforcement, and this is totally contrary to the aim of the convention.

45 Happ and Wuschka (n 36).

46 Reinmar Wolff (ed), *New York Convention: Convention on the Recognition and Enforcement of Foreign Arbitral Awards of 10 June 1958* (Beck/Hart 2012)1.

47 See <https://www.newyorkconvention.org/english> accessed 20 May 2021.

48 *US: Ministry of Def. of the Islamic Republic of Iran v. Gould, Inc.*, XIV Y.B. Com. Arb. 763, 766 (1989) (C.D. Cal. 1988); see also van den Berg, XVI Y.B. Com. Arb. 449, 450 (1991).

49 Submission of the European Union and its Member States to UNCITRAL Working Group III, 'Establishing a Standing Mechanism for the Settlement of International Investment Disputes' (18 January 2019) <http://trade.ec.europa.eu/doclib/docs/2019/january/tradoc_157631.pdf> accessed 30 May 2021.

50 Happ and Wuschka (n 36).

51 ibid.

term 'members of tribunal' rather than judges.[52] In the NYC article, examples of permanent arbitral bodies may be aligned with the ICC International Court of Arbitration, the Singapore International Arbitration Centre, or the Ukrainian Chambers of Commerce and Industry.[53] MIC decisions are not final, but it cannot be asserted that this means they more or less correspond to the arbitral award form. Finality is important for the enforcement of arbitral awards under the NYC.

The issue is public policy obstacles in the national courts. If the UNCITRAL does not clarify the MIC tribunal is the same as the NYC Article I(2), this might cause many public policy issues and non-compliance with MIC awards in national courts. Enforcing state courts might decide on the form of the MIC tribunal if there is no mutual definition of the permanent arbitral body.

Consider the approach of domestic courts. French courts do not enforce the awards if there is an inequality of tribunal selection and claim it is against public policy. In the MIC, investor does not have a chance to appoint an arbitrator. Traditional ISDS mechanisms enable the investor and the state party to appoint on a case-by-case basis. This contrasts with the ICS system, where court members (subject to strict independence and impartiality requirements) are appointed in advance by a joint committee of state parties to the treaty. The court decisions can then be appealed before an appeal body.[54] In parallel, the MIC appeal tribunal is pre-selected, and this raises the question of if the parties' first consent will cover the appeal tribunal.

Moreover, Article I(3) of the NYC establishes two reservations (reciprocity and commercial)[55] that can be adopted by member states that accede to the convention, and this could create problems for the enforcement of MIC awards. For example, it might restrict the scope of the convention, especially in the case of awards made in the territory of another contracting state (reciprocity) and commercial disputes.[56] But the scope of the commercial disputes was enlarged to encompass investment disputes covered by the (1985) UNCITRAL Model Law. In this circumstance, states may not be rejected for claiming commercial reservations.

The question of whether the MIC is a public or private entity has also been controversial. A number of authors have drawn parallels with the ICJ and European Court of Human Rights (ECtHR) to suggest that while a permanent investment tribunal would not be an institution of state justice, it would also not be a 'private' entity. Others refer to the IUSCT as a *sui generis* institution. One solution would be to give the MIC sufficient 'private' elements to enable it to be classified as an arbitral tribunal under the New York

52 ibid.

53 ibid.

54 Guillaume Croisant, 'Investment Court System' (*Jus Mundi* 18 June 2021) <https://jusmundi.com/en/document/wiki/eninvestmentcourtsystem?> accessed 1 August 2021. Another 'smaller' solution would be to establish a standalone multilateral investment appellate mechanism (MIAM). This would entail establishing a single-tier court system within a new independent international organisation. The organs of the MIAM would be identical to those of the MIC. This is particularly true of the judiciary and the plenary organ. The secretariat may however ultimately be smaller than the MIC. The applicable administrative and procedural law and the enforcement of MIAM decisions could correspond to the design proposed for the MIC. Bungenberg and Reinisch, *From Bilateral Arbitral Tribunals and Investment Courts to a Multilateral Investment Court* (n 35) 7.

55 For example, Turkey has two reservations: the reciprocity reservation and commercial reservation. See <https://newyorkconvention1958.org/index.php?lvl=cmspage&pageid=11&menu=852&opac_view=-1> accessed 8 May 2021.

56 Wolff (n 46) 13.

Convention. For example, a permanent judiciary might conflict with its characterisation as a private entity. But a list of specific candidates used in the judicial bench's election procedure could help to solve this problem. But in this instance, this element of arbitration overlaps with the fourth element, namely the arbitrators selected by the parties. The MIC is not likely to be a less private entity than the IUSCT, whose nature as a state or private institution has not been addressed during enforcement procedures under the NYC. In states that act in accordance with the NYC and enforce IUSCT decisions as arbitral awards, this element should not therefore create a problem. In general, it is the case that this third element cannot be evaluated independently, but should instead be clarified by referring to the overlap and elaboration of the other elements.[57]

Finally, the NYC can be amended so that it covers the MIC, which is in accordance with the VCLT. But an additional protocol may be drafted that removes the public policy exception for MIC member states. These options are the same as the ICSID proposal. But this is not an innovation in the current ISDS. It is also not easy to amend the whole convention to link the MIC, and on this basis it can be asserted that a new MIC statue may be more feasible and beneficial in terms of improving the current system. Although the EU considers the application of the NYC to be a short-term solution, the drawbacks of non-compliance will need to be taken into account, because enforcing states will decide if the MIC award is arbitral or if it is like the permanent arbitral bodies established by the NYC. While this may not create an obstacle for MIC member states in terms of enforcement, it is a big problem in third states. The best option may be a new, fresh, and different enforcement mechanism that remedies the current enforcement obstacles by drafting an MIC treaty. This might be a more attractive option for states that have more effective enforcement mechanisms that have greater legitimacy in the field. A phased enforcement regime of this kind would allow the MIC regime to enter into force as quickly as possible, with the greatest level of effectiveness, and would also offset the risk of any enforcement gaps. The working group should consider the risk of divergent approaches and interpretations in treaty obligations and, in so doing, should focus on public policy exceptions in particular.[58]

3.2.3 Creation of a new international convention

A closer consideration of the risks associated with applying the ICSID Convention and the NYC to MIC decisions would therefore appear to suggest the drafting of an additional protocol. But scholars and practitioners do not support this because they believe it will not be suitable. The best option seems to be a new treaty for the MIC that covers procedural and substantive rules. The new treaty would identify the organs of the MIC and their authorities, deadlines and dispute settlement proceedings, and this would in turn provide more clarity and transparency. This would enable parties to predict the court process and they can compare the court application and the classic arbitration when choosing their dispute settlement system. When an international court or institution is established, a treaty should be drafted by the offerors. There are many examples, including the ICJ of

57 Reinisch (n 34) 769.

58 Alvarez, Bhatty, Lavranos, and Leventhal (n 13).

the United Nations, , the ECtHR of the European Convention of Human Rights, and the ICSID from the Washington Convention.[59]

A new treaty also ensures there is a more independent and objective court system for investment disputes, and this is because the treaty covers the immunities of judges, ensures equal financial treatment, establishes the framework of their power, and provides transparency. In this field, transparency is of fundamental importance because of the role and significance of foreign investment. Judges may feel more independent because their rights and authority would be in the treaty; and staff rights and liabilities would also be in the statute. The United Nations Convention on Privileges and Immunities might also provide a model for judicial immunity in the MIC statute.[60]

When considered as an international organisation, the MIC would have a legal personality in both international and national law. This would give the court immunity from jurisdiction, and so the national courts cannot claim jurisdiction because states would already waive their jurisdiction by signing the MIC treaty.

One of the most important points is to select the permanent seat of the court. The seat of the court is generally where the secretariat works and the plenary body meets, and it would be decided in the treaty. But it should not be considered as just one seat of the MIC. If the treaty is more accepted at the international level, there can be several seats. It can also be linked with existing international organisations such as the WTO in Geneva.[61] When deciding the seat of the MIC, the court should try to access a large number of members, the court should pay attention to the members' geographical distance, and take their economic and security concerns into account. This will enable the MIC to work more effectively.[62] Bungenberg and Reinisch observe:

> The MIC Statute, which could already incorporate immunity rules, should therefore be supplemented with further seat and immunity agreements that are concluded with, *inter alia*, the MIC host state.[63] It should also be determined in relation to the seat – the President of the Court could, for example, be required to live at the seat of the MIC.[64]

Finally, enforcement of the MIC mechanism is the central pillar. It has already been noted that the emphasis is on using the ICSID enforcement mechanism by amending the ICSID Convention. If this is not done, the NYC would be the second option for the MIC. But they may be both partial and temporary. Borlini and Silingardi observe:

> Doubts about the compatibility of the MIC decisions with the ICSID Convention and the NYC clearly demonstrate they are no longer fully sufficient for the field. The international commercial and FDI realms have developed exponentially over the past few years as a result of a series of unexpected and sudden challenges, and this means that only a rapid change in the conventions may secure their survival in the investment dispute area.[65]

59 Bungenberg and Reinisch, *From Bilateral Arbitral Tribunals and investment Courts to a Multilateral Investment Court* (n 35) 179.

60 ibid.

61 ibid.

62 ibid.

63 ibid.

64 ibid.

65 Leonardo S Borlini and Stefano Siligardi, 'Enforcement of Investment Arbitration Awards' (2020) Bocconi Legal Studies Research Paper 3730569.

In parallel, the MIC uses its own enforcement mechanism to attack the ICSID and NYC. Its enforcement mechanism should be more effective than others, and so drafters should consider the shortcomings of existing mechanisms and arrange the new one accordingly. Scholars and practitioners have put forward a number of recommendations for the MIC's enforcement article.

These include Article 56 (Enforcement within MIC members).[66] The draft article is very similar to the ICSID Convention, which may provide insight into why parties apply to the MIC rather than the ICSID. If the answer is only the ICSID's lack of legitimacy, then it should be remembered there are many concerns with the MIC, and repoliticisation of the ISDS in particular. While considered from this perspective, both dispute settlement mechanisms seem equal, which raises the question of why the MIC is needed in practice. The MIC can only be a competitor to the ICSID in this regard. Repoliticisation may therefore lead states to withdraw from the ICSID because states have criticised the current ISDS, which is assumed to favour investors. The beginning of the MIC therefore marks the end of the ICSID.

With the exception of the ICSID Convention, the MIC may cover the enforcement mechanism in non-member third states. It is crucial because the assets of states or investors are not just located in one territory. The winning party may seek the failing party's assets in third countries, and the MIC may expedite the enforcement process.

3.3 Potential risk for enforcement of MIC awards in third states

With regard to third states that are not MIC members, the situation is increasingly complicated. Here it should be remembered that investors usually seek the assets of the host states in third states if the state does not voluntarily comply with the award. The third state therefore applies its municipal law to enforce the arbitral award. In this circumstance, the third state should determine the award, and should establish if enforcement is an arbitral award or a judgment decision by referring to its national law. The kind of enforcement methods can then be used. If the third state does not assume an arbitral award, the court of the third state can use its own recognition and enforcement proceedings to ensure it has effect in its territory. This means the award may tackle the public policy obstacle or any other national

66 Article 58 of the Draft MIC Statute:

> Each Member of the MIC shall recognise a decision rendered pursuant to this Statute as binding and enforce the pecuniary obligations imposed by that decision within its territories as if it were a final judgment of a court in that State or international entity. A Member of the MIC with a federal constitution may choose to enforce such a decision in or through its federal courts and may provide that such courts shall treat the decision as if it were a final judgment of the courts of a constituent State or international entity. A party seeking recognition or enforcement in the territories of a Member of the MIC shall furnish to a competent court or other authority which such Member shall have designated for this purpose a copy of the decision certified by the Director-General. Each Member of the MIC shall notify the Director-General of the designation of the competent court or other authority for this purpose and of any subsequent change in such designation. Execution of a decision shall be governed by the laws concerning the execution of judgments in force in the State in whose territories such execution is sought. Third States which are not Parties to this Statute may commit themselves to recognise and enforce decisions rendered by the MIC in accordance with the rules set out in this Statute. The declaration of commitment may be made at any time to the Secretariat of the MIC.

Marc Bungenberg and August Reinisch, 'Draft Statute of the Multilateral Investment Court' (November 2020) <https://uncitral.un.org/sites/uncitral.un.org/files/mediadocuments/uncitral/en/bungenberg_reinisch_draft_statute_of_the_mic.pdf> accessed 30 August 2021.

borders in practice. This is because there is no mutual frame of public policy and each state is able to interpret the term itself. Chapter 2 notes that states approach public policy on a national rather than international basis, and suggests that this may result in unfair treatment in the field. Investors will not only seek the assets, but will also seek to identify the state's public policy approach to the international decision. And their lawyers or consultants will also work hard to find a state that is available to receive the financial award.

The decision on the MIC's final awards will be assumed to be an arbitral award, and so will be enforced under the NYC. It will also always be linked to the power of the national courts where enforcement is sought.[67] The preceding discussion of the ICSID Convention also demonstrates that, in accordance with Article 34 of the VCLT, the CETA, TTIP proposal, and draft EU–Vietnam FTA cannot bind any non-member states. Although the NYC or ICSID Convention might be applied by using the VCLT for member states, Article 57 of the draft MIC statute enables enforcement in non-MIC members:

> The enforcement of MIC decisions in non-MIC Members will be governed by a separate treaty. The MIC Members are working towards the creation of such a treaty and are seeking to encourage the accession of third parties to that treaty in their international relations.[68]

With regard to accessing the rest of the world, the drafting of a separate treaty may sound like a good option, but it should be asked which states will benefit from being members. This is important because any state that becomes a member will waive or restrict its sovereignty. It would not be elegant or beneficial to draft two different treaties so they have a strong enforcement mechanism.

When two different treaties have an effective enforcement mechanism, it might be more beneficial to use a fund system under the MIC statute. This has already been considered in ICSID disputes, but it has not been put into effect because of the many drawbacks that are discussed in the next chapter. But the MIC can use the mechanism and so it does not have to seek enforcement in third states. Also, when third states agree to sign the separate treaty, they may find the award conflicts with their sovereignty and national law. The fund system can resolve the enforcement issue at the beginning of the dispute.

3.3.1 An alternative approach: Fund system of the MIC

The fund system seems a practical way to receive award compensation for the parties, and foreign investors in particular. And this is because the system allows the winning party to demand compensation from the MIC in certain conditions. The court then has recourse to the respondent state. The fund will obtain money from the contracting states of the MIC statute, which will be held as a deposit before the disputes. The winning party will not have to seek enforcement in third states or infringe on the sovereignty of respondent states. This fund system is similar to the IUSCT approach because Iranian assets in a US bank (about US$1 billion) were transferred to a 'security account' at the time of the Iranian hostage crisis.[69] The compensation was paid from the account and additional pay-

67 Happ and Wuschka (n 36).

68 Bungenberg and Reinisch, 'Draft Statute of the Multilateral Investment Court' (n 66).

69 Bungenberg and Holzer (n 4). Charles Nelson Brower and Jason D. Brueschke, *The Iran-United States Claims Tribunal* (Martinus Nijhoff Publishers 1998) 1. Bungenberg and Reinisch, *From Bilateral Arbitral Tribunals and Investment Courts to a Multilateral Investment Court* (n 35).

ment was requested from Iran. The fund system is more effective than other proposals, including establishing a link to the ICSID and the NYC. In this circumstance the question arises of if the fund mechanism should be included in the MIC as an organ or should instead be an independent organisation. If the latter is accepted, a new statute should be drafted or the general approach of a subsidiary secretariat can be established.[70] The secretariat should of course be financially independent, and this will help the enforcement system to be more neutral and objective. The provision of adequate funds could also be a problem because investment awards are generally high-cost:[71] if several respondent states do not voluntarily comply with the MIC decisions, then this question asserts itself even more strongly. It may also be unclear if the fund will pay in accordance with the decision date or the first application for payment. And it may also be linked to an existing international organisation, such as the Multilateral Investment Guarantee Agency (MIGA), the International Monetary Fund (IMF), or WTO. The MIGA was established in 1988, with the aim of promoting FDI into developing countries, supporting economic growth, reducing poverty, and improving people's lives. MIGA upholds its mandate by providing political risk insurance (guarantees) to investors and lenders.

MIGA provides dispute resolution services for guaranteed investment, and thereby prevents disruption to projects that benefit development.[72] MIGA insures FDI against losses incurred as a result of various factors (currency inconvertibility, transfer restrictions, expropriation, war, civil disturbance, terrorism and sabotage) and it also encompasses breaches of contract and the non-honouring of financial obligations. Article 18(a) of the MIGA Convention establishes:

> [I]f the MIGA pays compensation to the holder of the guarantee with this payment, the original claim against the host country is transferred from him/her to the MIGA. Article 18(a) of the MIGA Convention therefore provides for an automatic subrogation. An automatic subrogation should also be included in the MIC Statute, in case the Fund satisfies an investor's claim.[73]

But this remedy also raises several issues in practice.[74] It should also be recognised that the MIC cannot be accessed all over the world because there are developing and undeveloped states that cannot afford the fund, and so are not members of the statute. This might also be viewed as a violation of the right to fair trial: if you have insufficient money to afford the fund, you will not be able to bring your dispute before the MIC.

In the case of the IMF or World Bank, it should be remembered that activating the world bank in order to guarantee the enforcement of the MIC awards, the related articles must be amended accordingly . Article III, and specifically its assertion that 'the resources … of the Bank shall be used exclusively for the benefit of members,' appears to be foremost in

70 Bungenberg and Holzer (n 4). Bungenberg and Reinisch, *From Bilateral Arbitral Tribunals and Investment Courts to a Multilateral Investment Court* (n 35).

71 Bungenberg and Holzer (n 4) 100. 'According to the statistics issued by the UNCTAD, in 2017, an average of 28% of the amount originally claimed was awarded to successful plaintiffs. With an average amount claimed of approximately $454 million, the statistic shows an average amount awarded of about $125 million.'

72 See <https://www.miga.org/Documents/Dispute_Resolution_and_Claims.pdf> accessed 26 May 2021.

73 Bungenberg and Holzer (n 4).

74 ibid.

this respect.[75] It should also be noted that losing party states may view bank enforcement as an infringement of this obligation.[76]

It could also be considered if it is worthwhile to grant all WTO members the right to suspend concessions or collect duties/tariffs on imports that originate in the respondent state that is unwilling to pay. This would of course have a particularly strong effect on private enterprises in the respective state, and this raises the question of if an approach of this kind could be limited to state-owned enterprises.[77] Article 58 (Enforcement Fund) is the draft article that refers to the fund system.[78]

If the fund system provides an effective remedy for all enforcement mechanisms and the MIC uses it, it will become increasingly attractive.

3.4 Evaluating the significance of the MIC in practice

Despite the aforementioned institutional and procedural innovations, the ICS has been criticised by various scholars and practitioners. This section considers some of these criticisms in more detail. The establishment of an independent investment court is still discussed in the field and is criticised as a throwback. After World War II, states waived their sovereignty by signing the BIT with the intention of attacking FDI. They would then have brought their investment disputes before arbitral tribunals rather than their national courts. But over time, this ISDS failed to meet the need of host states for legitimacy, and the system changed into one that favoured foreign investors. Accordingly, many states brought a number of disputes before the ICSID and they started to withdraw their BITs. Finally, the establishment of a permanent court also raises the fundamental risk of repoliticisation. Here it is important to acknowledge a new trend in investment courts that mixes arbitration and adjudication. Although the EU is willing to establish a new system, a considerable number of states and actors are less enthusiastic. Some suggest judges appointed to the MIC could be politically biased, and raise the concern this could discourage investors and negatively impact the development of investments.[79] States including Chile, Japan, Russia, and the United States also oppose systemic reform and would prefer to fix the current defaults of ISDS.[80] The UNCITRAL Working Group has therefore

75 Joseph M Cardosi, 'Precluding the Treasure Hunt: How the World Bank Group Can Help Investors Circumnavigate Sovereign Immunity Obstacles to ICSID Award Execution' (2014) 41 Pepperdine Law Review 3.

76 ibid 152.

77 Bungenberg and Holzer (n 4).

78 Bungenberg and Reinisch, 'Draft Statute of the Multilateral Investment Court' (n 66). Article 58:

> A fund for the enforcement of MIC decisions ('the Fund') is hereby established. The Fund shall be governed by administrative regulations to be adopted by the Plenary Body. Upon accession to the MIC, MIC Members are obliged to contribute to the Fund. The minimum contribution will be determined by the Plenary Body. In accordance with the administrative regulations governing the Fund, the Fund shall satisfy an MIC Member's obligation under an MIC decision by payment to a successful claimant up to a sum of XXX USD per case upon request, if the claimant can demonstrate need for urgency of immediate payment of an awarded sum. Upon satisfying or agreeing to satisfy a Member's obligation under an MIC decision by payment to the benefitting claimant, the MIC shall be subrogated to such rights or claims related to the respective decision as the holder of the decision may have had against the Member and other obligors. The subrogation shall be effected in the form of assignment.

79 Dietz, Dotzauer, and Cohen (n 1). Croisant (n 54).

80 Croisant (n 54).

considered different remedies, including the creation of a multilateral advisory centre and the establishment of a standalone review mechanism.[81]

The MIC has sought to tackle the problems associated with the lack of impartiality in the system by preventing parties from participating in the appointment of the panel that will oversee their case. But this actually results in the opposite of what it is trying to achieve (depoliticisation). The random composition of judges who hear the case does not only remove the chance of parties to appoint a neutral tribunal but also enables a politically orientated organ to assume control of the selection process under the (dis)guise of impartiality.[82]

The risk of repoliticisation is not confined to the first step, but also extends to the appeal stage ('[t]here is concern that host state governments are likely to appeal every case lost at first instance, in order to gain favour with their constituents').[83] There is also a concern that the political agenda of governments would lead them to appeal. Supporters of the proposal have sought to address this by demanding securities as a form of deposit or bond. This would then make it possible to access the appeal facility.

When considering the party autonomy of international arbitration, the new court system will probably remove the interests of the parties. However, it is only the investor party that would lose the right to appoint the arbitrator who will help to resolve the dispute. This is because the opposing party (the host state) already has selected a judge in the court system, although he/she cannot settle the dispute. Although a greater level of legitimacy may be provided, balance may be removed.

When considered from the perspective of state parties, the geographical composition of judges also presents a clear challenge to a fair dispute settlement system. State parties have limited autonomy because there are not many full-time judges. Making the court system more fair and representative (and not dominated by the EU) may be viewed as a matter of primary importance.[84] Although it might be claimed to be fair for both parties, this is not the case. Here it could be asked: 'If the concern was that private business lawyers serving as arbitrators have a natural bias towards enterprises, could government-appointed judges not also be suspected of having a natural bias towards the state, in particular their own?'[85] Asking if the MIC award is arbitral is meaningless because when the party loses autonomy, the system will not permit an arbitration proceeding.

The shortcomings of the current ISDS have not been fixed and a new court has instead been proposed. When considered in detail, this means that the current mechanisms are not satisfied but they still exist. Foreign investors may therefore be subject to pressure from host states that will force them to settle the future dispute before the MIC in preference to arbitration. And arbitration and the ICSID in particular may no longer affect dispute resolution. States also may no longer have a good reason to be a member of the ICSID Convention.

Finally, it should be first recognised that the MIC enforcement mechanism should be different from its predecessors. However, in all other respects, it is better to fix the current

81 ibid.
82 Charris-Benedetti (n 27).
83 ibid.
84 Ning and Qi (n 23).
85 Charris-Benedetti (n 27).

ISDS than establish a new one. The MIC will not bring the new enforcement mechanism and will instead use the existing one, and so this approach makes sense for the enforcement of an arbitral award. However, there are problems: first, it is another burden on the enforcement of the award in third states. Second, the MIC causes the problem of repoliticisation, which arises in its proposal to overcome the legitimacy crisis of the current ISDS by establishing an appeal body. Foreign investors will not therefore voluntarily comply with the MIC awards because of the repoliticisation effect. This will probably result in repetition in the ISDS.

3.5 Conclusion

Negotiations that seek to establish an MIC occurred within Working Group III of the 40th session of UNCITRAL (Investor–State Dispute Settlement Reform), which was held in Vienna on 4–5 May 2021. In these proceedings, it was identified that the establishment of an international investment court was one of the options for reforming ISDS. However, this raised a number of issues, including regulatory chill, the exhaustion of local remedies and enforcement, costs and allocations, and the immunity of respondent states against enforcement.[86]

Of these, the enforcement of decisions across the globe emerged as the most important one. The EU and supporters of the MIC have complained the current system lacks legitimacy, and it is probable that the proposed court system will reach the same conclusion. This applies because MIC judges may feel the responsibility of their states weighing down on them, and they will act accordingly. And if this comes to pass, the new system will favour respondent states rather than foreign investors.

Repoliticisation is the largest potential problem of the proposed court, and if judgments are dominated by the states, the investor will frequently be the victim. This is also the exact opposite of what the arbitration method tries to achieve. The enforcement of the MIC's decisions is also problematic. All the proposed reforms are based on the ICSID Convention, and a state sovereignty issue therefore also arises in the execution of these decisions. And related reforms are therefore small in number. This raises the question of how this situation can be addressed and overcome. This chapter suggests that making the existing ISDS more legitimate can help to achieve this, in a way that does not result in a loss of balance. If this is not done, there are good grounds for believing that it will not be an effective court in the future.

It cannot be denied that the current ISDS has several shortcomings, including legitimacy. However, it is not necessary to establish a new system that is relatively similar. The MIC adopts enforcement rules from existing conventions, and this raises the question of why the field requires it. Indeed, the only difference is that party autonomy (especially of investors and the appellate body) is removed.

In addition, the ICSID debates currently envisage that the appeal body will include a system that addresses claims about a lack of legitimacy. The institution has tried to update itself in response to the demands of the parties. The ICSID mechanism is well-known

86 See <https://uncitral.un.org/sites/uncitral.un.org/files/letter_from_chair_of_wg_iii_-_resumed_40th_session_12_april.pdf> accessed 3 August 2021.

and established, and so it might be best to fix the current system and continue with it.[87] If states agree to establish an MIC to replace ICSID Convention arbitration, then the question of what institutional role the ICSID should fulfil arises, especially in disputes related to investment treaties.

Bibliography

Alvarez G, Bhatty S, Lavranos N, and Leventhal A, 'Ensuring the Effective Recognition and Enforcement of MIC Decisions To The UNCITRAL Working Group No. III on ISDS Reforms' (2020) *EFILA* <https://uncitral.un.org/sites/uncitral.un.org/files/mediadocuments/uncitral/en/efila_submission_to_uncitral_wg_iii.pdf> accessed 25 June 2021

Borlini L S and Siligardi S, 'Enforcement of Investment Arbitration Awards' (2020) Bocconi Legal Studies Research Paper 3730569

Briefing European Parliamentary Research Service, From Arbitration to Investment Court System: The Evolution of CETA Rules (June 2017). <https://www.europarl.europa.eu/RegData/etudes/IDAN/2017/607251/EPRS_IDA(2017)607251_EN.pdf> accessed 25 June 2021

Brower C N and Brueschke J D, *The Iran-United States Claims Tribunal* (Martinus Nijhoff Publishers 1998) 1.

Bungenberg M and Holzer A M, 'Potential Enforcement Mechanisms for Decisions of a Multilateral Investment Court' in Gunes Unuvar, Joanna Lam, Shai Dothan (eds), *Permanent Investment Courts: The European Experiment* (Springer 2020) 75–117.

Bungenberg M and Reinisch A, *From Bilateral Arbitral Tribunals and Investment Courts to a Multilateral Investment Court: Options Regarding the Institutionalization of Investor-state Dispute Settlement* (Springer Nature 2020).

Bungenberg M and Reinisch A, 'Draft Statute of the Multilateral Investment Court' (November 2020) <https://uncitral.un.org/sites/uncitral.un.org/files/mediadocuments/uncitral/en/bungenberg_reinisch_draft_statute_of_the_mic.pdf> accessed 30 August 2021

Calamita N J, 'The Challenge of Establishing a Multilateral Investment Tribunal at ICSID' (2017) 32 *ICSID Review* 611–624.

Cardosi J M, 'Precluding the Treasure Hunt: How the World Bank Group Can Help Investors Circumnavigate Sovereign Immunity Obstacles to ICSID Award Execution' (2014) 41 Pepp. L. Rev. 3.

Charris-Benedetti P J, 'The Proposed Investment Court System: Does It Really Solve The Problems?' (2019) 42 *Revista Derecho del Estado* 83–115.

Croisant G, 'Investment Court System' (*Jus Mundi*, 18 June 2021) <https://jusmundi.com/en/document/wiki/eninvestmentcourtsystem?> accessed 1 August 2021

Çalışkan Y and Dülger A, 'Time for the Appeal Tribunal in Investment Arbitration: Lessons from WTO' in Cigdem Nas and Mustafa Erkan (eds), *International Investment and Trade Agreements: Recent Developments and Problems* (Oniki levha 2021).

Dietz T, Dotzauer M, and Cohen E S, 'The Legitimacy Crisis of Investor-state Arbitration and the New EU Investment Court System' (2019) 26 *Rev. Int. Political Econ* 749–772.

Douma W, 'Investor-state Arbitration in the Light of EU Policy and Law after the Lisbon Treaty' (The Hague, The Netherlands, 16 April 2017).

Fanou M, 'The Independence and Impartiality of the Hybrid CETA Investment Court System: Reflections in the Aftermath of Opinion 1/17' (2020) 4 *Europe and the World: A Law Review* 1.

87 N Jansen Calamita, 'The Challenge of Establishing a Multilateral Investment Tribunal at ICSID' (2017) 32 ICSID Review–Foreign Investment Law Journal 611–24.

<https://ucl.scienceopen.com/hosted-document?doi=10.14324/111.444.ewlj.2020.26> accessed 7 May 2021

Happ R and Wuschka S, 'From the Jay Treaty Commissions towards a Multilateral Investment Court: Addressing the Enforcement Dilemma' (2017) 6 *Indian J Arb L* 113.

Hoffmann R T, 'The Multilateral Investment Court: A Stumbling Block for Comprehensive and Sustainable Investment Law Reform' (2018) *ESIL* 1. <https://papers.ssrn.com/sol3/papers.cfm?abstract_id=3363926> accessed 10 July 2021

Horn N and Kröll S, *Arbitrating Foreign Investment Disputes* (KIL 2004) 1.

Lenk H, 'An Investment Court System for the New Generation of EU Trade and Investment Agreements: A Discussion of the Free Trade Agreement with Vietnam and the Comprehensive Economic and Trade Agreement with Canada, <http://www.europeanpapers.eu/en/system/files/pdf_version/EP_EF_2016_I_033_Hannes_Lenk. pdf> accessed 14 November 2017

MIGA <https://www.miga.org/Documents/Dispute_Resolution_and_Claims.pdf> accessed 26 May 2021

Ning H and Qi T, 'Multilateral Investment Court: The Gap Between the EU and China' (2018) 4 *CJGG* 154–175.

Poulsen L, *Bounded Rationality and Economic Diplomacy: The Politics of Investment Treaties in Developing Countries* (CUP, 2015)

Reinisch A, 'The European Union and Investor-State Dispute Settlement: From Investor-State Arbitration To A Permanent Investment Court' (2016) 2 *CIGI* 1.

Reinisch A, 'Will the EU's Proposal Concerning an Investment Court System for CETA and TTIP Lead to Enforceable Awards?—The Limits of Modifying the ICSID Convention and the Nature of Investment Arbitration' (2016) 19 *J. Int. Econ. Law* 761.

Submission of the European Union and its Member States to UNCITRAL Working Group III, Establishing a Standing Mechanism for the Settlement of International Investment Disputes (18 January 2019) http://trade.ec.europa.eu/doclib/docs/2019/january/tradoc_157631.pdf accessed 30 May 2021

UNCITRAL Working Group <https://uncitral.un.org/en/working_groups/3/investor-state> accessed 10 August 2021

UNCITRAL <https://uncitral.un.org/sites/uncitral.un.org/files/letter_from_chair_of_wg_iii__resumed_40th_session_12_april.pdf> accessed 3 August 2021

Unuvar G, 'Reforming Investor-State Dispute Settlement: Reflections on the UNCITRAL Working Group III and Beyond' (2019) *Turkish Law Blog* 9 May 2019. <https://turkishlawblog.com/read/article/120/reforming-investor-state-dispute-settlement-reflections-on-the-uncitral-working-group-iii-and-beyond> accessed 14 June 2021

Wollf R (ed), 'New York Convention: Convention on the Recognition and Enforcement of Foreign Arbitral Awards of 10 June 1958' New York Convention, Convention on the Recognition and Enforcement of Foreign Arbitral Awards of. Vol. 10. 1958.

CHAPTER 4

Practical remedies to reduce execution issues in the investment dispute settlement system

4.1 Introduction

'If it ain't broke, don't fix it' often is very good advice.[1]

It should be initially recognised that investment treaty arbitration was not created as a universal solution for business disputes in foreign countries.[2] The dispute resolution mechanism has been used to depoliticise disputes and provide an independent, impartial judgment at the interstate level. Investment treaty arbitration is not only intended to create an objective platform to settle disputes; it also aims at facilitating the enforcement of arbitral awards in multiple jurisdictions.[3] Upon this basis, it can be inferred that investment treaty arbitration has not become completely detached from domestic laws. To put it slightly differently, it is not a supranational legal system.

The International Centre for Settlement of Investment Disputes (ICSID) mechanism established an innovative path by creating a system insulated from municipal laws and courts involvement, putting in place an utterly self-contained treaty which established obligations involving the commencement of arbitration and conciliation proceedings,[4] provisions governing the procedure, possible post-award remedies, and provisions on recognition and enforcement. The main purpose of this mechanism was to establish a balance between the rights and obligations of states and foreign investors, while putting in place the rights and obligations of a state party to the conflict relative to other member states of ICSID.[5] There is no possibility of reviewing the recognition and enforcement of its enforceability. The technique for the enforcement of arbitral awards can be traced back to Article 192 of the Treaty of Rome, the legal foundation of the European Economic Community (EEC), which establishes the foundation for the enforcement of the decisions of the EEC Commission, thus imposing a pecuniary obligation on non-state parties.[6] However, the next stage of the execution process is governed by the law of the state where execution is sought, specifically its laws on immunity from execution. At the

1 O Thomas Johnson and Catherine H Gibson, 'The Objections of Developed and Developing States to Investor-State Dispute Settlement, and What They Are Doing about Them' in Arthur W Rovine (ed) *Contemporary Issues in International Arbitration and Mediation* (Chapter 14/Fordham Papers 2013) 251–69. See <http://booksandjournals.brillonline.com/content/books/b9789004274945_016> accessed 17 October 2016.

2 ibid.

3 Graham Coop, Alvaro Nistal, Robert G Volterra, and Volterra Fietta, 'Sovereign Immunities and Investor-State Awards: Specificities of Enforcing Awards Based on Investment Treaties' in Julien Fouret (ed) *Enforcement of Investment Treaty Arbitration Awards* (Globe Business Publishing Ltd. 2015) 1.

4 ibid.

5 Ruqiya B H Musa, Martina Polasek, and ICSID, 'The Origins and Specificities of the ICSID Enforcement Mechanism' in Fouret (n 3).

6 Treaty Establishing the European Economic Community, 25 March 1957, 298 UNTS 11, Article 192.

DOI: 10.4324/9781003216919-5

time when the ICSID Convention was drafted, there was no real concern about execution against the state—this was because the convention's drafting committee believed that state parties would voluntarily comply with the award.[7] As has already been noted, there was also an additional concern with regard to the imbalance between host states and foreign investors,[8] an imbalance which was particularly pronounced at the execution stage. Generally, execution was considered with reference to host states; execution against investors was considered to a much lesser extent. To put it differently, most investment treaties enable foreign investors to bring their claims before the international platform; conversely, they do not expressly permit reciprocal claims by the state against a foreign investor on the basis of applicable treaty provisions.[9] It is, however, generally possible to bring counterclaims against investors.

The New York Convention (NYC) relies upon the support of the member states, with a view to establishing a fully functional system for the enforcement of arbitral awards. The convention enables a national legislative framework to be established for this purpose, enabling contracting states to enact domestic legislation, with a view to giving effect to the rules and principles of the New York Convention.[10] The convention includes exceptions for the refusal of enforcement of foreign awards. As the previous chapter has noted, various jurisdictions have recognised that public policy is the most controversial exception in this respect. Even though the concept of state sovereignty is not clearly articulated in the convention, it is widely recognised that it is a bar to the honouring of arbitral awards.[11]

There has recently been a growing sense that investment awards are subject to challenge by national courts.[12] This phenomenon is not only confined to investment disputes arising under the ICSID Convention; it has also arisen in relation to non-ICSID states. Closer analysis reveals that investment treaty awards are subject to unwarranted challenges at the enforcement stage of awards. Even though statistics establish that there is no serious issue at this stage, it is reasonable to suggest that the effectiveness of investment treaty awards should be increased in practice and the limitation of award enforcement should be reduced. It has already been noted that Article 54(3) of the ICSID Convention establishes that the execution of an award is governed by the enforcing state. Article 55 clarifies that the convention did not seek to modify the laws of contracting states with respect to immunity from execution. As a result of this provision, the convention's Act of Ratification (which is widely viewed as a waiver of immunity from jurisdiction) cannot be interpreted to be a waiver of immunity from execution.[13] The presence of a defence of sovereign immunity has been criticised upon the basis that it weakens the enforcement system, with this feature being referred to as the 'Achilles heel of the Convention.'[14] The majority of respondent states have voluntarily compiled with adverse investment treaty arbitral

7 According to Choi, state immunity is a crucial issue in enforcing ICSID awards, given that two out of three ICSID awards have not been enforced because of immunity from execution. Susan Choi, 'Judicial Enforcement of Arbitration Awards under the ICSID and New York Conventions' (1995–6) 28 NYU J Intl Law & Pol 175.

8 Musa, Polasek, and ICSID (n 5) 16.

9 S R Subramanian, 'BITs and Pieces in International Investment Law: Enforcement of Investment Treaty Arbitration Awards in the Non-ICSID States: The Case of India' (2013) 14 JWIT 198–239.

10 ibid.

11 ibid.

12 ibid.

13 Musa, Polasek, and ICSID (n 5) 28.

14 ibid. Christoph H Schreuer, *The ICSID Convention: A Commentary* (CUP 2009) 1.

awards.[15] There are, however, cases in which a respondent state has failed to honour the award, and the claimant investor has initiated enforcement proceedings before the local courts of one or more countries where the state's assets are situated (forum shopping).[16] Recent cases (such as the *Sedelmayer* case,[17] and cases against Argentina/Kazakhstan and Russia) have reiterated this ongoing problem within investment arbitration.[18] The main international legal instruments that regulate the enforcement of arbitral awards explicitly require member states to be positively predisposed towards the effective enforcement of the awards in their jurisdictions. Meanwhile, sovereign immunity from execution remains an issue for national courts to decide.[19]

Historically, sovereign immunity has impeded the exercise of jurisdiction and execution against states. Over time, however, a trend has emerged in which national courts seek to exercise jurisdiction over states and execution against certain state assets. Despite this, the theory of restrictive sovereign immunity, in particular sovereign immunity from execution, has not yet been universally applied.[20] The United Nations Convention on Jurisdictional Immunities of States and Their Property (UNCSI), adopted in 2004,[21] was the first international legal instrument to issue the law on sovereign immunity—however, it has not yet entered into force. Sovereign immunity therefore persists as a significant consideration when identifying assets that may be seized with a view to complying with an arbitral award.

As a consequence, it is difficult to establish a clear picture of the effectiveness of the ICSID mechanism, with a view to establishing whether the recent instances of states deciding not to comply is only a 'micro-wave' or whether a tsunami is approaching in the aftermath of Argentina and a couple of other countries.[22] However, this issue has not received adequate attention in investor–state arbitration.[23] This is particularly important because the significance of the disadvantages and their effects should not be underestimated.

With a view to addressing this crisis and reducing execution issues, commentators have suggested various reforms, including the reduction of state immunity from execution. The suggestion that the system of reciprocal enforcement of award should be included within the convention draft ultimately foundered, with no conclusion being reached.[24] Other prac-

15 OECD, 'Public Consultation on Investor–State Dispute Settlement' (16 May–9 July 2012) paras 62–75.

16 Coop, Nistal, Volterra, and Fietta (n 3) 69.

17 As touched on in Chapter 2, Sedelmayer reportedly attempted to enforce a non-ICSID award against Russia for 16 years in over 80 sets of legal enforcement proceedings in several different states such as Germany and Sweden, with only limited success. Nytt Juridiskt Arkiv [NJA] [Supreme Court] 2011-07-01 Ö 170-10 (Swed.) (*Sedelmayer v. Russian Federation*) (unofficial translation), available at <http://www.arbitration.sccinstitute.com/Views/Pages/GetFile.ashx?portalId=89&cat=95788&docId=1081823&propId=1578> accessed 13 July 2015.

18 Coop, Nistal, Volterra, and Fietta (n 3) 69.

19 ibid 73.

20 ibid 74. For example, the Hong Kong Court of Final Appeal emphasised that absolute sovereign immunity applies in the Hong Kong Special Administrative Region. *Democratic Republic of the Congo v. FG Hemisphere Associates* [2011] HKCFAR 41.

21 United Nations Convention on Jurisdictional Immunities of States and Their Property, adopted in New York, 2 December 2004, UN Doc A /59/508, Annex (not yet in force).

22 Anna Joubin-Bret and Cabinet Joubin-Bret, 'The Effectiveness of the ICSID Mechanism Regarding the Enforcement of Arbitral Awards' in Fouret (n 3) 99–113.

23 Subramanian (n 9) 198–239.

24 'At the African Regional Meeting held in December 1963, delegates discussed the possible conflict between the enforcement provision of the convention and internal laws and other international treaties. One delegate recalled that another draft provision required each contracting state to declare that it had "taken all

tical solutions have also been proposed—these include redrafting the sovereignty acts, cutting World Bank benefits[25] for failing states, and suspending World Trade Organization (WTO) concessions. It has also been suggested that the ICSID could play an active role by refusing the failing party's next ICSID application. This raises the question of what kind of barriers will be faced. It also highlights the issue of the process through which investors can reduce the effectiveness of state sovereignty at the execution stage. In addition, it raises the question of how the winning state will receive payments derived from the arbitration process.

The primary objective of this book is to examine how the execution of the ICSID awards can be practically facilitated. Up until now, the primary obstacles that impede the enforcement of ICSID awards have been examined from two angles, specifically the failure of the state and the failure of the investor. In this chapter, the advantages and disadvantages of specific practical proposals will be analysed in more depth, with specific attention to their advantages and disadvantages. In addition, this chapter will also evaluate whether the ICSID can play a more active role. One possibility in this respect is that the ICSID Administrative Council could review award compliance, focusing in particular upon nationals of the member states that have not paid awards, possibly with a view to preventing them from bringing new claims against other states. These possibilities will be examined with reference to both advantages and disadvantages and also the illustrated treatment by the enforcement mechanism. It will be suggested that solutions suggested to date have not been assimilated into the ICSID system because they potentially threaten the underpinning principle of depoliticisation. This raises the question of how reform can be engendered without inflicting harm upon the ICSID's foundational principle. If it is possible to introduce a political angle, then this course of action may well inspire future reforms. If this proves not to be the case, the law of countermeasures [as exemplified in Article 27 of the ICSID Convention, the 2001 International Law Commission's (ILC's) Articles on State Responsibility, and Article 60 of the Vienna Convention on the Law of Treaties] may provide a more sustainable alternative.

4.2 The general progress of enforcement of an international arbitral award

If an international arbitral award is to be executed in a state, several prerequisites need to be met by the state's national courts. These include recognition and enforcement that is governed by national law. Once recognition is in place, the award can be applied in the territories. The difference between the recognition and enforcement stages is that each foreign award must be recognised before the enforcement stage, however, it does not have to be enforced after recognition of the award. This may be further conceptualised with reference to the following example:

steps necessary to enable it to carry out all of its obligations under the convention," allowing the reciprocal enforcement of awards in all contracting states, without possibility of challenging the award (subject to the doctrine of immunity from execution). No conclusion was reached on the issue. The first tentative draft of the ICSID Convention, the working paper in the form of a draft convention was drawn up in 1962.' See History of the ICSID Convention: Documents Concerning the Origin and Formulation of the Convention, Vol. II (1968).

25 'An investor holding an unpaid ICSID award may attempt to convince its home state to try to put pressure on the non-compliant state at the World Bank, such as in the form of suspension of loans to that state.' Edward Baldwin, Mark Kantor, and Michael Nolan, 'Limits to Enforcement of ICSID Awards' (2006) 23 J Intl Arb 1.

> A brings arbitration against B for a sum of money and A loses. A then brings court proceedings against B seeking payment. B is entitled to argue (in front of an English court) that there is a binding award and that A's claim should be dismissed. B is therefore asking the English court to recognise the award, not to enforce it.

The principle of state sovereignty underpins each of the respective stages. States do not accept to enforce any foreign awards (whether rendered by other state's courts or international tribunals) in the absence of a review by their own national court. This is because, during any forced enforcement proceedings,[26] the state will pay its debts without being required to do so. If this was not the case, there would be a clear breach of state sovereignty. The majority of states have a similar process in place with regard to the enforcement of international arbitral awards. With a view to illustrating this point, this chapter will now consider the Turkish provisions for ICSID, the New York Convention, and enforcement provisions within investment treaty arbitration.

4.2.1 The Republic of Turkey

Turkey is a member of a number of international agreements that concern the recognition and enforcement of foreign arbitral awards—the ICSID Convention and New York Convention are just two prominent examples in this respect.[27] It should also be noted that Turkey adopted the reciprocity reservation of the New York Convention [see Article I(3)] when signing it. The reservation restricts the Turkish application of the convention to the recognition and enforcement of arbitral awards made within the territory of another state party.[28] If the awards do not fall within the convention, they can be enforced through the Turkish International Private and Procedural Code (hereafter TIPPIC), whose provisions are similar to the convention. It should be noted that Article V of the New York Convention establishes that the enforcement may be refused where grounds for the refusal of enforcement exists; Article 62 of the Turkish Private International Law Act 2007 further reiterates that the court should deny enforcement in this instance.[29] In addition, Turkey has also adopted the commercial reservation under Article I(3) of the New York Convention. In other words, the convention is only applicable to the disputes that Turkish law deems to be 'commercial.'[30] Turkish courts cannot extend their jurisdictional authority when recognition or execution of arbitral awards is sought; similarly, it is not possible to revise tribunal awards, and the court's examination is limited to the determination of whether the award meets the requirements for recognition and enforcement.[31] In state practice, the General Assembly of the Court of Appeals has recently clarified that 'public policy is the entire set of rules and institutions, which determines the foundation structure and protects the

26 Ziya Akinci, 'Turkey' in Fouret (n 3) 455–68.

27 ibid 460.

28 The Turkish Supreme Court has approved that the convention applies only to any awards made within the territory of a state that is party to the convention.

29 Bennar Balkaya, 'IBA Recognition and Enforcement of Arbitral Awards—Study on Public Policy' (2015) <http://www.ibanet.org/LPD/Dispute_Resolution_Section/Arbitration/Recogntn_Enfrcemnt_Arbitl_Awrd/publicpolicy15.aspx> Turkey part, accessed 17 February 2016.

30 ibid.

31 Akinci (n 26) 460.

fundamental interests of the society from the political, social, economic, ethical and legal perspectives within a specific period of time.'[32]

In a further decision pertaining to the enforcement of a foreign court judgment, the court further clarified that 'public policy is the set of rules, which protects the foundation structure and fundamental interests of the society.'[33]

These two recent decisions are important because they clearly demonstrate how the concept of 'public policy' has been defined by national courts. To the same extent, they also highlight how national courts have, with specific reference to the aforementioned concept of 'public policy,' approached the enforcement of foreign arbitral awards and court judgments.[34]

With particular pertinence to the issuance of awards within Turkey, Article 90 of the Turkish constitution establishes the general principle of Turkish law that governs the application and effects of international treaties.[35] The principle clearly establishes that 'international treaties that have taken effect in accordance with the procedure have the force of law.' This means that the ICSID Convention is applicable as part of Turkey's national law. Article 54 of the ICSID Convention establishes the basis for the direct enforcement of convention awards, meaning that no additional domestic procedures need to follow.

The enforcement of international arbitral awards is also governed by Turkish law, which sets out the required conditions of recognition and enforcement in Turkey. However, if the award falls within the scope of the New York Convention, the TIPPIC will not apply. Therefore, it is crucial to determine if the award meets the conditions for grounds for refusal of enforcement, as established by Articles 60–62 of the TIPPIC. On the other hand, as has already been noted, public policy is an impediment to the enforcement process. However, it is important to recognise that only a few decisions of refusal of enforcement have been rendered on these grounds. With regard to sovereign immunity, it has been deemed that, in giving consent to arbitration, a state agrees to waive the defence of judicial immunity. Turkish law establishes that state assets cannot be attached. The new Enforcement and Bankruptcy Law (No 2004)[36] further clarifies that the scope of state sovereignty does not extend to another state's assets. Furthermore, it is also established that a foreign state's assets cannot be seized if they are used for public purposes; if the assets are used for commercial purposes, the *lex fori* (Turkish law) applies in determining the legal nature of the assets.[37] Turkish court practice therefore confirms that commercial assets can be seized.[38] The reason for the current focus upon Turkish cases derives from

32 Decision of the General Assembly of the Court of Appeals dated 8 February 2012, E. 2011/13-568 K. 2012/47.

33 Decision of the General Assembly of the Court of Appeals dated 10 February 2012, E. 2010/1, K. 2012/1.

34 Balkaya (n 29).

35 Article 90, para 5 of the Constitution of the Republic of Turkey says: 'International agreements duly put into effect bear the force of law. No appeal to the constitutional court shall be made with regard to these agreements, on the grounds that fundamental rights and freedoms duly put into effect and the domestic laws due to differences in provisions on the same matter, the provisions of international agreements shall prevail.'

36 Akinci (n 26) 462.

37 Ergin Nomer, *Devletler Hususi Hukuku* (20 edn, Beta 2013) 1.

38 Article 82(1) of the Bankruptcy and Enforcement Law providing 'for the non-seizability of state property applies to the Turkish state's properties and not to foreign state properties. Additionally, in Turkish domestic law there is not any other provision on the immunity for the assets of another state. Foreign states' assets situated in Turkey which are not allocated to the service of public officials may be subject to attachment. For instance, if a state has commercial activities in the territory of another state and if it has assets there for this

the fact that it is one of the few states which voluntarily complies with arbitral awards in the absence of initiated enforcement proceedings.[39] As the Uzan family cases demonstrate, the reverse does not apply; there are several awards in favour of Turkey in which the losing investors have not yet been paid.[40] This book focuses upon non-compliance of ICSID awards, and directly focuses upon the investor and host state. It is upon this basis that the current research can claim to be original.

When the unpaid host states are taken into account, Turkey appears to be the main victim. In this circumstance, it might be more suitable to analyse the state's experience of unpaid ICSID awards by the Uzan Group. By 2011, seven cases had been brought before the ICSID tribunal and addressed to the Turkish Republic. They are *Motorola,*[41] *PSEG,*[42] *Europe Cement,*[43] *Cementownia "Nowa Huta,"*[44] *Saba Fakes,*[45] *Libananco,*[46] *and Alapli.*[47] The majority of these cases belong to the same group of cases that were brought against Turkey. The *PSEG* case tribunal was the only one that ordered Turkey to pay costs. In addition, the *CEAS* and *Kepez* cases can be added to the Uzan Group of cases brought against Turkey in non-ICSID proceedings.

With a view to establishing how a state can be negatively impacted by a foreign investor, several selected cases will now be examined. In *Europe Cement Investment & Trade SA v. Republic of Turkey*, Europe Cement, a Polish company, maintained its owned stakes in two Turkish electricity companies (CEAS and Kepez). Both of the companies belong to the Uzan Group.

The fundamental question which the ICSID tribunal sought to address was whether Europe Cement had acquired shares prior to the claimed termination of the electricity concessions. However, the documentary evidence that the claimant provided did not sufficiently prove these claims to the tribunal.[48] In the final instance, the claimant's claim was dismissed (in its entirety) due to a lack of jurisdiction. The tribunal ordered the claimant to pay Turkey $3,907,383.14 for representing the respondent's legal costs and expenses; in addition, it was also required to meet the respondent's share of the costs of the arbitration (a total amount of $129,740). The tribunal, however, declined to decide whether moral damages had been inflicted upon Turkey.[49] In addition, the tribunal decided simple

purpose, attachment may occur.' Turkish Supreme Court, 12th Civil Circuit, Decision 6469/13007 of May 24 2004.

39 Akinci (n 26) 463.

40 In *Libananco,* the tribunal joined the opinion expressed in *Maffezini* and held that the right whose protection is sought is hypothetical in that ICSID tribunals at that time would typically split the costs (pay-your-own-way approach) rather than order the losing party to pay the costs of the winning party, a trend which has started to change gradually. *Libananco v. Turkey*, Decision on preliminary issues, (ICSID Case No. ARB/06/8) para 59. Additionally, in this case, the respondent had based its petition on the mere assertion that the claimant is a 'shell company.' In rejecting the request, the tribunal did not find this sufficient reason since many investments are made through an investment vehicle.

41 *Motorola Credit Corporation, Inc v. Republic of Turkey* (ICSID Case No ARB/04/21).

42 *PSEG Global Inc. and Konya Ilgin Elektrik Üretim ve Ticaret Limited Sirketi v. Republic of Turkey* (ICSID Case No ARB/02/5).

43 *Europe Cement Investment and Trade S.A. v. Republic of Turkey* (ICSID Case No ARB(AF)/07/2).

44 *Cementownia "Nowa Huta" S.A. v. Republic of Turkey* (ICSID Case No ARB(AF)/06/2).

45 *Saba Fakes v. Republic of Turkey* (ICSID Case No. ARB/07/20).

46 *Libananco Holdings Co. Limited v. Republic of Turkey* (n 40).

47 *Alapli Elektrik B.V. v. Republic of Turkey* (ICSID Case No ARB/08/13).

48 Akinci (n 26) 464.

49 ibid.

interest (at the rate of 5 per cent) should, in the event of non-payment of any amounts within 30 days, be paid.[50]

Cementownia "Nowa Huta" SA v. Republic of Turkey provides a similar situation. In this instance, the investor was also a Polish company which began arbitration proceedings against Turkey after claiming the Energy Charter Treaty (ECT) had been breached.[51] The main similarity with the preceding case is that the claimant also claimed to own shares in CEAS and Kepez, the same Turkish electricity companies. In addition, the jurisdictional question was also the same, namely whether Cementownia had acquired shares prior to the alleged termination of the concession agreements.[52] The tribunal found the claimant's proposition to be 'manifestly ill-founded,' and noted that the claimant 'internationally and in bad faith abused the arbitration (process).'[53] These observations reflected the tribunal's recognition that, prior to the date of the alleged sale and purchase of the shares, the Turkish state and Turkish nationals were the only objects of complaint.[54] Ultimately, the tribunal concluded, in applying discretionary power:

> The Claimant is to bear all ICSID costs (the fees and expenses of the Members of the Tribunal and of the ICSID Secretariat) which are estimated to USD 400,000.00. The Claimant is to pay to the Respondent USD 325,000.00, which represents the Respondent's contribution to ICSID. The Tribunal further finds that the Respondent's legal fees and expenses are not unreasonable having regard to the course of these proceedings and that, therefore, the Claimant is to bear such costs in the amount of USD 4,904,822.06.[55]

Saba Fakes v. Republic of Turkey provides an additional point of reference. In this case, the Uzan Group was required to bear $182,500 (corresponding to the respondent's share of the costs of the arbitration) and $1,496,248.49 (representing the respondent's legal costs and expenses).[56] The award has, however, not been enforced.[57] The final ICSID case within the Uzan Group is *Libananco Holdings Co Limited v. Republic of Turkey.* In this case the dispute related to the termination of concession agreements for the CEAS and Kepez companies. The Uzan Group has Turkish citizenship and it could not, therefore, initiate arbitration proceedings against Turkey in ICSID; accordingly, Libananco, which claimed to be a shareholder of the CEAS and Kepez corporations, was registered in southern Cyprus.[58] However, the tribunal found that it has no jurisdiction over the case. This applied because Libananco had not, prior to 12 June 2003 (the date of the alleged expropriation), proven that it owned shares in CEAS and Kepez.[59] Upon this basis:

> The Claimant is ordered to pay the Respondent US$ 602,500 in reimbursement of the expended portion of the Respondent's advance on costs as well as US$ 15,000,000 in respect of the Respondent's legal fees and out of pocket expenses; such amounts to bear interest on the outstanding amount thereafter at the rate of three-month LIBOR plus one per cent per annum,

50 ibid.
51 ibid.
52 ibid.
53 ibid.
54 See <https://www.italaw.com/sites/default/files/case-documents/ita0138.pdf> accessed 11 October 2017.
55 ibid para 178.
56 Akinci (n 26) 464–5.
57 ibid.
58 ibid.
59 *Libananco Holdings Co. Limited v. Republic of Turkey* (n 40) para 570.1.

> such interest to run from the 31st day after the date of despatch of this Award on the unpaid portion of the amounts due on this Award.[60]

The claimant also tried to annul the award, but this was dismissed by the annulment committee.[61] The cases clearly demonstrate that Turkey, the host state, has always been negatively impacted in its interactions with investors. This victimisation is a heavy burden of the state due to

> costs in response to the nature of the claim and the manner in which the claimant conducted itself over the lengthy period of the proceedings, in particular that it commenced and prosecuted an abusive claim. According to the Respondent [Turkey], the Claimant repeatedly altered its case theory and narrative, which forced the Respondent to gather evidence from multiple jurisdictions and engage counsel and experts to investigate, evaluate and refute the claimant's contentions. The Respondent referred, in addition, to the considerable burden of having to translate documents and submissions out of and into Turkish.[62]

Even though the tribunal ordered reasonable interest be paid to the respondent, non-compliance with the awards is the central issue. In these cases, the awards include mostly legal expenses, and therefore pertain to costs and interests.

In all cases, the investors did not honour the awards; however, this did not prevent them from bringing another arbitration case against Turkey, which was the respondent state. This situation provides another dimension to the enforcement issue of ICSID awards. It generally seems easier to enforce an award against the investors by the host state; however, if the investor moves its assets from the state or has already gone bankrupt, this might not prove to be the case.

It should also be recognised that Turkey has just won another arbitration against itself, which was brought by the Uzan Group in the Stockholm Chamber of Commerce (SCC) in 2016.[63] However, the received benefits have not been considered. It has already been noted that non-compliance by the losing investors is not purely anecdotal evidence.[64] It has also been observed that parties do not only bring their case arising under investment agreement, they also initiate ICSID proceedings under their contracts. In practice, there have only been two cases which were brought under the ICSID Convention upon the basis of contracts by the host states.[65] However, they both lost the contractual cases under the convention. It is therefore the case that failing investors generally do not comply with the award regarding the legal fees and costs of the arbitration.[66] This can sometimes create a deeply unenviable situation for host states such as Turkey, as both obvious bad faith and the innumerable negative consequences derived from this bad faith attest.

---

60 ibid para 569.

61 Akinci (n 26) 465.

62 See <https://www.italaw.com/sites/default/files/case-documents/ita0466.pdf> accessed 11 October 2017.

63 See <https://www.italaw.com/sites/default/files/case-documents/italaw8642.pdf> accessed 10 October 2017.

64 Joubin-Bret (n 22) 111.

65 *Republic of Peru v. Caravelí Cotaruse Transmisora de Energía S.A.C.* (ICSID Case No. ARB/13/24). Joubin-Bret (n 22) 111.

66 Joubin-Bret (n 22) 111.

4.3 Previous practical proposals to reduce enforcement issues

After the ICSID Convention was drafted, the attendant state authorities recognised the shortcomings of the arbitration system, recognising that the enforceability of arbitral awards was a particular point of concern. The president of the World Bank, in seeking to offset these concerns, argued that this was not a central issue.[67] It was suggested that only sovereign immunity should be considered as a limitation of enforcement against the states, with it being added that the states had evidenced reliability in their voluntary compliance with international arbitral awards. It was also clearly discernible that there was, with regard to the status of award creditors, a clear imbalance between a state and foreign investor.[68] For this reason, the convention's enforcement provisions could be said to be of more interest to states than to foreign investors. It might therefore be suggested that the imbalance between the parties was a key oversight—while the principle of sovereignty provides state actors with the opportunity not to attach their properties, this privilege is not provided to private parties, who do not have any basis upon which to limit the enforcement of arbitral awards against themselves. When the ICSID Convention was in the process of being prepared, its drafting committee openly acknowledged this shortcoming.[69] As has already been noted, private parties may have the right to limit enforcement—in this respect, the attachment of the investors' assets may be restricted. On the contrary, it should be acknowledged that the winning state receives the payment of the arbitral award, even if the investor is already bankrupt. These issues may, however, be resolved in that the Convention has, throughout its history, been developed in accordance with a dominant approach.[70]

4.3.1 Creating a uniform state sovereignty law

State immunity is a hybrid of customary international law, domestic law, and, to a lesser extent, treaty law.[71] The trend of state sovereignty law began with the introduction of the US Foreign Sovereign Immunities Act in 1976.[72] The United Kingdom, Australia, and other states then followed the example set by the United States.[73] Many countries that use the common law system have codified state immunity law; in contrast, civil law countries have instead tended to develop the law on a case-by-case basis.[74] As has already been noted, there are only two international conventions on immunity,[75] only one of which is in force. Both conventions distinguish between immunity from jurisdiction and immunity from execution.[76]

67 Aron Broches, 'Awards Rendered Pursuant to the ICSID Convention: Binding Force, Finality, Recognition, Enforcement, Execution' (1987) ICSID Review 318.

68 Joubin-Bret (n 22) 111.

69 Musa, Polasek, and ICSID (n 5) 17.

70 ibid.

71 Andrea K Bjorklund, 'State Immunity and the Enforcement of Investor-State Arbitral Awards' (2008) Practice 858.

72 ibid 837.

73 ibid.

74 ibid.

75 The United Nations Convention on Jurisdictional Immunities of States and Their Property 2004 (UNCSI) <https://treaties.un.org/doc/source/recenttexts/english_3_13.pdf> accessed 21 November 2016. It has not yet entered into force.

76 European Convention Article 23; UN Convention Article 19.

The question of the importance of state sovereignty in the enforcement of arbitral awards is outlined within three articles (53–55) of the ICSID Convention. These articles clearly clarify how the principle of state sovereignty significantly impacts on the arbitral awards enforcement process. Article 54 establishes that the execution of the award shall be governed in accordance with the municipal laws that are in force within the state where execution is sought.[77] Domestic court jurisprudence establishes the central role that the domestic application of sovereign immunity plays in determining the outcome of enforcement applications for investment treaty arbitration.[78] This point is further reiterated by legislation and case law on sovereign immunity in three of the world's leading financial centres, providing further insight by virtue of instances in which claimant investors have sought the enforcement of arbitral awards against respondent states. The individual state's sovereignty laws are essential to execute the awards because these laws decide whether or not the assets can be attached. They define the nature of properties and assets in accordance with their sovereignty acts.

In addition to these points, it should also be recognised that sovereign immunity is only concerned about measures of execution against certain assets. Article 55 of the ICSID Convention explains that the domestic law on sovereign immunity of the ICSID member states may be considered to limit the forced execution of ICSID awards (both against a foreign state and within the state in which execution is sought). When states apply, in the course of the execution stage, their sovereign power against foreign investors, they should take into account national investors investing in other states at the same time. To put it slightly differently, they should seek to work towards a balance, doing so in the knowledge that, if this is not the case, national investors run the risk of incurring the same wrongful action from other member states. This has an indirect impact upon host states breaching the obligations.

This duality creates clear potential conflicts of interest. Accordingly, states must draft provisions that simultaneously protect their sovereign regulatory powers and the investments of their citizens abroad.[79] The insertion of national law into the execution process adds a further degree of unpredictability, although it should be recognised that provision has been made to ensure that investment arbitration awards will be executed in national courts by the conventions. State practice, however, suggests a perceptible movement towards the theory of restrictive immunity from execution. As Christoph Schreuer has noted:

> Allowing plaintiffs to proceed against foreign States and then to withhold from them the fruits of successful litigation through immunity from execution may put them into the doubly frustrating position of having been lured into expensive and seemingly successful lawsuits only to be left with an unenforceable judgment plus legal costs.[80]

Therefore, one of key questions that confront states is how to transfer power to a tribunal in a way that upholds both of these interests.[81] In approaching this question from a dif-

77 Coop, Nistal, Volterra, and Fietta (n 3) 70.

78 ibid 69.

79 Julia Hueckel, 'Rebalancing Legitimacy and Sovereignty in International Investment Agreements' (2011–2) 61 Emory L J 601.

80 Andrea K Bjorklund, 'Arbitration and National Courts: Conflict and Cooperation: Sovereign Immunity as a Barrier to the Enforcement of Investor-State Arbitral Awards: The Re-Politicization of International Investment Disputes' (2010) 21 Am Rev Intl Arb 211–315.

81 ibid.

ferent angle, it might be said that the central issue is how states can establish a legitimate system which obliges them to adhere to international investment agreements (IIAs) without violating their sovereignty.[82] The influence of legitimacy and sovereignty pulls the state in opposite directions. The system is currently structured in a way that upholds state sovereignty and facilitates the execution of arbitral awards. In instances where there is a preponderance of state sovereignty, it is therefore incumbent upon states to revise their domestic law.

Successful investors firstly need to find the state's assets and then establish whether the assets can be categorised as commercial. In practice, this is a significant burden for foreign investors, often contributing to the phenomenon of forum shopping. In instances where the property is not categorised as commercial, a waiver of immunity (which makes explicit reference to the property) will be required before attachment is permitted.[83]

4.3.1.1 States' consent to waive immunity from execution in their agreement

In addressing themselves to the state immunity issue, some commentators argue that the creation of a model law provides the optimal recourse of action, enabling complications such as those encountered in the Lady Fox case[84] to be overcome. Others instead suggest that states should, waive their immunity from execution in their agreements. This latter recommendation is the most widely accepted one because, when recognising the ICSID Convention's shortcomings with regard to the execution of its awards,[85] the ICSID suggests that the following model clause should, with the intention of waiving immunity from execution, be adopted for bilateral investment treaties (BITs) and other consensual agreements:

> The [Name of Contracting State] hereby irrevocably waives any claim to immunity in regard to any proceedings to enforce any arbitral award rendered by a Tribunal constituted pursuant to this agreement, including immunity from service of process, immunity from jurisdiction of any court, and immunity of any of its property from execution.[86]

It may be argued that this is why the ICSID does not cover the clause in its text and give a model clause. The answer is relatively straightforward because, as previously explained, the president of the World Bank did not express concern with regard to non-compliance with the awards nor the possibility that member states would not sign the convention. The depoliticised character of the ICSID was, however, a stronger concern. While political pressure might conceivably ensure the effective execution of awards, it is important to recognise that the situation is complex: in instances where the host state does not comply with the award, there is clear risk that the interests of its national investors may be adversely impacted by the home state's retaliatory action. This also applies to third states that may be reluctant to waive their immunity for the host state's debt which is held in their territories. A better option may, therefore, be to negotiate bilaterally, while including a waiver of execution clause. On the other hand, it can be assumed, as some commentators have

82 ibid.

83 ibid.

84 Bjorklund, 'State Immunity and the Enforcement of Investor-State Arbitral Awards' (n 71) 858.

85 Albert Jan van den Berg, 'Some Recent Problems in the Practice of Enforcement under the New York and ICSID Conventions' (1987) 2 ICSID Review–Foreign Investment Law Journal 439.

86 ibid.

observed, that the ICSID Convention extends the immunity to execution.[87] However, the consensus opinion holds that Article 54 safeguards states against execution by investors, but not vice versa. On closer reading of the convention, it appears that the latter interpretation is the correct one. It cannot be denied that the waiver of immunity from execution will be a difficult issue to address in the negotiation process, presenting a formidable challenge to any investment agreement with state parties.[88] Under these circumstances, the central issue appears to be that the bargaining power of the foreign investor will, by virtue of the fact that some states have already accepted the waiver of state immunity, be substantially increased. In registering this point, it should be acknowledged that the bargaining power of foreign investors is ultimately contingent upon the kind of investment that is being contemplated.[89]

It should also be recognised that, outside of the financial field, waivers of immunity are quite rare—this means that private parties may be in a better bargaining position when demanding a waiver of immunity from execution.[90] It is also not uncommon for economic development agreements to include a waiver of immunity clause.[91] In addition, the business relationship between the investor and the state party to the agreement must be taken into account. If the third state shelters the debtor state's assets, then the question of whether the third state should, setting aside the fact that it is the enforcing state, be permitted to attach the debtor state's assets. This question arises because the third state's sovereign immunity act may directly contradict the said clauses. Article 54(3) of the ICSID Convention therefore establishes that '[e]xecution of the award shall be governed by the laws concerning the execution of judgments in force in the State in whose territories such execution is sought.'[92]

In responding to the preceding questions, the third state will establish its own sovereignty act. If the third state's sovereignty act does not allow waiver immunity from execution, a foreign investor cannot seize the assets of the debtor state that are held within the third state's territory, even though the debtor state has already waived its immunity from execution; or the third state will allow the investor to seize the debtor state's assets in its territories, though the debtor state's own act does not permit the waiver clause from immunity.[93] French examples sufficiently demonstrate that the host state can waive its immunity from execution if it indicates certain assets.[94] In the French case, this outcome developed over time. In the first instance, the French government found that the state could not seek immunity from execution when the targeted assets are purely commercial in character. In the absence of an explicit and specific waiver, states could also rely upon sovereign immunity from execution against diplomatic assets. In 2013, in the *NML Capital Ltd et al.*

87 Schreuer, *The ICSID Convention: A Commentary* (n 14).

88 ibid.

89 Vincent O Nmehielle, 'Enforcing Arbitration Awards under the International Convention for the Settlement of Investment Disputes (ICSID Convention)' (2001) 7 Ann Surv Intl & Comp L 21.

90 Georges R Delaume, 'Economic Development and Sovereign Immunity' (1985) 79 AJIL 319–46.

91 ibid.

92 According to ICSID Convention Article 54. Convention on the Settlement of Investment Disputes Between States and Nationals of Other States (1965) <https://icsid.worldbank.org/ICSID/StaticFiles/basicdoc/CRR_English-final.pdf> accessed 18 December 2015.

93 ibid.

94 Coop, Nistal, Volterra, and Fietta (n 3) 75–6.

v. the Republic Argentina saga,[95] the French Court of Cassation, in acknowledging the fact that the Argentinian government had already waived its immunity from execution, sought to protect the general principle of state sovereignty. By as early as 1991, the International Law Commission had already established that

> [a] general waiver or a waiver in respect of all property in the territory of the State of the forum, without mention of any of the specific categories, would not be sufficient to allow measures of constraint against property in the categories listed in paragraph 1.[96]

A new milestone within the French approach was established in a ruling that the French Court of Cassation issued on 13 May 2015. In engaging with a long-running dispute between the Republic of Congo and the Congolese company Commissions Import Export SA (or Commisimpex),[97] the International Chamber of Commerce (ICC) ruled upon behalf of the latter, finding in its favour on two occasions (2000 and 2013). The awards related to several contracts for public works that were concluded in the 1980s. The ICC ruled that Congo had failed to pay, also finding that it had failed in the payment of its debts. Commisimpex sought to enforce the first award against Congo by attaching a number of bank accounts held in Paris in the name of the Congo's diplomatic mission and delegation to UNESCO.[98]

In 2012, the Versailles Court of Appeal ruled that states can benefit from diplomatic missions against execution, adding the caveat that this did not apply if the state had waived in an explicit and specific manner. Congo expressly indicated that it had waived its right to invoke any immunity of jurisdiction as well as any immunity of execution. The court, however, did not find the absence of specificity to be a sufficient basis upon which to waive. Commisimpex then brought the case before the first Chamber of the Court of Cassation. This was the same chamber that had ruled, in 2013, that 'international customary law does not require a waiver of the execution immunity to be anything else than express.'[99]

This lenient approach meant that the French Court of Cassation overlooked the requirement of a specific manner and found the express manner to be a sufficient basis upon which to waive the state's immunity from execution.[100] Upon this basis, it will be assumed that the French courts acted in accordance with UNCSI rules, which will be set out in more detail later.[101] Each of these examples demonstrates that states can waive their immunity from execution while also waiving immunity from execution in their own courts as well. However, if this course of action is to be fulfilled, then states need to first specify the assets which will be seized in their agreements.

In addition, it should also be recognised that there is often an imbalance of political and economic power between BIT signatory states. Capital-importing states, therefore,

95 *Société NML Capital (Iles Caïmans) v. Etat d'Argentine,* Cour de Cassation (1ère Chambre Civile), no 10-25.938, 11-10.450, and 11-13.323, 28 March 2013.

96 International Law Commission, Report of the Commission to the General Assembly on the work of its forty-third session, A/CN.4/SER.A/1991/Add.1 (Part 2).

97 *Republic of Congo ('Congo') and the Congolese company Commissions Import Export SA ('Commisimpex'), Cour de cassation,* Chambre civile 1, 13 May 2015, no 13-17751.

98 ibid.

99 ibid.

100 Gregory Travaini, 'State 1 – Investor 1: Bring It On!' 1 April 2016 <http://kluwerarbitrationblog.com/2016/04/01/state-1-investor-1-bring-it-on/> accessed 6 December 2016.

101 Philippe Pinsolle and Thomas Voisin, 'Enforcement of Interim Relief in Investor-State Arbitration' in Fouret (n 3) 67–83.

only guarantee the protection of investor properties and the provision of facilities; capital-exporting countries, in contrast, demand more expansive insurance, encompassing expropriation or the arbitrary treatment of investments.[102] Taking these circumstances into account, it may be inappropriate to provide a loan to capital-importing states upon the basis that they have waived their immunity from execution.[103] This should be provided by the signatory states of BITs, not the investor or the host state. If this is not the case, then the solution may be problematic in the future.

In spite of the fact that the ICSID Convention remains hugely significant within the field, the convention still struggles to address issues of sovereign immunity. By virtue of this feature, the best option for the investor is to engage in forum shopping, with a view to finding a restrictive application of the immunity doctrine.[104] Unfortunately, as has already been noted,[105] many countries still seek to maintain the doctrine of absolute immunity from execution. Even in states with narrow immunity doctrines, it may be difficult for private investors to prove that attached assets are not immune from execution.[106] This is why a number of scholars support a uniform convention, upon which the basis that will provide balance and an enhanced degree of certainty with regard to the immunity from execution issue. However, these contributions appear to have overlooked the fact that bilateral treaties and agreements provide a more appropriate basis upon which waiver immunity from execution can be negotiated. This is because states may not want to enable the same facility for each state or bargain at the same level. Under these circumstances, it may be suggested that bilateral agreements provide a preferable alternative to multinational agreements. With a view to highlighting the relative advantages of bilateral agreements, the UNCSI will now be examined in more detail.

4.3.1.2 Enter into force of the United Nations Convention on Jurisdictional Immunities of States and Their Property (UNCSI)

The UNCSI operates in accordance with the general rule which holds that 'a state enjoys immunity, in respect of itself and its property, from the jurisdiction of the courts of another state.'[107] There are a number of exceptions to the rule, foremost among which is arbitration. Under the terms of the treaty, the state that has agreed to submit to arbitration (in disputes related to commercial transactions and investment) cannot invoke immunity from jurisdiction before the competent court of another state, citing the following objections: '(a) the validity, interpretation or application of the arbitration agreement; (b) the arbitration procedure; or (c) the confirmation or the setting aside of the award.'[108] The only exception in each of these respects is if the agreement provides otherwise. Articles 19 and 20 of the UNCSI also clearly establish that consent to arbitration does not imply a waiver of immunity from execution measures (in reiterating this point, the UNCSI refers

102 Johanna Kalb, 'Creating an ICSID Appellate Body' (2005) 10 UCLA Journal International Law & Foreign Affirmation 179.

103 Gary W Larson, 'Default on Foreign Sovereign Debt: A Question for the Courts' (1985) 18 Ind L Rev 18 959.

104 Nmehielle (n 89) 47.

105 See Chapter 1, Section 1.3.2.2 'Immunity against execution.'

106 Nmehielle (n 89) 47.

107 UNCSI (n 75) Article 5.

108 ibid.

to said measures as 'post-award measures of constraint').[109] State immunity from execution is regulated separately in Article 19, where it is clearly established that state assets may not generally be attached during proceedings before another state's court. However, there are three exceptions to this fundamental rule: firstly, if the state has, in a consensual agreement or arbitration contract, explicitly agreed to waive immunity from execution; secondly, if the state has specifically reserved certain assets for the honour of the relevant court claim; and thirdly, if it has been established that the state is using—or intends to use—the relevant assets for commercial purposes. This last exception, however, has an important caveat: execution measures may only be used against property that has 'a connection with the entity against which the proceeding was directed.'[110] In addition to outlining this third condition, the UNCSI also lists properties that cannot, under any circumstances, be considered as property used for non-governmental purposes:

> (a) property, including any bank account, which is used or intended for use in the performance of the functions of the diplomatic mission of the State or its consular posts, special missions, missions to international organizations or delegations to organs of international organizations or to international conferences;
> (b) property of a military character or used or intended for use in the performance of military functions;
> (c) property of the central bank or other monetary authority of the State;
> (d) property forming part of the cultural heritage of the State or part of its archives and not placed or intended to be placed on sale;
> (e) property forming part of an exhibition of objects of scientific, cultural or historical interest and not placed or intended to be placed on sale.[111] [Unless the state agrees otherwise.]

In addition, the UNCSI also clearly establishes that privileges and immunities are not affected.[112] In other words, the convention provides a uniform system for states: it therefore helps in reducing time and increasing the practical significance of ICSID awards.

As its name clearly demonstrates, the UNCSI's central aim is to 'enhance the rule of law and legal certainty, particularly in dealings of States with natural or juridical persons, and … contribute to the codification and development of international law and the harmonization of practice in [the law on state immunity].'[113] However, more than a decade after it was first drafted, the UNCSI has still not entered into force. In order for each article to enter into force, the UNCSI requires the assent of at least 30 state parties; however, at the time of this writing, only 21 states have met this condition.[114] Due to the absence of uniform rules on execution (such as those drafted in the UNCSI), the issue of sovereign immunity can easily arise. From the perspective of the award-holder, variations within national laws on state immunity have become important, even overriding points of reference, clearly helping to determine which forum will be most conducive to the execution of an award. This development, which has been generally categorised as forum shopping, presents a

109 ibid Articles 19–20.
110 ibid Article 19.
111 UNCSI (n 75) Article 21.
112 ibid Article 3.
113 Claudio Matute, 'Forum Shopping in the Execution of ICSID Awards: Is It Time to Revive the UN Convention on State Immunity?' (2016) June 24 <http://kluwerarbitrationblog.com/2016/06/24/preventing-forum-shopping-in-the-execution-of-icsid-awards-is-it-time-to-revive-the-un-convention-on-state-immunity/> accessed 21 November 2016.
114 UNCSI (n 75).

clear threat to the ICSID Convention's ostensible objective of establishing a simple and effective mechanism for the recognition and enforcement of arbitral awards.[115] The law on state immunity evidences considerable variation, something in large part attributable to the fact that it is governed by different national laws. As a direct consequence, state assets are provided with diverse scopes of immunity and, by implication, different levels of protection.[116] It is only necessary, with reference to the issue of immunity from execution, to review a handful of national court decisions. This is sufficient to gain an appreciation of the vast differences that distinguish various municipal laws. The issue of waiver of immunity from execution is, to take one example, brought out in clear detail by *Creighton v. Ministre des Finances de l'État du Qatar* (2000),[117] a particularly well-known case in which the French supreme court confirmed the theory of implicit waiver of immunity from execution, making specific reference to an ICC arbitration clause in the process. In a separate ruling, the Hong Kong Final Court of Appeal [in *DRC v. FG Hemisphere* (2011)][118] established that an agreement to arbitrate under the ICC rules does not, in itself, imply a waiver of immunity from execution. Several scholars have drawn attention to the conceptual parallels between the aforementioned ICC arbitration clause and Article 53 of the ICSID Convention, with a number suggesting that the latter could be 'a back door to thwarting sovereign immunity from execution.'[119] The French supreme court (in the *NML v. Rep. Argentine* case, which took place in 2011),[120] held that the waiver of immunity must both be explicit and relate specifically to diplomatic property. In 2013, the same court, in a separate NML case,[121] exceeded the specificity requirement and issued a ruling that extended to all assets used for public purposes.[122]

Domestic court decisions also appear to be divided on the so-called commerciality exception, which consists of allowing state assets to be subject to execution when these assets are used for commercial purposes (this is also categorised as a restrictive approach). This approach is not uniformly accepted. Even in instances where it is approved, its scope tends to vary tremendously, a point which is reiterated by specific examples: Hong Kong's courts do not accept the commerciality exception to immunity.[123] Brazil, Ecuador, Venezuela, Poland, and Japan all adhere to the absolutist approach to state immunity.[124] In contrast, other domestic courts have adopted the restrictive approach, accepting that state assets with a commercial purpose are seized, the ruling that was issued in the 2011 *Russian Federation v. Franz J. Sedelmayer* case[125] being a particularly important reference point in this respect. In this instance, the Swedish supreme court not only accepted the commercial purpose exception, but also requested that the state assume the burden of proving that the property against which enforcement was sought was only used for public

115 Matute (n 113).

116 ibid.

117 *Creighton v. Ministre des Finances de l'État du Qatar*, Cass 1 e civ 6, 6 July 2000.

118 *Democratic Republic of the Congo v. FG Hemisphere Associates* [2011] HKCFAR 41.

119 Matute (n 113).

120 *Société NML Capital Ltd v. République Argentine*, Cour de Cassation (1ère Chambre Civile), no 09-72.057, 28 September 2011.

121 ibid.

122 ibid.

123 See, e.g., *DRC v. FG Hemisphere* (2011) (n 118).

124 Matute (n 113).

125 *Sedelmayer v. Russian Federation* (n 17).

purposes.[126] In the same year, the French supreme court, which operates in a restrictive approach state, ruled in exactly the opposite direction (in *NML*). In this ruling, the French court established that embassy bank accounts enjoy a presumption of public utility, shifting the burden of proof in favour of the foreign investors.[127]

As demonstrated earlier, while some of the decisions are investor-friendly, others are more protective of the state assets that are subject to execution. The decisions closely depend on the jurisdictions and associated national laws on state immunity. This divergence incentivises forum shopping, simultaneously undermining the automatic and independent enforcement mechanism that is at the heart of the ICSID Convention.[128]

This phenomenon could be addressed by reviving seemingly defunct efforts to provide uniformity and clarity to immunity laws. The UNCSI does not only draft the exception but also addresses specific categories of assets that are to be safeguarded from execution—these include the bank accounts of diplomatic missions, the property of the restrictive central banks, and the monetary authorities of the debtor state.[129] In clarifying the waiver of immunity issue, Articles 17–19 of the UNCSI clearly establish that a waiver of jurisdictional immunity does not imply a waiver of immunity from enforcement (in an additional clarification, it is also made clear that any such waiver must be explicitly expressed). Equally significantly, the UNCSI does not include a specificity requirement.[130]

It is broadly accepted that the UNCSI's entry into force could produce a number of benefits for states. Firstly, it will create a balance solution for sovereign debtors and sovereign creditors. In addition, sovereign states will also attain considerable influence over the rules that will govern potential attachment of their assets—this would mean that they would no longer be reliant upon third-state municipal laws, no matter how unusual or investor-friendly these rules may be. This means that the forum shopping originated by the fragmentation of the law on state immunity could force states to shift their assets from one state to another, imposing substantial transaction costs and further exacerbating the problems that a uniform mechanism would be intended to resolve.[131]

Over the past year, five countries (Czech Republic, Iraq, Liechtenstein, Mexico, and Slovakia) have ratified or acceded to the UNCSI, but nine additional ratifications are required if the UNCSI is to enter into force. Significantly, the United Kingdom, which is one of the most important commercial centres of the world and one of the financial hubs where assets of foreign states are most often placed, is currently considering whether to become a member.[132]

Christoph Schreuer notes, with reference to the issue of differences in national law on state immunity, that '[i]t would be a pity if the law of state immunity were to fall apart and become a matter of comparative law rather than international law.'[133] Even though the UNCSI is by no means a perfect solution to the enforcement of ICSID awards, it would nonetheless, from the perspective of the field, represent a step in the right direction. It

126 Matute (n 113).
127 ibid.
128 ibid.
129 UNCSI (n 75) Article 21(1)(a)(b).
130 Matute (n 113).
131 ibid.
132 ibid.
133 Christoph H Schreuer, 'Review: State Immunity: Some Recent Developments' (1991) 39 Am J Comp L 213–21.

would, even if only to a partial extent, address a situation in which the fragmentation of state immunity obligations undermines the spirit of the ICSID Convention and also harms the interests of investors and states.[134]

It should be noted that, while states retain a strong attachment to sovereign control, they may, in waiving immunity from jurisdiction, be more predisposed to allow it to be restricted by treaty. However, it cannot be assumed that waivers of immunity from execution will operate in practice, even if national courts accept the principle in advance.

The intention in this respect may be to permit states to retain their immunities while leaving them open to the pressure of the World Bank. As previous statistics clearly reiterate, the ICSID has significant mechanisms that enable the awards to be voluntarily enforced. However, over recent decades, a number of execution issues have arisen, some of which pertain to the definition of assets and some of which relate to more general economic crises. By virtue of the fact that each state has its own jurisdiction, award-holders struggle to identify the most suitable jurisdiction in which to seize the assets of the debtor state. This reduces the efficiency and power, meaning that creditors have to commit substantial resources of money and time to the enforcement of the award. The UNCSI establishes clear rules that frame the execution of arbitral awards. However, it has not proven to be sufficiently persuasive, and the UNCSI, by virtue of the lack of state members, has still to enter into force.

4.3.2 Activating the World Bank

The World Bank, in directly addressing itself to many of the aforementioned difficulties, may offer a potential recourse of action. It is important to remember that the convention was drafted by the executive directors of the International Bank for Reconstruction and Development (the World Bank), a feature which adorned the convention with the requisite level of 'institutional gravitas.'[135] This represented something of a departure for the World Bank, which is predominantly focused upon granting loans to developing countries. It is a crucial source of financial and technical assistance to developing countries around the world, functioning, in many respects, as more than a bank. Upon closer inspection, it more closely resembles a unique partnership that enables states to prosper and develop.[136] The World Bank also has extensive experience in settling disputes between bank member governments (or subdivisions or agencies of members) and foreign investors.[137] During 1951–2, the World Bank attempted to settle a dispute that related to Iran's expropriation of the Anglo Iranian Oil Company's assets.[138] In responding to Egypt's 1956 nationalisation of the Suez Canal Company, the World Bank also successfully mediated the dispute by intervening between the company's shareholders and the state.[139] In 1985, the World Bank,

134 Matute (n 113).

135 Susan D Franck, 'Foreign Direct Investment, Investment Treaty Arbitration, and the Rule of Law' (2006) 19 McGeorge Global Bus & Dev L J 337. See also Allee Todd and Clint Peinhardt, 'Contingent Credibility: The Reputational Effects of Investment Treaty Disputes on Foreign Direct Investment' (2008) 51 Urbana 61801.

136 See <http://www.worldbank.org/en/about/what-we-do> accessed 16 December 2016.

137 Ibrahim F I Shihata, 'The Settlement of Disputes Regarding Foreign Investment: The Role of the World Bank, with Particular Reference to ICSID and MIGA' (1986) 1 Am U J Intl L & Poly 97.

138 ibid 99.

139 ibid.

in providing technical advice during a dispute between an Argentine state gas company and a Dutch company, helped both parties to settle their differences.[140] Despite the World Bank's involvement, a number of practical obstacles and the limits of its own mandate, strongly militated against the assumption of this role.[141] In addition, from a country's perspective, it was also conceivable that non-compliance with the World Bank's advice would negatively impact its overall relationship with this institution.[142] However, because ICSID operates upon a voluntary basis, states that are eligible to sign the ICSID Convention are obviously free to decline to do so.[143] By extended implication, any decision to act otherwise will not deleteriously impact relations with the World Bank.[144] Unfortunately, this kind of 'self-enforcement' did not survive into the 21st century, and pragmatic omissions from the ICSID Convention have contributed to a new reality.[145] It is therefore widely accepted that the World Bank can only assume an active role again in addressing non-compliance with ICSID awards.

The World Bank Group consists of five different organisations which are managed by its member states: The International Bank for Reconstruction and Development (IBRD) lends to governments of middle-income and creditworthy low-income countries. The International Development Association (IDA) provides interest-free loans, which it defines as credits and grants, to governments of the poorest countries. In combination, the IBRD and IDA constitute the World Bank. The International Finance Corporation (IFC) is a global development institution that exclusively focuses upon the private sector. It assists developing countries to achieve sustainable growth. Its activities include the financing of investment, the mobilisation of capital in international financial markets, and the provision of advisory services to businesses and governments. The Multilateral Investment Guarantee Agency (MIGA) was established in 1988, with a view to promoting foreign direct investment (FDI) into developing countries and ultimately supporting economic growth, reducing poverty, and improving people's lives. MIGA upholds this mandate by providing political risk insurance (guarantees) to investors and lenders. MIGA provides dispute resolution services for guaranteed investment, thereby preventing disruption to projects that benefit development.[146] MIGA insures FDI against losses that are incurred as a result of currency inconvertibility and transfer restrictions, expropriation, war, civil disturbance, terrorism, and sabotage; it also encompasses the breach of contract and the non-honouring of financial obligations. The International Centre for the Settlement of Investment Disputes (ICSID) provides international facilities for the conciliation and arbitration of investment disputes. It has its own enforcement mechanism, a feature which clearly distinguishes it from other institutions.[147]

A number of commentators have argued that the execution issue can be overcome in-house. This assertion is grounded within the fact that the World Bank has considerable

---

140 ibid.

141 ibid.

142 Ibid.

143 ibid 100.

144 ibid.

145 J Martin Hunter and Javier Garcia Olmedo, 'Enforcement/Execution of ICSID Awards against Reluctant States' (2011) 12 JWIT 307.

146 See <https://www.miga.org/Documents/Dispute_Resolution_and_Claims.pdf> accessed 26 December 2016.

147 See <http://www.worldbank.org/en/about> accessed 16 December 2016.

impact upon the domestic economies of individual states. Conceivably, it could influence the actions of the debtor state by adjusting or even cutting loans, thereby potentially assuming a central role within the arbitration process.[148] This coercive component would, however, be contrary to the character (independent and objective) and purpose of the ICSID. Even though it is not expected that states will fail to abide by their obligations, the ICSID Convention puts in place two dispute settlement mechanisms, thus establishing the basis upon which the arbitration process can be initiated, assuming that the home state, in operationalising Article 27, espouses the investor's claim. This article enables the home state to provide diplomatic protection on the investor's behalf, which can be upheld before the International Court of Justice (ICJ) and against the host state that has failed to pay an award. In addition to these two solutions, pressure can conceivably be exerted through the ICSID's connection to the World Bank.[149] It has already been noted that the ICSID institution is no longer an active consideration within the case after the award is rendered. If the losing state fails to honour the award, the only option is to communicate officially with the non-paying party, with a view to reminding it of its 'international obligation to respect the result of a process to which they have given their consent.'[150] However, it should be recognised that this communication does not have any sanction against the losing party. Several commentators have therefore suggested that the simplest and most effective solution may be to overcome the issue 'in-house' by supplementing the ICSID enforcement system with a World Bank group execution mechanism.[151] The World Bank's operational policies explicitly allow it to block new loans to member countries or to refrain from providing them in the first instance. This course of action can be adopted in instances when member countries are unwilling to pay external debts or are not making reasonable efforts to settle disputes relating to the unlawful expropriation of property belonging to aliens.[152] The World Bank Operations Manual provides the bank with the discretion to apply these prerogatives and also regulates the procedures through which they are exercised.[153]

The United Nations Conference on Trade and Development (UNCTAD) has suggested a distinction between compliant and non-compliant states, originating this as something that can be applied when it is a developed country that has rebuffed an award.[154] Indeed the identified states are all either developing or transitioning economies to be found in Africa (Liberia, Senegal, Congo, Zimbabwe), Asia (Laos, Thailand, Kazakhstan, Kyrgyzstan,

148 Sylvia T Tonova, Baiju S. Vasani, and Jones Day, 'Enforcement of Investment Treaty Awards against Assets of States, State Entities and State-Owned Companies' in Fouret (n 3) 83–97.

149 Bjorklund, 'State Immunity and the Enforcement of Investor-State Arbitral Awards' (n 71) 834.

150 Jan Paulsson, 'ICSID's Achievements and Prospects' (1991) 6 ICSID Review–Foreign Investment Law Journal 380.

151 Joseph M Cardosi, 'Precluding the Treasure Hunt: How the World Bank Group Can Help Investors Circumnavigate Sovereign Immunity Obstacles to ICSID Award Execution' (2014) 41 Pepperdine Law Review 3. Joubin-Bret (n 22) 99–112; Tonova, Vasani, and Day (n 148) 83–97; Baldwin, Kantor, and Nolanmake (n 25) 22. Antonio R Parra, 'The Enforcement of ICSID Arbitral Awards' in R. D. Bishop (ed.), *Enforcement of Awards against Sovereigns* (Juris 2009) 131. The Arbitral Awards' in D Bishop (ed)(2009). World Bank, 'Disputes over Defaults on External Debt, Expropriation, and Breach of Contract' (2012) <https://policies.worldbank.org/sites/ppf3/PPFDocuments/090224b08231b9e1.pdf> accessed 10 October 2017.

152 World Bank Group, 'The World Bank Operations Manual,' Operational Policies, OP 7.40, July 2001.

153 ibid.

154 UNCTAD, 'World Investment Report 2012: Towards a New Generation of Investment Policies,' 84–86, U.N. Doc. UNCTAD/WIR/2012 <http://www.unctad-docs.org/files/UNCTAD-WIR2012-Full-en.pdf> accessed 12 December 2016.

Russia), and South America (Argentina, Bolivia, Ecuador, Venezuela).[155] These countries are all members of the IBRD.[156] The majority of non-compliant states are developing or transitioning economies that have outstanding loans with the IBRD or the IDA.[157] It has previously been noted that the World Bank Group contains five institutions which work together with a view to promoting economic growth and eradicating poverty.[158] The bank's diversity of services and depth of financial power place it within a unique position, meaning that it is best placed to remove sovereign immunity obstacles that hinder the free flow of FDI.[159] It has created prophylactic and remedial measures, with a view to reducing the risk of non-compliance with arbitral awards. However, this has been held to be inadequate, because it is believed that the World Bank Group can do more to achieve a multilateral execution mechanism, especially in relation to awards that have been rendered by ICSID.[160]

It may be appropriate to delegate duties among the World Bank institutions. One example would be to ensure that MIGA insures against the non-payment of arbitral awards.[161] This option is particularly important because it provides a readily available execution mechanism, simultaneously providing a clear alternative to forum shopping. Although this course of action may cause increases within insurance premiums, the costs will ultimately be lower than those associated with judicial attachment and execution proceedings. Under ideal circumstances, MIGA can serve as a dispute settlement mechanism, enabling losses incurred by expropriation to be reimbursed and reassuring investors that higher damages can be achieved through arbitration.[162] If this eventuality does come to pass, it appears likely that ICSID awards will only be presented to MIGA for ex *post facto* relief.[163]

The IBRD and IDA work together with the aim of 'promoting sustainable economic development and reducing poverty in its developing member countries.'[164] While the IBRD provides low-interest loans and guarantees to middle-income and creditworthy lower-income countries, the IDA offers no-interest loans and donations to the poorest bank members.[165] The IBRD Articles of Agreement lead the World Bank's policies.[166] It is important to note that World Bank policy relating to overdue and non-performing loans is characterised by a number of rigid measures. For example, if the member country fails to pay, disbursements on all loans for the country are suspended and no new loans will

155 ibid 86, at Annex Table I.1 (FDI Flows, by Region and Economy, for the Period of 2006–2011).

156 Cardosi (n 151) 147.

157 ibid.

158 See <http://www.worldbank.org/en/about/leadership> accessed 10 October 2017.

159 ibid 148.

160 ibid.

161 Multilateral Investment Guarantee Agency, World Bank, 'World Investment and Political Risk' (2011) <http://www.miga.org/documents/WIPR11.pdf> 15 December 2016. 'PRI protects against losses arising from a host government's breach or repudiation of a contractual agreement with an investor. Claims are usually payable only after an investor has invoked a dispute resolution mechanism (such as arbitration), has obtained an award for damages, and the host government has failed to honour the award.'

162 Shihata, 'The Settlement of Disputes Regarding Foreign Investment' (n 137) 97. See Tonova, Vasani, and Day (n 148) 83–97.

163 Cardosi (n 151) 150.

164 ibid.

165 ibid.

166 ibid 150–1.

be available to this member country until all arrears are paid.[167] If a member seeks to withdraw from the World Bank, or if the World Bank suspends membership and does not restore the membership within one year, the World Bank can use funds from a member state's account to settle debts. The World Bank understands remaining losses from default to be 'country credit risk,' and covers losses with equity that it keeps in store.[168]

Thirteen countries are members and shareholders, each of whom benefits from loans and credits provided by the IBRD and IDA. However, under certain circumstances these countries have refused to comply with the arbitral awards in practice. This raises the question of whether the World Bank can use its unique ability to honour the unpaid awards.[169]

Closer examination of this question suggests that the World Bank can target non-compliance with ICSID arbitration awards by suspending financing to the debtor country—this is similar to the penalties imposed upon members for unpaid bank loans.[170] With regard to ICSID awards, implying that Article 53 of the ICSID Convention establishes an obligation to the World Bank would enable it to enforce the same penalties that are imposed on members of the World Bank who fail to honour awards.[171] In addition, the World Bank can honour the awards which are applied by the party and then add this—whether to the non-compliant state's capital account or as an additional obligation owed to the Bank–to the outstanding loans taken out by the losing party.[172] However, it should not be overlooked that activating the World Bank in this manner may require amendments to be made to the Articles of Agreement. Article III, which establishes that 'the resources … of the Bank shall be used exclusively for the benefit of members,' appears to be foremost in this respect.[173] It should also be noted that losing party states may regard World Bank enforcement to be an infringement of this obligation.[174] In addition, this action may also be construed to be a violation of the ICSID Convention. This is attributable to the fact that the ICSID was established as a self-executing institution;[175] in addition, the World Bank agreement also establishes that each organisation of the World Bank is separate and associated with different liabilities. In addition, it should also be acknowledged that the ICSID was established with a view to creating an independent and impartial platform that would be immune to both political pressure and the influence of national courts. ICSID Convention Article 54(3) establishes that execution is governed by the state in which execution is sought.

> As a counterargument, it may be suggested that the satisfaction of the awards by the World Bank can contribute to increases in FDI (also it should be recognised that the reverse consequence is just as likely).[176] However, it is clearly insufficient to focus upon the benefits that

167 ibid 151.

168 IBRD, World Bank, Management's Discussion & Analysis and Financial Statements 55–58 (2012) [hereinafter IBRD MDA], <http://treasury.worldbank.org/cmd/pdf/IBRD_MDA_and_Financial_Statements_June_2012.pdf> accessed 22 March 2017.

169 Cardosi (n 151) 150.

170 ibid.

171 ibid 151.

172 ibid.

173 ibid 152.

174 ibid.

175 Baldwin, Kantor, and Nolanmake (n 25) in Subramanian (n 9) 200.

176 Cardosi (n 151) 152. See also George K Foster, 'Collecting from Sovereigns: The Current Legal Framework for Enforcing Arbitral Awards and Court Judgments against States and Their Instrumentalities, and Some Proposals for Its Reform' (2008) 25 Ariz J Intl & Comp L 665–732. (discussing the likelihood of

> accrue to individual member states; after all, activating the bank in the preceding manner may require the establishment of a multilateral agreement.[177] While the World Bank is free, when considering whether to provide a loan or guarantee to a borrower, to take other variables into account (such as the level of political risk within the country), it is ultimately the case that it may require a multilateral agreement.[178]

As Joseph M. Cardosi demonstrates, the practical lessons which emerge from the *AIG v. Kazakhstan* case[179] may contribute to a greater degree of comprehension. This example clearly illustrates how the World Bank can, in working with other institutions, effectuate ICSID awards. As has been previously noted, AIG is an American foreign investor that invested in Kazakhstan. If AIG had purchased political risk insurance from MIGA with a view to recovering the risk of expropriation, it would have benefited from two courses of potential action. Firstly, it could have filed a claim with MIGA, seeking compensation for losses incurred under the MIGA insurance policy. Secondly, it could have filed a claim with MIGA after the ICSID arbitration, seeking compensation for the non-honoured award.[180]

With regard to the IBRD, Kazakhstan also has approximately 3000 shares in the IBRD, which have been purchased at a total cost of almost $20 million.[181] In addition, the state is also currently borrowing almost $5 million from the IBRD.[182] The World Bank could therefore justifiably consider suspending all future loans, pending Kazakhstan's payment of the award to AIG. Notwithstanding this possibility, if the state does not comply with the award, the World Bank could pay the award out of its equity and so debit the state's capital account. The Kazakhstan example clearly reiterates that the World Bank could seek to resolve sovereign immunity in a number of different ways; however, it should be taken into account that the World Bank may be significantly eroded if it pays out ICSID

---

increased investment flows following the creation of an execution mechanism that assured investors their losses would be recoverable).

177 ibid 156.

178 ibid 15

1. World Bank Operating Policy 7.40 provides:
2. If the Bank receives notice that a member country is unwilling to take steps to resolve a dispute over its failure to service external debt and if the Bank deems such failure to have a significant effect on the member's creditworthiness or on its ability to implement Bank-financed projects/programs or service Bank loans, the Bank examines the procedures followed by the parties in addressing the issue and determines what action, if any, it should take.
3. If the Bank is seriously dissatisfied with the position taken by the member country, it may, at its discretion, decide not to make new loans to or with the guarantee of the member country until the country takes certain actions to rectify the situation. In making its decision, the Bank considers whether the circumstances of the default give rise to concerns about the member country's creditworthiness for continued Bank lending.

World Bank, 'Disputes over Defaults on External Debt, Expropriation, and Breach of Contract' (March 2012) [hereinafter WBOP], <http://go.worldbank.org/WBOMT5JTU0> accessed 3 January 2017. In addition to this, according to Cardosi (n 151) 152–3: 'The Bank's Executive Directors handle disputes regarding interpretation of the Articles of Agreement; if the clearinghouse function proved to be ultra vires, a vote of three-fifths of Bank members carrying eighty-five percent of the voting power could amend the Articles of Agreement to allow the new function.'

179 *AIG Capital Partners, Inc. v. Republic of Kazakhstan (AIG, Inc.)*, [2005] EWHC (Comm) 2239, [1], [2006] 1 W.L.R. 1420 (Eng.). (Noting that the ICSID award held that the actions of the Republic of Kazakhstan amounted to expropriation.)

180 Cardosi (n 151) 153.

181 IBRD MDA (n 168).

182 ibid.

awards for undeveloped countries.[183] Zimbabwe is a particularly instructive example in this respect—the country has already defaulted on bank loans. The unpaid loans are over 20 times greater than the amount that Zimbabwe has paid in capital.[184] At the same time, even if the World Bank continues to pay developing countries' ICSID award payments, it may prove to be the case that the countries paying in capital Could withdraw from the World Bank, upon the basis that they are significantly impaired by the loan obligations.[185]

On the other hand, it should be recognised that the recommended solution can be applied by individual countries, such as the United States. The United States has a 1961 Foreign Aid Act that, when combined with the Helms Amendment of 1994, restricts foreign aid to any state that has 'nationalized or expropriated the property of any United States person' and has not provided 'adequate and effective compensation [...], as required by international law.'[186] According to the act, the suspension of aid will occur if the disputes have not been resolved within three years of the date on which the claims were filed (or other dates depending on the process)—under these circumstances, the prohibition on funding would resume.[187] However, if the expropriating state has either compensated the US investor or has accepted to initiate the ICSID process or other forms of arbitration, the prohibition will not be valid for this situation.[188] The act also establishes that the president

> shall instruct the United States Executive Directors of each multilateral development bank and international financial institution to vote against any loan or other utilization of the funds of such bank or institution for the benefit of any country that is subject to the suspension of US foreign aid under the sections' provisions.[189]

The most well-known example in this respect is provided by the Argentina case, with the US attempting to vote against[190] the World Bank's extension of loans to Argentina in September 2011.[191] However, it should be recognised that investors must have a strong and close relation to their home states if they are to protect them at the international level, primarily by exerting pressure on international organisations or by manipulating existing business ties and relations. This latter possibility is, should it be recognised, somewhat remote—states will invariably be reluctant to damage diplomatic and business relations with host states.[192] In addition, given variations within these relations, there are also likely to be comparable variations in practice.

Under these circumstances, it is clear that the withdrawal of bank membership creates a number of disadvantages for member states. The best alternative is probably to withdraw ICSID membership.[193] This is due to the fact that states can settle their cases in various

183 Cardosi (n 151) 153.
184 IBRD MDA (n 168) 53–8.
185 Cardosi (n 151) 154.
186 US Foreign Aid Act of 1961, 22 USC section 2370a(a)(1)(A), (a)(2)(B).
187 ibid.
188 Bjorklund, 'State Immunity and the Enforcement of Investor-State Arbitral Awards' (n 71) 835.
189 ibid.
190 Charles B Rosenberg, 'The Intersection of International Trade and International Arbitration: The Use of Trade Benefits to Secure Compliance with Arbitral Awards' 2 (2013) 44 Geo J Intl L 503–30.
191 Tonova, Vasani, and Day (n 148) 92. Joubin-Bret (n 22) 104. Also there is the approach of 'peer pressure.' In *Santa Elena v. Costa Rica*, 'the US government put diplomatic pressure on Costa Rica, notably on attending the OECD, to ensure that it would not resist an ICSID arbitration over the amount of compensation after an expropriation.'
192 Cardosi (n 151) 145.
193 ibid 154.

systems. The New York Convention can also be substituted. In practice, the connection of the World Bank Group organisations has a number of clear benefits and drawbacks. It might be suggested that the latter is why the bank sought to establish a depoliticised system for investment dispute settlement. It should also be recognised that the establishment of connections between bank institutions will require amendments to be agreed—it may be difficult to establish agreement among member states on this issue.[194] In setting this potential obstacle aside, some scholars have argued that the issue of sovereign immunity can only be resolved through multilateral means.[195] In operating within this framework, the bank will help investors to facilitate the execution of awards; in operating in this manner, the bank will simultaneously complete a number of different goals, thus promoting sustainable economic growth, eradicating poverty and minimising the sovereign immunity obstacle.[196] As has already been noted, it is possible that this solution may damage the bank, inflicting with particular severity upon the ICSID institution and potentially making the situation even worse than it currently is. At the beginning of this chapter it was noted that each of the World Bank Group organisations is 'legally and financially independent, with separate assets and liabilities.'[197] This established the basis for a discussion of whether these organisations could be made to work together more effectively. However, another alternative would be to consider whether the execution of arbitral awards could resolved in ICSID itself, thus offsetting the need for help from other institutions or organisations. This would also mean that it would no longer be necessary for member states to withdraw World Bank membership. In addition, it would also overcome potential confusion as to whether the clause that enables the host state to waive its sovereignty from execution is valid within the enforcing state.

4.3.3 *Refusal of the next ICSID application of non-compliant states or investors (new proposal)*

Within the legal field, there is a strong belief that ICSID awards have been voluntarily honoured since the ICSID Convention was drafted. By virtue of the fact that states signed the convention, it is assumed, in accordance with *pacta sunt servanda*, that they will obey the provisions without any political or economic force being necessitated.[198] However, current ICSID cases demonstrate that there is a risk of non-compliance with the awards, with state sovereignty arising as a perennial concern. Although this right does not immediately appear to be an issue in the execution of ICSID awards, in practice there is a clear problem that pertains to the categorisation of state assets. It could be argued that a number of states have used the right as a pretext, with a view to preventing execution. The state's municipal laws, which determine whether the assets are connected with public or commercial activities, are a particularly important reference point in this regard. At this point, the convention enters and enables the enforcing state's jurisdiction. It might be helpful to recall that the ICSID does not completely disappear after the award is rendered—in

194 Cardosi (n 151) 152.

195 ibid 156.

196 ibid.

197 See <https://openknowledge.worldbank.org/bitstream/handle/10986/22550/WBAR2015FinancialStatements.pdf> accessed 30 December 2016.

198 Nmehielle (n 89) 21–48.

this respect, the institution offers a number of post-award remedies which allow for the interpretation, revision, or annulment of awards. However, it should be noted that these remedies are restricted on a number of grounds. To take one example, Article 52's annulment requirements are narrow and primarily procedural in character. Indeed, the review process is internal and does not extend to further appeals.

Up until this point, this chapter has presented investor–state arbitration as being semi-commercial, semi-public, and associated with a clear political risk. Although it can be assumed that the ICSID is a depoliticised, independent, and impartial dispute settlement system, it is clear that there is political or economic pressure in reality, especially at the execution stage—the vote cutting World Bank benefits being a particularly instructive reference point in this respect.[199] Even if these political or economic influences are not clearly evidenced during the ICSID process, they may nonetheless become apparent after the awards are rendered. For example, one state can retaliate against a counterpart upon the basis that it has failed to fulfil its treaty obligations. The applicant state could initiate countermeasures against the violating state, possibly deliberately breaching its own investment treaty obligations in the process. Conceivably, this course of action could be excused by the law of countermeasures.

However, the crucial purpose of this resolution proposal is to balance the disputing sides.[200] Before attending to the new suggestion, it might therefore be more instructive to touch upon Amazu A. Asouzu's suggestion of a balanced provision which establishes that when an arbitral award favours a state, the state of the individual party must endeavour, within the scope of its national law, to assist in the implementation of the award.[201] It is particularly well established that the home state should be liable in instances where the investor refuses to satisfy an award in favour of the host state.[202] Even though this proposal appears to balance the disputing parties, it might still be impossible to achieve this outcome; this is because current investors are multinationals and defining their nationality has been debated in practice. It may therefore be the case that related home states may fail to incur the payment with an appropriate sense of responsibility.

As a relatively recent innovation, the ICSID itself could not be used to retaliate against a state that has violated its ICSID Convention obligations. This point is further reiterated by the Draft Articles on the Responsibility of International Organizations (DARIO). The convention imposes obligations on an international organisation; refusing to register an investor's claim would, under ICSID, be considered a violation of those obligations.[203] It will be now analysed whether the ICSID has the right to retaliate. Alternately, is it instead the home state of the unpaid investor that would have a sound basis for retaliation? The convention imposes obligations on an international organisation (ICSID); refusing to register an investor's claim would, under the terms established by ICSID, be considered

199 Tonova, Vasani, and Day (n 148) 92.

200 Amazu A Asouzu, 'African States and the Enforcement of Arbitral Awards: Some Key Issues' (1999) 15 Arbitration International 1–52.

201 ibid 47. See also ICSID, 'History of the Convention: Documents Concerning the Origin and Formulation of the Convention' (1968) Vol. II, Part 1, at para 31 (Doc. 13).

202 ibid.

203 Yet, perhaps this violation could be justified under Article 22 of the ILC's Draft Articles on Responsibility of International Organisations (DARIO). It would fulfil the conditions in Part Four, Chapter II of DARIO. Draft Articles on the Responsibility of International Organizations (DARIO) <http://legal.un.org/ilc/texts/instruments/english/draft_articles/9_11_2011.pdfdar> accessed 12 February 2017.

a violation of those obligations. However, it is perhaps the case that this violation could be justified under Article 22 of the ILC's draft articles on DARIO. This in turn raises the question of whether the conditions set out in the relevant part of DARIO (Part Four, Chapter II) would be fulfilled.

This chapter has previously suggested that the World Bank could play an important role in ensuring compliance with ICSID awards, with several roles being set out for the World Bank. However, this chapter focuses upon the ICSID's institutional role—it will accordingly be evaluated whether the ICSID could initiate an action against the non-compliant parties, taking their next application to the institution into account. With a view to analysing the proposed solution, this chapter will now consider the ICSID's application process.

The ICSID Administrative Council is the main organ that is related to the disputing parties' application, consisting of one representative of each contracting state. Its mandate and authority are set out in Articles 4–8 of the ICSID Convention. The World Bank Group's president is *ex officio* chairman of the Administrative Council but has no vote. Article 6 establishes that the council is the central decision-making mechanism that guides the implementation of institutional procedures.

When a contracting state or a contracting state's national brings a dispute before the ICSID, their written application is initially received by the secretariat. The secretary-general is the legal representative and the principal officer of the ICSID, being responsible for administration and ensuring that the council operates in accordance with the convention and the rules that it has established. It performs the function of registrar, retaining the power to authenticate arbitral awards rendered pursuant to the convention and retaining the power to certify copies. The general secretariat is also responsible for sending a copy of the request to the opposing party. The request contains information pertaining to the issues in dispute and the identity of the respective parties, along with their consent to engage in arbitration in accordance with the rules of procedure for the institution of conciliation and arbitration proceedings. Subsequent to the receipt of the request, the secretary-general is responsible for registering it, presuming that it is not found, upon the basis of information contained in the request, that the dispute falls outside the ICSID's jurisdiction. It is also responsible for notifying the respective parties of registration or refusal to register.[204]

In the terms established by the proposal, the secretariat could refuse the application by the losing party if previous ICSID award debts remain unpaid. The council could monitor compliance with the awards, making note of failures to honour obligations before then forwarding the relevant documentation to the general secretariat. When the secretariat receives a request to apply to ICSID arbitration by one of the parties on this list, this organ could then, as a precondition, request that this party comply with the previous award debt. It is open to debate whether this action can be justified under Article 22 of the ILC's draft articles on DARIO.

It should be acknowledged that the ICSID is an international organisation,[205] a truth clearly established by the World Bank's official website.[206] In addition, the ICSID has the

204 ICSID Convention Articles 9–12.

205 Sergio Puig, 'Emergence & Dynamism in International Organizations: ICSID, Investor-State Arbitration & International Investment Law' (2012) 44 Geo J Intl L 531.

206 ibid. For more information regarding the development of international organisations, see Guy Fiti Sinclair, *To Reform the World: International Organizations and the Making of Modern States* (OUP 2017) 1.

ability to initiate action against the losing party under Article 22 of DARIO.[207] DARIO also clearly establishes that an international organisation cannot initiate countermeasures against a responsible member state unless the countermeasures are consistent with the rules of the organisation. In addition, it is also clearly established that countermeasures may not be taken by an international organisation against a member state in response to breach of an international obligation unless such countermeasures are provided for within the organisation's rules.[208]

With regard to the ICSID, there are no rules related to countermeasures, clearly establishing the steps to be taken when a member state breaches its obligations. However, Article 27 establishes another option to use countermeasures.[209] It also clearly establishes that sanctions which an organisation adopts against its members are *per se* lawful measures, meaning that they cannot be appropriately categorised as countermeasures.[210] The obligations of the injured party may restrict or forbid, albeit implicitly, the organisation's application of countermeasures against its members.[211] However, it remains open to question whether countermeasures may be applied in the absence of explicit or implicit rules.[212] DARIO establishes two requirements that pertain to the application of countermeasures. First, countermeasures cannot be 'inconsistent with the rules of the organization.' Second, there should not be other available alternatives that may qualify as 'appropriate means [...] for otherwise inducing compliance with the obligations of the responsible State or international organization concerning cessation of the breach and reparation.'[213] In this circumstance, it appears that countermeasures will only be permitted if the organisation's rules establish clear relations between the international organisation and its members. The ICSID does not appear to possess this attribute; in addition, its depoliticised character also raises further questions. In conclusion, it therefore appears that the DARIO cannot be applied by the ICSID, with a view to resolving non-compliance arbitral awards.

Setting these shortcomings aside, it also appears that a number of other issues could potentially arise. The situation would be substantially complicated if the losing state made a partial payment. Similar difficulties would also arise if, in the course of the opposing party seeking to bring a case before the ICSID, the ICSID rejected the request, citing the losing state's previous breach as a justification. In rejecting the innocent member state's investor, the ICSID would therefore appear to have breached its own convention. However, if the ICSID invokes these rules, it is best placed to achieve a rebalancing of the parties. In this circumstance, the home state does not intervene in the dispute, and it is therefore placed in diametric opposition to the host state. In this instance, the purpose is to balance the parties and guarantee the payment of the award.

Taking these potential difficulties into account, it may be more beneficial not to activate the institution. This raises the question of whether there are other lawful means through

207 DARIO (n 203).

208 DARIO Article 22(2)(b).

209 Martins Paparinskis, 'Investment Arbitration and the Law of Countermeasures' (2008) 79 British Yearbook of International Law 264.

210 International Law Commission, Draft Articles on the Responsibility of International Organizations, with Commentaries (2011) <http://legal.un.org/ilc/texts/instruments/english/commentaries/9_11_2011.pdf> accessed 12 February 2017.

211 ibid.

212 ibid Article 22.

213 ibid.

which compliance with ICSID awards can be achieved. This question has not received extensive treatment in the literature, an oversight which justifies the following discussion of the applicability of the law of countermeasures and challenges in practice.

4.3.4 Proposal to reform ICSID rules

The most frequently proposed remedy to the problems of the current investor–state dispute settlement (ISDS) is the establishment of an appellate body within the ICSID system, which is preferred to multilateral solutions. This in large part reflects the current international political environment, as it is clear that neither the US nor other active countries such as Russia will be able to effectively initiate a multinational investment statute.[214]

In the current system, there are a number of issues, including the need for an appeal body whose interventions will provide coherence, consistency, predictability, and objectivity. It could also, in assessing procedural and substantive correctness, overturn or amend incorrect awards,[215] and this would enhance the legitimacy of the whole ICSID system. This reform would also help to overcome the enforcement issue of ICSID awards. It was previously noted that current problems are linked to enforcement issues; these have arisen because some states are not satisfied with the legitimacy and correctness of ICSID awards. This is why they have refused to comply with its arbitral awards and have even used the state sovereignty guard in practice.

This reform was actually debated in 2004 by the ICSID Secretariat when it drafted the ICSID Appeals Facility Rules after reviewing ICSID awards. The secretariat said the facility rules 'would best be designed for use in conjunction with both forms of ICSID arbitration, UNCITRAL Rules arbitration and any other form of arbitration provided for in the investor-to-State dispute-settlement provisions of investment treaties.'[216]

But in 2005, the secretariat abandoned the proposal after receiving an unenthusiastic response from members.[217] This reflected a general consensus that while an amendment was legally possible, it would not work in practice. Opponents also claimed that the appeal body would take too long to make a decision,[218] meaning that enforcing the award could take as much time. At this time, the establishment of an appellate mechanism continued to be discussed. The United Nations Commission on International Trade Law (UNCITRAL) is now considering an appeal mechanism that will overcome ongoing problems with ISDS and is also examining a multilateral investment court (MIC).

It is essential to take the advantages and disadvantages of an appellate mechanism into account when considering the ICSID Convention. It is clear that an appellate body would

214 Yusuf Çalışkan and Ahmet Dülger, 'Time for the Appeal Tribunal in Investment Arbitration: Lessons from WTO' in Cigdem Nas and Mustafa Erkan (eds), *International Investment and Trade Agreements: Recent Developments and Problems* (Oniki levha 2021).

215 Alexander J Marcopoulos, 'Revisiting the Risk of Undesired Appeal in Investment Treaty Arbitration: Is Deference to the Tribunal's Award Still Less Likely in the ICSID Context?' (2021) Arbitration International <https://academic.oup.com/arbitration/advance-article-abstract/doi/10.1093/arbint/aiab005/6209780> accessed 2 May 2021.

216 ICSID Secretariat Discussion Paper, 'Possible Improvements of the Framework for ICSID Arbitration' (Washington 2004). <https://icsid.worldbank.org/sites/default/files/Possible%20Improvements%20of%20the%20Framework%20of%20ICSID%20Arbitration.pdf> accessed 20 May 2021.

217 Antonio Parra, *The History of ICSID* (1st edn, OUP 2012) 1.

218 Albert Jan van den Berg, 'Appeal Mechanism for ISDS Awards: Interaction with the New York and ICSID Conventions' (2019) 34 ICSID Review 156–89.

provide consistency, coherence, legitimacy, and precedent to be followed by future tribunals. It is acknowledged that it is possible to confront a contradictory arbitral decision in investment arbitration when disputing parties are not happy.[219] Precedent is not binding in the field and is not considered to be appropriately adjusted to the current structure of investment arbitration. An appellate body with hierarchical superiority can impose binding decisions on first instance arbitral tribunals.[220] State decisions can also provide predictability, consistency, and legitimacy in the field. If an appellate mechanism is established under the ICSID Convention, it will have been inspired by the success of the WTO's Dispute Settlement Body.[221] The WTO Appellate Body would have the legal power to realise global consistency of the law.[222] Here it should be remembered that amendment of the ICSID Convention is highly complex in practice.

First, it has been noted that 'an appeal mechanism could fragment the ICSID arbitral regimes: ICSID arbitrations would in some instances be subject to the mechanism and in other cases remain free of the mechanism.'[223] The parties might therefore cover the appellate mechanism in their BITs, but others might not. This produces different legal regimes in the ICSID system and creates delays for enforcement by extending the time required to produce a final award.[224] But if the award rendered by the first instance tribunal is wrong, the results are graver than delayed enforcement.[225] In this circumstance, the correctness of the award is related to the actual interpretation of the treaty.[226] Strictly speaking, there are no wrong awards, but rather wrong interpretations.

Second, there is also a concern that appeal may be an option for the failing party, and this must be recognised as a limitation on the mechanism's application.[227] An appeal body imposes high costs and will take time to reach a final decision.

Third, establishing an appellate mechanism under the ICSID requires some technical conditions to be addressed. For example, Article 53(1) of the convention would contradict review of ICSID awards.[228] In order to amend the article in accordance with the appeal, 164 member states would need to accept the amendment and this would be quite hard to achieve. But it has already been noted that Article 41 of the Vienna Convention on the Law of Treaties (VCLT) can establish a way for certain parties to amend the convention. But if this approach is adopted, other member states will not be affected by the

219 *SGS v. Pakistan*, ICSID Case No. ARB/01/13; and *SGS v. Republic of Philippines*, ICSID Case No. ARB/02/6, sister cases.

220 Christoph Schreuer and Matthew Weiniger, 'A Doctrine of Precedent?' in Peter Muchlinski, Federico Ortino, and Christoph Schreuer (eds), *The Oxford Handbook of International Investment Law* (OUP 2008) 1.

221 Çalışkan and Dülger (n 214) 114–5.

222 Thomas Dietz, Marius Dotzauer, and Edward S Cohen, 'The Legitimacy Crisis of Investor-State Arbitration and the New EU Investment Court System' (2019) 26 Review of International Political Economy.

223 ICSID Secretariat Discussion Paper (n 216) 15.

224 ibid.

225 Note by the UNCITRAL Secretariat, Possible Future Work in the Field of Dispute Settlement: Reforms of ISDS (20 April 2017) <https://undocs.org/en/A/CN.9/917> accessed 11 August 2020 para 22.

226 ibid.

227 The UK has restrictions to apply the mechanism. See Nikolay Popov, 'The Effectiveness of the Grounds for the Annulment of ICSID Awards' (LLM thesis, Uppsala University 2020).

228 Article 53 of the ICSID Convention: 'The provisions of these Rules shall apply mutatis mutandis to any procedure relating to the interpretation, revision or annulment of an award and to the decision of the Tribunal or Committee.'

reform.[229] But an appealed award should also be enforced in the third states of (which do not accept the amendment related to appeal body section of the ICSID Convention) the ICSID Convention. In order to enforce the appeal award in third states, the appeal award can be considered an award for the purposes of Article 54 of the ICSID Convention.[230] But the ICSID treaty only permits one award to be rendered and others (such as partial or interim) are considered to be 'decisions.'[231]

In considering ICSID's one-award scheme, we see that one remedy may be to view all decisions by the first instance and the appellate body as a 'decision,' and to only see the last decision (on appeal) as an 'award.' Another possibility is that the appeal decision goes back to the first instance tribunal that endorsed it as an award, and it then becomes enforceable under the ICSID Convention. In addition, the award of the ICSID appellate body could be enforced under the New York Convention.[232] However, the disadvantage of the latteralternative is that the appealed award cannot be benefited from the ICSID's automatic enforcement mechanism.

One further issue arises when the decision rendered by the appellate body is subject to annulment or setting aside under the terms established by the ICSID. It is possible to appeal under Article 52 of the ICSID Convention, although this does not apply if an *inter se* amendment provides otherwise. This would also be a fragmentation of ICSID arbitration.

To summarise, the necessity of legitimacy in the field has resulted in the establishment of an appeal mechanism. But it is not certain how an appeal body and its framework can be drafted under ICSID arbitration. There are still a number of factors to take into account, including the aforementioned questions and the clear incentive for the ICSID to reform itself, lest it be replaced by the MIC. The resolution of the legitimacy issue will require the interests of states to be taken into account.

Amendment of an ICSID award via *inter se* can result in fragmentation and the other mentioned problems, and so one alternative might be to revise the model BITs, such as the 2018 Dutch Model Investment Agreement.[233] Arbitrators would no longer be appointed by parties but rather by an appointing authority from a panel; however, a number of provisions would need to be put in place, including serious ethical provisions, the prohibition of 'double hatting,' and the establishment of one fee for all that corresponds to the ICSID fee schedule.[234] These and similar measures can correct many of the shortcomings in

229 Gabrielle Kaufmann-Kohler and Michele Potestà, 'Can the Mauritius Convention Serve as a Model for the Reform of Investor-State Arbitration in Connection with the Introduction of a Permanent Investment Tribunal or an Appeal Mechanism?' (CIDS, 3 June 2016) paras 141, 200, 237–45 <http://www.uncitral.org/pdf/english/CIDS_Research_Paper_Mauritius.pdf> accessed 15 May 2019. Gabrielle Kaufmann-Kohler and Michele Potestà, 'The Composition of a Multilateral Investment Court and of an Appeal Mechanism for Investment Awards (CIDS Supplemental Report, 15 November 2017) <http://www.uncitral.org/pdf/english/workinggroups/wg_3/CIDS_Supplemental_Report.pdf> accessed 15 May 2019. See also August Reinisch, 'Will the EU's Proposal Concerning an Investment Court System for CETA and TTIP Lead to Enforceable Awards?—The Limits of Modifying the ICSID Convention and the Nature of Investment Arbitration' (2016) 19 J Intl Economic L 761, 772–3. ICSID Secretariat Discussion Paper (n 216) 15.

230 Berg, 'Appeal Mechanism for ISDS Awards' (n 218) 170.

231 Schreuer, *The ICSID Convention: A Commentary* (n 14) 812.

232 Berg, 'Appeal Mechanism for ISDS Awards' (n 218) 176.

233 Dutch Model Investment Agreement (2018) Article 20, available at <https://www.rijksoverheid.nl/documenten/publicaties/2018/10/26/modeltekst-voor-bilaterale-investeringsakkoorden> accessed 15 January 2019, in Berg, 'Appeal Mechanism for ISDS Awards' (n 218) 189.

234 ibid.

the current ISDS and can even be considered to create an ISDS. The resolution of the legitimacy crisis may not therefore require a time-consuming appeal mechanism. This applies because each FDI has distinct characteristics that are based on cultural, economic, geographical, and political differences between host states.[235] Accordingly, if the intention is to develop a multilateral or ICSID *inter se* appeal mechanism, this may not be the best approach.

4.3.5 Securing compliance of ICSID awards with countermeasures under the law of state responsibility

The contemporary law of foreign investment protection rests on a number of different legal arguments and foundations.[236] The acceptance of traditional legal rules reflects a situation in which attempts to devise new solutions and frameworks have proven, to varying degrees and extents, to be ineffective.[237] Aside from providing a clear foundation, this sometimes allows separate approaches to develop in parallel.[238] The current chapter will compare classic and modern approaches to investment disputes, placing particular emphasis upon the law of countermeasures.[239] Much of the discussion of this issue has begun with the premise of voluntary compliance with arbitral awards, however, contemporary debates and developments have reiterated the salience of non-compliance. A number of recommendations that have sought to overcome this obstacle have already been engaged, however, closer examination has revealed that their disadvantages outweigh their advantages. A number of insufficiently recognised articles enable us to approach this central issue within the investment arbitration field from a different angle. In the ensuing discussion, the chapter will examine how countermeasures might be, during the ICSID arbitration process, applied to instances of non-compliance. While the discussion works towards solutions, it will also highlight a number of associated drawbacks.

Countermeasures are established as one of the basic rules of decentralised international legal order, providing injured states with the right of self-help.[240] Countermeasures are unilaterally affirmed by states, operating outside of multilateral institutions.[241] Countermeasures are voluntarily used as a reaction to acts that are internationally recognised to be wrong.[242] Wrongfulness can be conceived with reference to procedural and substantive criteria. While wrongfulness functions at an objective level of analysis, states ultimately formulate it in accordance with their own perspective.[243] As preconditions, an internationally wrongful act must occur and the injured state must call upon the injuring party to comply with its obligations.[244] In addition, the proposed countermeasures must be proportionate to the injury.[245]

235 Çalışkan and Dülger (n 214).
236 Paparinskis, 'Investment Arbitration and the Law of Countermeasures' (n 209).
237 ibid.
238 ibid 265.
239 ibid.
240 Derek W Bowett, 'Economic Coercion and Reprisals by States' (1972) 13 Va J Intl L in Paparinskis, 'Investment Arbitration and the Law of Countermeasures' (n 209) 324.
241 Paparinskis, 'Investment Arbitration and the Law of Countermeasures' (n 209) 269.
242 ibid.
243 ibid.
244 ibid.
245 ibid.

The application of countermeasures to investor–state disputes is a long-established and widely recognised practice within the international legal order.[246] With a view to ascertaining the significance of countermeasures, it will be instructive to refer to the Sicilian Sulphur dispute (which occurred between the years 1837 and 1842).[247] In the course of this dispute, Great Britain claimed that the Two Sicilies had breached the 1816 treaty of commerce (which, *inter alia*, protected the property rights of British nationals) by granting sulphur monopoly rights to a company of French merchants. As a result, Great Britain embargoed Sicilian ships, maintaining this course of action until, subsequent to French mediation, the grant of the monopoly was withdrawn in 1840.[248] In the course of this dispute, the British countermeasures were adopted with a view to compelling 'consent [upon the part of the Two Sicilies] to a satisfactory settlement of a difference created by its own international delinquency.'[249]

However, it is clear that countermeasures and FDI can be applied in the opposite direction, that is, against the foreign investor.[250] Oppenheim therefore observes that '[a]n act of reprisal can be performed against anything and everything that belongs or is due to the delinquent State and its citizens.'[251] As the preceding quotation was strict. More recent developments have brought about an important change in this respect, aligning it with the prerequisites of a modern rule and enabling it to function as an ICSID mechanism. The tribunal overseeing one case (*Banro American Resources, Inc. and Société Aurifère du Kivu et du Maniema S.A.R.L. v. DRC*)[252] explained that

> [o]ne of the main objectives of the mechanisms instituted by the Washington [ICSID] Convention was to put an end to international tension and crises, leading sometimes to the use of force, generated in the past by the diplomatic protection accorded to an investor by the State of which it was a national.[253]

With regard to the reduction of tensions and crises, the investor's home state does not enter the equation at all; on the contrary, it only applies countermeasures in defence of its investor, citing grounds of wrongfulness in the process.[254]

The WTO Dispute Settlement Understanding (WTO DSU) is a particularly well-known and effective mechanism, being applied with a view to ensuring that countermeasures comply with the provisions of the overarching treaty.[255] Article 22 of the WTO DSU establishes that the applicant can suspend concessions that have been made to the state that has violated the obligations. However, this step can only be undertaken if it is consistent with prior criteria. The WTO agreement drafted an important limitation to the use of trade-related countermeasures in the investment field.[256] Any suspension should first

246 ibid.

247 Great Britain, *State Papers 1839–1840*, Volume 28 (Harrison and Sons, London, 1857) 1163–1242.

248 ibid.

249 Paparinskis, 'Investment Arbitration and the Law of Countermeasures' (n 209) 266.

250 ibid.

251 ibid.

252 *Banro American Resources, Inc. and Société Aurifère du Kivu et du Maniema S.A.R.L. v. Democratic Republic of the Congo*, ICSID Case No. ARB/98/7, 1998.

253 ibid para 15.

254 Paparinskis, 'Investment Arbitration and the Law of Countermeasures' (n 209) 266.

255 Joubin-Bret (n 22) 109.

256 Roberto Echandi, 'Non-Compliance with Awards: The Remedies of Customary International Law' (2012) 106 Am Socy Intl L Proc.

look to engage with the sectors in question;[257] however, if the party considers that this is not an effective and practicable course of action, then other sectors may be considered.[258] In addition, the injured state is also entitled to seek the suspension of concessions or the upholding of other obligations through another agreement.[259]

Although countermeasures are the most effective means through which losing states can be forced to comply with investment awards, ICJ proceedings have not, to date, (under Article 64 of the ICSID Convention) sought to institute them, establishing a clear point of practical reference in instances where a state refuses to comply with an ICSID award.[260] With a view to understanding why this is the case, it should be first sought to establish the procedural conditions of the countermeasures. It should first be recognised that multinational treaties (and the ICSID is a good example in this respect) do not contain explicit provisions that pertain to countermeasures. In addition, the convention does not clearly indicate a solution that can be initiated in response to wrongful acts—this is despite the fact that it was originally established with a view to ending the strict application of countermeasures to foreign investors. The ILC's Articles on State Responsibility summarises the most up-to-date thinking on the subject of countermeasures.[261] This document clearly establishes that countermeasures can be applied within two conceptual frameworks: firstly, respectively precluding wrongfulness (Article 22); and secondly, implementation of the international responsibility of the state (Articles 49–54).[262] The application of countermeasures in investor–state arbitration disputes can therefore be conceived with reference to two situations—in the words of Martins Paparinskis—a 'shield' and a 'sword.'[263] In the first instance of investment law, countermeasures appear as a shield, meaning that the host state, in addressing itself to primary obligations under investment protection law, prevents a wrongful violation.[264] In the second instance of investment law, countermeasures appear as a sword, meaning that the home state actively strives to guarantee the implementation of investment protection obligations.[265] This chapter will focus upon the question of how countermeasures are used as a sword in the course of ICSID arbitration. It will demonstrate how countermeasures are, under the ICSID arbitration process, connected to non-compliance awards.

The previous case examples have clearly illustrated how countermeasures have been historically connected with the treatment and protection of foreigners' interests. Although the investment treaties include diplomatic protections that settle the dispute and protect individuals, countermeasures have not been sufficiently discussed.[266] One reason why

257 WTO Dispute Settlement Understanding, WTO DSU Article 22(3)(a).

258 WTO DSU Article 22(3)(b).

259 WTO DSU Article 22(3)(c).

260 Joubin-Bret (n 22) 109. Paparinskis, 'Investment Arbitration and the Law of Countermeasures' (n 209) 276. 'There is so far no publicly available information about States going further and using countermeasures to ensure the implementation of investment treaty obligations. At the same time, the lack of practice may simply reflect the so-far generally satisfactory compliance by host States with the awards, giving no practical incentive for home States to interfere in the dispute.'

261 Paparinskis, 'Investment Arbitration and the Law of Countermeasures' (n 209) 270.

262 The International Law Commission's (ILC) Articles on State Responsibility Articles 22, 49, 54. See <http://legal.un.org/ilc/texts/instruments/english/commentaries/9_6_2001.pdf> accessed 25 February 2017.

263 Paparinskis, 'Investment Arbitration and the Law of Countermeasures' (n 209) 270.

264 ibid.

265 ibid.

266 ibid 277.

countermeasures have not been used as a sword may be that investor–state arbitration, as a prior condition, has been 'depoliticised.' However, ongoing economic developments, in addition to the significant amount of risk that characterises pending arbitrations, may result in states increasingly failing to honour investment awards. Under these circumstances, it will be near-impossible to ascertain whether the failure originates within inability or reluctance.[267] This suggests that there needs to be a more sustained engagement with the home state's position with regard to countermeasures. Mexico is the best example in this regard, having, on two separate occasions, explicitly invoked countermeasures with a view to preventing wrongful breaches of investment protection rules.[268] Argentina has also, in response to economic crises, undertaken voluntary courses of action which breach its international obligations.[269] Taking these examples into account, it can be inferred that countermeasures against foreign property or investments are not, by virtue of the fact that they have a clear contemporary resonance, a purely historical phenomenon.[270]

However, it should be acknowledged that the role of countermeasures is not expressly addressed in any of the aforementioned documents, including the ICSID Convention. This means that their legal effect is indirect and must be extracted from the established right of diplomatic protection. This right is clearly spelt out within Article 1 of the 2006 ILC Draft Articles on Diplomatic Protection:

> diplomatic protection consists of the invocation by a State, through diplomatic action or other means of peaceful settlement, of the responsibility of another State for an injury caused by an internationally wrongful act of that State to a natural or legal person that is a national of the former State with a view to the implementation of such responsibility.[271]

Both diplomatic protection and the cited countermeasures can be traced back to secondary rules of international law that come into play when a primary rule is violated, but which are only put into effect under specific circumstances.[272] The law of diplomatic protection addresses the invocation of state responsibility, coming into force if the primary rule is breached. It establishes the treatment of the home state as a secondary rule.[273] The law of countermeasures comes under the law of state responsibility (see the ILC Articles on State Responsibility), establishing that countermeasures would be used as a defence against a claim that the state breached a treaty.[274]

Article 44 of the 2001 ILC Articles on State Responsibility puts in place a clear rubric of admissibility that references diplomatic protection rules of nationality. It outlines clear remedies that can be applied to injuries, clearly establishing how diplomatic protection can be initiated after local courses of action have been exhausted. Disputes between states

267 ibid 276.

268 ibid.

269 ibid.

270 ibid. As an example, 'Arangio-Ruiz pointed to the 1958 Indonesian expropriation of Dutch property, the 1959–1960 Cuban expropriation of property belonging to the Americans and the 1971 Libyan expropriation of the investment belonging to British Petroleum as examples of such countermeasures. Bank accounts of foreign nationals have also been frozen as apparent countermeasures against their home States.' G Arangio-Ruiz, 'Fourth Report on State Responsibility' in Yearbook of the ILC 1992, Vol. II.

271 2006 ILC Draft Articles on Diplomatic Protection <http://legal.un.org/ilc/texts/instruments/english/draft_articles/9_8_2006.pdf> accessed 28 February 2017.

272 Paparinskis, 'Investment Arbitration and the Law of Countermeasures' (n 209) 279.

273 ibid.

274 ibid.

are clearly referenced within the ICSID Convention and most investment protection treaties. The ICSID procedural framework permits recourse to countermeasures only after the inefficiency of all formalised methods of dispute settlement has been established.[275] By implication, third-party intervention by a neutral party should be pursued before countermeasures are initiated against the state that has failed to uphold its obligations. This point is, however, hotly debated within the ICL's work on state responsibility. Particular attention has been dedicated to the exhaustion of peaceful dispute settlement mechanisms and the existence of compromise clauses. Attention has also focused upon the issue of whether dispute settlement should be considered to be a co-requisite, as opposed to prerequisite, on countermeasures.[276] Thinking on this issue has incrementally shifted over time. While early drafts required the home state to exhaust all available measures of peaceful settlement of disputes, Article 48 of the ILCDraft (1996) established that 'the injured State may take countermeasures without any prior resort to third party dispute settlement procedures.'[277] Meanwhile, Article 52 of the ILC Draft (2001) established that the initiation of countermeasures does not rest upon preconditions.[278] In each of these respects, this chapter will assume that the ILC operated within the terms established by the Air Service Agreement case,[279] a particularly important case within the post-war period. This legal reference point, it is anticipated, will help to clarify the concepts of 'notification' and 'negotiation,' both of which have important implications for the topic of countermeasures.[280] In this case, the tribunal concluded that the US was entitled to use countermeasures (even though there was an obligation of negotiation and the possibility to submit the dispute to arbitration); however, it simultaneously established that the right would end when the dispute came before a tribunal.[281] While the case represented a crucial progression within thinking on state responsibility, this development was not embodied within a treaty; as such, the classical requirements that precede the adoption of countermeasures continue to be in practice.[282]

The most common approach to BITs is to allocate 6 months (although the precise period varies—it can be as short as 2 months or as long as 12 months) for negotiations or consultations.[283] Once this period is concluded, the dispute is then brought before the tribunal. The duration of this negotiation process may overlap with customary law obligations; however, this should not preclude the subsequent application of the countermeasure to a stage in advance of the time limitations.[284] This is attributable to the fact that the

275 ibid 302.

276 James Crawford, 'Counter-Measures as Interim Measures' (1994) 5 EJIL 65, 66. See also Paparinskis, 'Investment Arbitration and the Law of Countermeasures' (n 209) 303.

277 1996 Draft Articles on State Responsibility with Commentaries Thereto Adopted by the International Law Commission on First Reading. See <http://untreaty.un.org/ilc/texts/instruments/english/commentaries/9_6_1996.pdf> accessed 28 February 2017.

278 2001 ILC on State responsibility (n 262) Article 52.

279 Air Service Agreement case <http://legal.un.org/ilc/texts/instruments/english/commentaries/9_6_2001.pdf> accessed 28 February 2017.

280 ibid 136.

281 ibid.

282 ibid.

283 Paparinskis, 'Investment Arbitration and the Law of Countermeasures' (n 209) 304.

284 ibid.

obligation to negotiate has a strong meaning. The offer to negotiate, in contrast, has a weaker connotation.[285]

A number of accounts of non-compliance with ICSID awards have suggested that research pertaining to countermeasures in non-ICSID arbitrations can be applied verbatim to the ICSID arbitrations, thereby enabling the legal effect of Article 27 of the convention. Article 27(1) establishes the instances in which the provision does and does not apply, also setting out its *ratione materiae* scope.[286] In the terms that the provision establishes, it begins to apply when the investors complete their consent by submitting the claim. The article attains *dies a quo* when the host state consents to submit, that is, when mutual consent is established. Article 27(1) grants the home state the right to defend its national interest against the host state's non-compliance with awards.[287] There is still considerable controversy as to whether the article waivers or suspends applications that seek to achieve diplomatic protection for non-compliance ICSID awards.[288] *Waiver* means that the state and investor consent to initiate arbitration. In proceeding upon this basis, they will only preserve the home state's right to claim responsibility for the infringement of the primary rule with regard to the honouring of ICSID awards.[289] In this circumstance, the home state will only claim responsibility upon the basis that there has been a violation of non-compliance ICSID awards. The ILC Draft Article 45(a) (2001) establishes that the responsibility of a state may not be invoked if the injured state has validly waived the claim. Conversely, *suspension* means that the home state can exercise diplomatic protection over the main breach that has been lifted at a particular point in time.[290] Indeed, it should be recognised that failure to comply with the ICSID award is a different breach in and of itself. However, non-compliance may establish a continuation of the right to enjoy protection over the earlier breach. This point has, however, been significantly complicated by the fact that the differences between the two breaches have not been clearly and precisely spelt out.[291]

Broches, in directly addressing the article's lack of clarity on these points, sought to explain the notions of 'suspension' and 'revival of the right' by asserting (in the legal committee) that the

> closing phrase of [what was to become Article 27(1)] did not introduce a right of intervention by the investor's State but merely permitted such a right (if it existed) to revive if the State party to the dispute failed to comply with the award.[292]

In subsequent years, this argument gained considerable support, with the consequence that it is now widely assumed that a non-compliance award is not a new breach of the primary rule but a complete revival of the right to diplomatic protection, as it existed before

285 *Railway Traffic between Lithuania and Poland (Poland v. Lithuania)* [1931] PCIJ Rep Series A/B no 42 108, 116. John Collier and Vaughan Lowe, *The Settlement of Disputes in International Law; Institutions and Procedures* (OUP 1999) 73. 'An obligation to offer negotiation is weaker and would probably require only a good faith effort to create an opportunity of negotiations.'

286 Paparinskis, 'Investment Arbitration and the Law of Countermeasures' (n 209) 305.

287 Gauthier Vannieuwenhuyse, 'Bringing a Dispute Concerning ICSID Cases and the ICSID Convention before the International Court of Justice' (2009) LAPE 115–41.

288 Paparinskis, 'Investment Arbitration and the Law of Countermeasures' (n 209) 310.

289 ibid 280–1.

290 ibid 310.

291 ibid.

292 Vannieuwenhuyse (n 287).

the investor consented to arbitration.[293] It might be objected that this is not valid for the situation of non-compliance awards. It should, however, be noted that Article 26 of the ICSID Convention mentions the local remedies that have been exhausted in order to apply the diplomatic protection.[294]

It is also instructive to note how countermeasures are used to enforce international investment awards. This raises the possibility that any member state to the ICSID Convention (other than the injured state) can apply in situations when the breached obligations are owed to a group of states—in this instance, protection relates to a collective interest of the group.[295] It could also be argued, with specific reference to Article 54(1) of the ICSID Convention, and in the specific context of non-compliance with ICSID arbitral awards, that any third state which contracted to the ICSID Convention would be entitled to undertake countermeasures, with a view to ensuring compliance with international arbitral awards.[296]

Up until this point, the foundations of this view have not been questioned. However, in practice, even the injured state is reluctant to protect its own investor—for this reason, it appears to be weaker than any comparable third state. Even though investor–state dispute settlement mechanisms do not include specific provisions that are addressed to non-compliance with the international arbitral award, customary international law provides injured states with several effective remedies that can be addressed to this point. These countermeasures, when applied effectively, can be used to promote and uphold the honouring, and by extension the overall efficacy, of the international investment regime.[297]

When considering these questions, the attention of the observer continually comes back to the theme of depoliticisation. The depoliticised character of the ICSID is perhaps most clearly indicated in the applicable law and the fact that the foreign investor's home state is excluded from diplomatic protection once a dispute has been submitted to the ICSID.[298] However, it should not be overlooked that many of the issues with which the ICSID is concerned can easily become politicised—certainly, the ICSID did not anticipate a number of developments that occurred in the last quarter of the 20th century.[299] While the depolitical character of the ICSID was initially viewed positively by investors, it has since come to evidence a number of negative attributes, particularly with regard to execution issues. Although depoliticisation was necessary to achieve a peaceful settlement of investment disputes in the aftermath of the Second World War, it has since become clear that such disputes cannot, taking the broader context of international economic law and politics into account, be completely depoliticised.[300] Politics intrudes at all stages, from the drafting of BITs to the resolving of disputes. It should also be recognised that the non-compliance with ICSID awards is a breach of the ICSID Convention; however, the institution is currently silent on this issue. The ICSID only recommends the model clause to the states and member states' investor, with regard to the waiver of sovereign immunity from execution.

293 Paparinskis, 'Investment Arbitration and the Law of Countermeasures' (n 209) 311.
294 ibid.
295 Echandi (n 256) 122.
296 ibid.
297 ibid.
298 Ibironke T Odumosu, 'The Antinomies of the (Continued) Relevance of ICSID to the Third World' (2006) 8 SDILJ 345.
299 ibid.
300 ibid 354.

However, the convention does not cover the clause. It may be preferable to include the clauses inside, leaving member states to apply reservation rights at their own discretion. Upon closer reflection, it may be preferable for the institution to acknowledge and engage these political dimensions. In the absence of this development, investors will continue to seek losing state assets within each member state jurisdiction, incurring considerable expense in the process. The ongoing development of the ICSID suggests, however, no sustaining (re)balancing of depoliticisation and member state interests. This is despite the fact that, in practice, there is a quite transparent imbalance.[301]

The political dimensions of the process are further reiterated by the fact that, even though states are absent from the dispute settlement system, they can be brought back into the post-award process by countermeasures.[302] Charles Brower II has recently stated that investment arbitrations should be assumed to be political. Hersch Lauterpacht, in following this line of argument, maintains that every international law dispute is political; depoliticisation of these disputes is, therefore, by logical implication, *ab initio* problematic.[303] Upon this basis, it would appear appropriate to reiterate that investor–state arbitration is part of the international legal order and cannot, by virtue of this feature, be totally isolated from the political relations between states. Indeed, relations between states can be viewed as lawmaking or reinterpretative activities that affect applicable primary or secondary rules.[304] It is also important to note that during the ICSID arbitration process there are explicit limitations that restrict the application of diplomatic espousal.[305] However, it is debatable whether the home state can invoke responsibility in its own right. With regard to investor–state arbitration, states have used various means to try to persuade other states to consent to arbitration at the first stage. At the second stage, a clear incentive is provided by the fact that a failure of host state compliance could elicit countermeasures by the home state. Broches conveys the classical approach in the following terms:

> If the investor feels aggrieved by actions of the host government and has found no redress through the exercise of local remedies, he may seek the protection of his national government. … the investor's government may in fact not be willing to take up a meritorious claim of the investor because it fears that to do so would be regarded as an unfriendly act by the host government and interfere with bilateral relations on other matters. This political element is likely to weigh particularly heavily if the merits of the investor's case are not wholly clear in his government's view, thus withholding from the investor any opportunity to have his case judged by an impartial tribunal.[306]

The invocation of responsibility does not oblige the home state to undertake a specific action; it is only an entitlement that opens up space, thus allowing the home state to engage with various considerations, such as those set out earlier.[307] However, some of

---

301 Martins Paparinskis, 'The Limits of Depoliticisation in Contemporary Investor-State Arbitration' (2010) <http://ssrn.com/abstract=1716833> accessed 28 February 2017.

302 ibid 5.

303 ibid 6.

304 A Roberts, 'Power and Persuasion in Investment Treaty Interpretation: The Dual Role of States' (2010) 104 AJIL 179. See also Paparinskis, 'The Limits of Depoliticisation in Contemporary Investor-State Arbitration' (n 301) 11.

305 Paparinskis, 'The Limits of Depoliticisation in Contemporary Investor-State Arbitration' (n 301) 11.

306 Aron Broches, 'The Convention on the Settlement of Investment Disputes between States and Nationals of Other States' (1972) 136 Recueil des Cours 331 in Paparinskis, 'The Limits of Depoliticisation in Contemporary Investor-State Arbitration' (n 301) 12.

307 ibid.

the considerations are not valid for non-compliance of ICSID awards. This is the case in instances where the investor's case is clear and he or she has already won the case, meaning that the home state has no basis for questioning whether the different elements of the investor's case are strong or not. The ILC's Articles on Diplomatic Protection (2006) also recognise diplomatic protection as a right and only recommend that states consider the possibility of espousal.[308]

The ICSID Convention does not include the aforementioned provisions because it is grounded within the principle of depoliticisation—if these provisions were present, the underlying principle would be adversely impacted. If the investor's home state retaliates to a breach, it will be interfering with the dispute between the investor and the host state. The suspension of concessions would also be assumed to be an attribute of the system; if this was to be amended, it would be necessary to gain the support of two-thirds of the member states.[309]

If they do not seek to amend the ICSID Convention, states can initiate a countermeasure by drafting their BITs in accordance with any breach of provisions. This course of action was undertaken by Canada and Thailand,[310] neither of whom was a member of the ICSID Convention. Article XV(7) establishes that the

> contracting parties shall, within 60 days of the decision of a tribunal, reach agreement on the manner in which to resolve their dispute. Such agreement shall also be considered part of the tribunal's arbitral decision. If the contracting parties fail to reach agreement, the contracting party bringing the dispute shall be entitled or to suspend benefits of equivalent value to those awarded by the panel.[311]

This may be a more sustainable means through which to force the failing state to comply with the awards. This is attributable to the fact that it does not aspire to amend the ICSID Convention. If the state has not negotiated on countermeasures for non-compliance arbitral awards in their BITs, they then have the chance, under Article 27 of the ICSID and the law of countermeasures (refer to the 2001 ILC), to make use of diplomatic protection. The fact that the relationship between the ICJ and ICSID has never really been analysed in the literature should not negate a consideration of the relevant practice.

It should be accepted that direct access to arbitration by foreign investors does not logically imply that state-to-state arbitration disappears or investor–state claims are not priviliged to state-to-state claims.[312] However, there are some reasons that state-to-state arbitration is not currently used. Ibrahim Shihata, the longest-serving secretary-general of the ICSID, has therefore stressed that the goal of this approach is to protect the weaker

308 2006 ILC's Articles on Diplomatic Protection (n 271).

309 ICSID Convention Article 66. See <http://icsidfiles.worldbank.org/icsid/icsid/staticfiles/basicdoc/parta-chap09.htm> accessed 3 March 2017.

310 Joubin-Bret (n 22) 109. At that date both states were not contracting to the ICSID Convention. Thailand has not entered the Convention into force but has signed it. Canada is a contracting state from 2013 (signed in 2006)

311 ICSID Convention Article 15.

312 Cristoph Schreuer, 'Investment Protection and International Relations' in August Reinisch and Ursula Kreibaum (eds) *The Law of International Relations: Liber Amicorum Hanspeter Neuhold* (Eleven International Publishing 2007) 345–58. See <http://www.univie.ac.at/intlaw/wordpress/pdf/87_investment_protect.pdf> accessed 10 November 2017.

host state against the home state and, more specifically, its ability to exert diplomatic pressure and gunboat diplomacy.[313]

Developing countries resent pressure from developed countries, whether it is exercised bilaterally or multilaterally (e.g. in international lending institutions).[314] In extending diplomatic protection during the course of investor–state disputes, developed countries have frequently elicited irritation from their developing counterparts.[315] Although state-to-state arbitration has not been extensively used by foreign investors during BIT claims,[316] state-to-state arbitration is frequently used to commence arbitral proceedings against the other state, invariably with a view to settling any dispute that relates to the interpretation or application of the BIT.[317] However, the key and essential point is that investor–state arbitration was designed to create a depoliticised dispute settlement system; as such, it was envisaged that it would displace diplomatic protection and enable investors to seek redress for injury.[318] Therefore, during the drafting of the ILC Draft Articles, some claimed that there is no longer necessary diplomatic protection and that this is, to all intents and purposes, a legal fiction.[319] However, it appears that protecting its own nationals may be understood as a signal to other states that they should not ignore treaties and customary law obligations in the future.[320] In such circumstances, diplomatic protection is a crucial vehicle to promote international economic relations.[321]

Another possible permutation that needs to be taken into account is when the interests of the investor differ from its home state. When diplomatic protection is provided, the investor does not have considerable influence over proceedings—the home state, therefore, has considerable discretion to negotiate with the host state.[322] This brings about a transformation in the respective interests of the investor and home state.[323] This subject has given birth to considerable literature. A number of scholars claim that a home state must carefully balance its interest in protecting the rights of its nationals; see the case of *Philip Morris*,[324] which was brought against Australia by the Hong Kong–Australia BIT for its plain packaging of cigarettes.[325] This case was guided by the complaint that

313 Sergio Puig, 'Recasting ICSID's Legitimacy Debate: Towards a Goal-Based Empirical Agenda' 36 (2013) 2 Fordham Intl L J 465–504. See also Rudolf Dolzer and Christoph Schreuer, *Principles of International Investment Law* (OUP 2008) 4.

314 Schreuer, 'Investment Protection and International Relations' (n 312) 346.

315 ibid.

316 Francisco Orrego Vicuña, 'Changing Approaches to the Nationality of Claims in the Context of Diplomatic Protection and International Dispute Settlement' 15 (2000) 2 ICSID Review 340–61.

317 Schreuer, 'Investment Protection and International Relations' (n 312) 348.

318 Jarrod Wong, 'The Subversion of State-to-State Investment Treaty Arbitration' 6 (2014) 53 Colum J Transnatl L 1.

319 Anthea Roberts, 'State-to-State Investment Treaty Arbitration: A Hybrid Theory of Interdependent Rights and Shared Interpretive Authority' (2014) 55 Harv Intl L J.

320 Choi, 'The Present and Future of the Investor-State Dispute Settlement Paradigm' (n 119) 725–47.

321 ibid.

322 ICJ, Barcelona Traction, Light and Power Company, Ltd, 1970 ICJ 3, 44 (5 February): '[I]t is clear that by international law there is no legal duty incumbent upon the state to extend diplomatic protection. Whether such a duty exists towards the citizen is a matter of municipal law of his own country, the general rule being that even under municipal law the state is under no legal duty to extend diplomatic protection.'

323 Won-Mog Choi, 'The Present and Future of the Investor-State Dispute Settlement Paradigm' (2007) 10 J Intl Econ L 725–47.

324 *Philip Morris Asia Ltd. v. Austl., PCA* Case No. 2012-12, Notice of Claim (22 June 2011), Perm. Ct. Arb. (2011).

325 Roberts (n 319) 49.

investors were bound by state-to state awards, and as a result, they did not have opportunity to present arguments to the state-to-state tribunal.[326] Had this defect been acknowledged, then the increased input of the investor would have enabled state-to-state tribunals to fully consider the impact of their decisions on investors.[327] State-to-state arbitration brings about a fundamental shift in power, in which power is transferred from investors to treaty parties and from investor–state tribunals to state-to-state tribunals.[328] However, an additional concern relates to the question of whether host states can rely on interstate countermeasures in seeking a defence during investor–state claims.[329]

State-to-state arbitration before the ICJ would therefore touch upon a range of economic, political, and diplomatic issues; when considered in cumulative effect, these issues can be seen to exceed the scope of the interests at stake.[330] Conversely, it should also be recognised that diplomatic protection recommends itself upon the basis that it can screen out frivolous or dishonest claims by nationals of bad intent.[331] In addition, the process would also be time-consuming. The host state, as the respondent, should consent to the ICJ's jurisdiction and lend its support to the claim that the investor's state has made on behalf of its national. It is not, it should be noted, a duty for the respondent state to accept the ICJ's jurisdiction.[332] If diplomatic protection is provided, then the investor must have a close relationship with the home state (this relationship will be balanced against the home state's diplomatic and economic ties with the state that has failed to uphold the award).[333]

After all, if the respondent state accepts the jurisdiction, then the ICJ will take a considerable amount of time to examine the dispute in question. The average length of cases that are brought before the ICJ is four years.[334] In addition to this, the ICJ's direct involvement in a dispute that concerns a non-compliance ICSID award case may be seen as an essentially theoretical proposition that has little or no practical significance.[335]

Diplomatic protection may also be understood as having little relation to the investor's own interest; it appears, to this extent, to be much more clearly related to economic and geopolitical considerations.[336] Even for nationals from developed states, diplomatic protection has had its disadvantages—the fact that the home state has complete discretion over the claim is one example of this.[337] This state acts as the sole judge and is empowered

326 ibid 51.

327 ibid.

328 ibid 24.

329 ibid 70.

330 ibid.

331 Choi, 'The Present and Future of the Investor-State Dispute Settlement Paradigm' (n 323) 746.

332 Charles N Brower and Lee A Steven, 'Who Then Should Judge: Developing the International Rule of Law under NAFTA Chapter 11' (2001) 2 Chi J Intl L 193. See, for example, *Barcelona Traction, Light and Power Company, Ltd (Belgium v. Spain),* 1970 ICJ 3, 44 (5 February 1970), stating: 'The State must be viewed as the sole judge to decide whether its protection will be granted, to what extent it is granted, and when it will cease. It retains in this respect a discretionary power the exercise of which may be determined by considerations of a political or other nature, unrelated to the particular case.'

333 Roberts (n 319) 70.

334 See <https://www.wto.org/english/tratop_e/dispu_e/speech_agah_4mar10_e.htm> accessed 10 October 2017.

335 Paparinskis, 'Investment Arbitration and the Law of Countermeasures' (n 209) 335. ICJ decisions have a significant effect on the development of international law, though they are only enforced on the disputing states. Sean D Murphyt, 'The ELSI Case: An Investment Dispute at the International Court of Justice" (1991) 16 Yale J Intl L 391.

336 Joubin-Bret (n 22) 108–9.

337 Choi, 'The Present and Future of the Investor-State Dispute Settlement Paradigm' (n 323) 728.

to decide whether and to what extent such protection will be provided; it also has the ability to decide if and when the grant of protection will end.[338] In addition, there is no guarantee that the home state's exercise of this discretion will not be determined by political purposes or be unrelated to the particular case.[339] Finally, it should also be noted that the ISDS avoids the threat by substituting direct claims by nationals for the mechanism of diplomatic protection; it, therefore, reduces unnecessary diplomatic friction in the field between disputant countries by extending the legal context into a wider arena of global economic interest.[340]

4.3.6 Securing compliance of ICSID awards with VCLT Article 60: Termination or suspension of the operation of a treaty as a consequence of its breach

1. A material breach of a bilateral treaty by one of the parties entitles the other to invoke the breach as a ground for terminating the treaty or suspending its operation in whole or in part.
2. A material breach of a multilateral treaty by one of the parties entitles:
   (a) the other parties by unanimous agreement to suspend the operation of the treaty in whole or in part or to terminate it either:
      (i) in the relations between themselves and the defaulting State, or
      (ii) as between all the parties;
   (b) a party specially affected by the breach to invoke it as a ground for suspending the operation of the treaty in whole or in part in the relations between itself and the defaulting State;
   (c) any party other than the defaulting State to invoke the breach as a ground for suspending the operation of the treaty in whole or in part with respect to itself if the treaty is of such a character that a material breach of its provisions by one party radically changes the position of every party with respect to the further performance of its obligations under the treaty.
3. A material breach of a treaty, for the purposes of this article, consists in:
   (a) a repudiation of the treaty not sanctioned by the present Convention; or
   (b) the violation of a provision essential to the accomplishment of the object or purpose of the treaty.
4. The foregoing paragraphs are without prejudice to any provision in the treaty applicable in the event of a breach.
5. Paragraphs 1 to 3 do not apply to provisions relating to the protection of the human person contained in treaties of a humanitarian character, in particular to provisions prohibiting any form of reprisals against persons protected by such treaties.[341]

Setting aside the law of countermeasures, another possible option, with regard to security a compliance award, would be Article 60 of the VCLT.[342] As the preceding excerpts from the article clearly demonstrate, Article 60 of the VCLT establishes the right of the injured state (the investor's home state) to terminate or suspend the operation of a treaty in response to its breach by another contracting party (the host state). The VCLT even encompasses issues of security that pertain to international investment relations. It is

338 ibid.

339 ibid.

340 ibid 736.

341 Vienna Convention on the law of treaties (with annex) concluded at Vienna on 23 May 1969.

342 See <https://treaties.un.org/doc/publication/unts/volume%201155/volume-1155-i-18232-english.pdf> accessed 3 March 2017.

already hard to receive diplomatic protection from the home state, in large part due to the fact that this actor is responsible for, within an international forum, defending the investor against the other state party.[343] Terminating or suspending the treaty does not recover the original source of the dispute, for example, the compensation of the damages caused by the host state to the foreign investor.[344] In addition, the home state's action might be counterproductive as other investors remaining in the host state could be left unprotected.[345] In addition, it should also be recognised that many states are reluctant to provide diplomatic protection to their nationalities; as such, they will not accept a situation in which investment relations with the failing state are cut off—the national interest will predominate in practice. However, even the mere act of recognition may provide a deterrent of sorts; other investors will be reluctant to invest in the failing party when the host state continues to be categorised as a failure.[346]

The VCLT is not technically applicable to the ICSID Convention and BITs. However, the VCLT reflects customary international law on non-compliance awards if states make provision for this in their BITs. If the termination of the treaty is taken to be too drastic a step, then the suspension of the treaty, subject to compliance, may encourage the host state to honour the awards. In working upon this premise, states should amend their BITs, with a view to suspending benefits that derive from Article 60 of the VCLT, thus securing the rights of their national investors and providing another solution to the injured investor's state.

4.3.7 Securing compliance from losing investors

With regard to the failure of investors, there has been an increase in the number of cases in which the winnings of host states exceed incurred costs.[347] ICSID statistics demonstrate that states have consistently won about half of cases.[348] Non-compliance, generally relating to the costs associated with arbitration proceedings and legal fees, along with associated interest charges, have arisen as a particular concern for states. In some instances, investors who have abandoned the country in the aftermath of a failed investment operation have also withdrawn their assets from the country; in other instances, they have gone insolvent.

Several recent cases (*Libananco v. Turkey*, *Cementownia v. Turkey*, and *Saba Fakes v. Turkey*) have provided considerable insight into the increase of non-compliance actions against host states. In addition to countermeasures, security costs might conceivably be applied by the ICSID tribunal. An arbitral tribunal should aspire to a cost-effective security, with the aim of balancing the claimant's interest in accessing justice against the respondent's interest in recovering costs in instances where it is successful.[349] The situation

343 Echandi (n 256).

344 ibid 119.

345 ibid.

346 ibid.

347 Inna Uchkunova, and Oleg Temnikov, 'Security for Costs in ICSID Arbitration' (Kluwer Arbitration Blog 2015) <http://kluwerarbitrationblog.com/2015/02/10/security-for-costs-in-icsid-arbitration/> accessed 7 March 2017.

348 ibid.

349 Stavros Brekoulakis, Audley Sheppard, Susan Dunn, Mick Smith, and Jonas von Goeler, 'Draft Report of ICCA-Queen Mary Task Force on TPF in International Arbitration Subcommittee on Security for Costs

here is clearly distinct from the one that arises in commercial arbitration, as the respondent state has not signed an arbitration agreement with a particular claimant. However, it is noticeable that the host state is often claimed to have expropriated unlawfully, and therefore caused the claimant's impecuniosity. This clearly reiterates that accessing justice for claimants can often be a delicate issue in investment arbitration disputes. This possibly explains why investment tribunals are usually very unwilling to order security costs and thus enable the claim to proceed. Security costs fall under the category of 'provisional measures,' being regulated by Arbitration Rule 39 and Article 47 of the ICSID Convention. The aim of security is, *inter alia*, to insulate the award's effectiveness and preserve the integrity of the proceedings—this latter outcome can be ensured by preserving the requesting party's potential right to the reimbursement of costs. Although several security cost requests have been made by respondents, the ICSID tribunal has tended to react negatively.[350] The ICSID tribunals have required to see evidence of exceptional circumstances in order to decide on security for costs such as 'abusive conduct or some evidence of bad faith on the claimant side.'[351] While the failure of investors is interesting from an academic perspective, the practical consequences of investor non-compliance have been considerable, impacting with particular severity upon Turkey.[352] The first request came during the *Maffezini v. Spain*[353] case. The tribunal rejected the respondent's request, maintaining that the cited right, whose protection was sought, was hypothetical, lacking any real connection to the subject-matter in dispute.[354]

There are five requirements that precede and sustain the security of costs. These are (1) the existence of *prima facie* jurisdiction; (2) plausibility (the right that is to be protected must be plausible); (3) there must be a clear relation to the dispute in question; (4) the measure must be necessary; and (5) the measure must be urgent.[355] In advancing their case, the respondent must meet each of these requirements. The first security costs decision was issued during the *RSM Production Corporation v. Saint Lucia* case.[356] In this instance, the tribunal ordered the request. While the final decision helped to clarify key issues, it did little to establish the threshold for security—in large part, this was attributable to the fact that the circumstances of the case were highly specific. Firstly, the claimant had a history of non-compliance with prior decisions, having repeatedly failed to make advance payments; secondly, there was also evidence that the claimant had, in the initiation of its claim, been funded by a third party. As has been previously noted, the Uzan family group[357] has not paid the arbitral awards owing to Turkey; this has not prevented

and Costs Daft Report' (1 November 2015). See <http://www.arbitration-icca.org/media/6/09700416080661/tpf_taskforce_security_for_costs_and_costs_draft_report_november_2015.pdf> accessed 6 December 2017.

350 See <https://icnsid.worldbank.org/en/Pages/process/Decisions-on-Provisional-Measures.aspx> accessed 7 March 2017.

351 Brekoulakis, Sheppard, Dunn, Smith, and Goeler (n 349) 134.

352 *Libananco v. Turkey*, Decision (n 40). Additionally, in this case, the respondent had based its petition on the mere assertion that the claimant is a 'shell company.' In rejecting the request, the tribunal did not find this sufficient reason since many investments are made through an investment vehicle. There may be cases in which it is prima facie obvious that the claim is fabricated, for e.g. the claimant cannot present any original documents to prove the existence of investment (*Europe Cement v. Turkey*, Award of 13 August 2009, para 184).

353 *Maffezini v. Spain*, Procedural Order No. 2 of 28 October 1999, paras 18, 24–25.

354 ibid.

355 Uchkunova and Temnikov, 'Security for Costs in ICSID Arbitration' (n 347).

356 *RSM Production Corporation v Saint Lucia*, ICSID Case No. ARB/12/10, 2012.

357 Investor in Libenanco, Europe cement cases.

it from continuing to initiate arbitration proceedings against Turkey in other institutions. This decision can therefore, with reference to overcoming the non-compliance of the winning state's payment, be cited as a relevant example. The tribunal observed:

> The third party funding exacerbates the concern engendered by RSM's conduct in the Annulment Proceeding and the Treaty Proceeding. It places an unfunded RSM and the third party funder(s) in the inequitable position of benefiting from any award in their favour yet avoiding responsibility for a contrary award.[358]

The main objective of the order was to secure the respondent state's right to recover legal costs from a claimant who was unable to pay—this is a crucial benefit in instances where the latter has a proven history of defaulting on costs orders.[359] In addition, the tribunal should also accept the claimant's past conduct as sufficient evidence of bad faith when attempting to ascertain security for costs.[360]

However, decisions rendered on security for costs should be careful to balance the right to access justice with the requirement for an effective tribunal award.[361] It should also be recognised that provisional measure decisions are not final—by virtue of this feature, it is not possible for them to benefit from the ICSID's enforcement mechanisms that fall under member state jurisdiction. In other words, these decisions may be rejected in the recognition stage, with public policy concerns being cited as a relevant consideration. Finally, as one tribunal has already ruled, failure to comply with the award presents a systemic risk to the ICSID.[362]

This provides further impetus to the project which seeks to reform the ICSID Convention. Security for costs originates from Article 47 of the ICSID Convention, which was inspired by Article 41 of the Statute of the ICJ.[363] This establishes that the ICSID tribunal 'may, if it considers that the circumstances so require, recommend any provisional measures which should be taken to preserve the respective rights of either party.'[364] When a respondent demonstrates that the claimant is insolvent or cannot afford the award, the tribunal, thanks to the wide scope of Article 47, has the power to order financial measures.[365] It should be noted that the provisions of Article 47 of the ICSID Convention and Article 39 of the Arbitration Rules 'contain no indication or exact statement' that restricts the discretion of tribunals.[366] Article 44 of the ICSID Convention also further confirms the tribunal's procedural discretion.[367] In addition, tribunals also have the power to grant provisional measures (*proprio motu)* in ICSID arbitration, subject to the parties' consent to arbitration.[368] The existence of *proprio motu* rules lend further support to the idea that ICSID tribunals have broad authority over provisional measures. This applies, it should be

358 *RSM Production Corporation v. Saint Lucia* (n 356) para 76.

359 Brekoulakis, Sheppard, Dunn, Smith, and Goeler (n 349) 134–5.

360 ibid.

361 Uchkunova and Temnikov, 'Security for Costs in ICSID Arbitration' (n 347).

362 ibid.

363 Schreuer, *The ICSID Convention: A Commentary* (n 14) 764–6. See also Christine Sim, 'Security for Costs in Investor–State Arbitration' (2017) 33 Arbitration International 427–95.

364 ICSID Convention Article 47.

365 Schreuer, *The ICSID Convention: A Commentary* (n 14) 784. See also Sim (n 363) 433.

366 Sim (n 363) 433–4.

367 ibid.

368 ibid 434. See also Yves Fortier, 'Interim Measures: An Arbitrator's Provisional Views' (16 June 2008) Fordham Law School Conference Paper.

noted, in the absence of an explicit and specific provision that sets out security for costs for the benefit of the disputing parties.[369]

In practice, ICSID tribunals have proven to be unwilling to grant security for costs, or to ground it in assumptions about the outcome of the arbitration.[370] A wide number of decisions further reiterate this conclusion. *TANESCO v. IPTL*[371] is particularly important in this regard: in this instance, the tribunal rejected the respondent's request for provisional measures. In justification, it cited the fact that a substantial monetary award had been made against the claimant. In recognising the danger that this might not be honoured, the tribunal stated that 'conservatory or provisional measures under Rule 39 should not be recommended in order, in effect, to give security for the claim.'[372]

It was therefore clearly established that the ICSID should change the provisional measure provisions, as this would enable separate security for costs provisions to be issued with certain evidence. This was held to be particularly important for overcoming the issue of non-compliance awards. If there is a history of non-compliance, then the tribunal should not exercise discretion in ordering a security for costs. If this is not the case, then there is a clear danger that respondents will lose their rights. In helping to balance the interests of the respective parties, this reform could potentially make a crucial contribution. This is clearly open to question if the matter is left open to the discretion of the tribunal, as the example cases clearly illustrate. Lack of precedent, it should also be acknowledged, significantly exacerbates this uncertainty in ICSID arbitration.

The main point is that an arbitral tribunal should consider the balance between the investor's ability to access arbitration proceedings against the state's ability to enforce a costs award, because the risk for states increases when an investor is insolvent and its third-party funder dissents from any liability for costs.[373] Furthermore, for capital-importing states, despite winning, the arbitration case can impose a heavy burden in practice.[374] A recent case, *Herzig v. Turkmenistan*,[375] discussed the requirements of security for costs and also the third-party funder's responsibility. The minority of the tribunal advised that BITs or arbitration rules should be reformed to make third-party funding conditional on extending powers to tribunals to make costs orders against funders. Thus, access to justice for the investor is not affected. This case has also a different approach that despite some states accepting that security for costs should only be ordered against investors, the ICSID underlined its view is 'balanced and consistent with the purpose of security for costs.'[376]

369 Regis Bismuth, 'Anatomy of the Law and Practice of Interim Protective Measures in International Investment Arbitration' (2009) 26(6) J Intl Arb 773, 821. See also Sim (n 363) 434.

370 Sim (n 363) 434.

371 *Tanzania Electricity Supply Co. Ltd. (TANESCO) v. Independent Power Tanzania Ltd.* (ICSID Case No ARB/98/8), Decision on Request for Provisional Measures (20 December 1999) para 14.

372 Sim (n 363) 434.

373 Christina L Beharry, 'Case Comment: *Herzig v Turkmenistan* Requests for Security for Costs in ICSID Arbitrations Involving Third-Party Funded Insolvent Claimants' (2021) ICSID Review 1–10.

374 Matthew Hodgson and Alastair Campbell, 'Damages and Costs in Investment Treaty Arbitration Revisited' (14 December 2017) Global Arb Rev.

375 *Dirk Herzig as Insolvency Administrator over the Assets of Unionmatex Industrieanlagen GmbH v. Turkmenistan*, ICSID Case No ARB/18/35, Decision on the Respondent's Request for Security for Costs and the Claimant's Request for Security for Claim (27 January 2020).

376 See Proposals for Amendment of the ICSID Rules: Working Paper 4 (Vol. I, February 2020) 322.

However, it should be asserted that it is likely hard to show that the State is unwilling to pay the costs of defending against a counterclaim.[377]

4.4 Conclusion

The indication of a willingness to negotiate on a BIT and consent to ICSID proceedings provides a clear signal to foreign investors, indicating an intention to satisfy arbitral awards; the honouring of awards provides a state with credibility and reduces a number of the political risks associated with foreign investment.[378] In addition to these positive benefits, the reputation of the state significantly benefits, perhaps providing a clearer incentive to other states to uphold awards.[379] In failing to honour the award, a state will expose itself to a loss of credibility in the eyes of foreign investors.[380]

Although the ICSID's own enforcement mechanism mostly categorises appropriately, a number of execution issues have arisen as a result of the way that state assets have been labelled. Article 55 of the ICSID Convention, which permits member states not to enforce the awards by claiming the defence of state sovereignty, is a particularly important reference point in this respect. Although this article clearly establishes that this defence should not be understood as derogating, the convention ultimately leaves the execution process to the states' own jurisdictions, meaning that each state has the opportunity to define its own assets. Investors, in seeking to seize the state's assets in various jurisdictions, must therefore take amorphous sovereign immunity laws into account, underlining a more practical solution to the challenge of award non-compliance.[381]

When a state refuses to comply with an arbitral award, investors must begin a worldwide search, with a view to identifying the state's assets; in the event that they successfully achieve this, they must then overcome the sovereign immunity laws that govern access to those assets.[382] A number of recommendations have been put forward with a view to facilitating the enforcement of arbitral awards under the ICSID Convention: establishment of an appeal body under the ICSID by amending the convention, the cutting of World Bank loan benefits, the principle of reciprocity (as embodied by the WTO), and the redrafting of state sovereign laws (in accordance with restrictive immunity from execution). As has already been noted, this was in large part attributable to the fact that there was a strong belief that member states would voluntarily comply. This chapter has engaged with three practical approaches that have sought to reduce the execution issue. The first approach has sought to redraft the state's sovereignty, putting in place a hybrid structure with a view to facilitating the execution process for foreign investors. However, it will be noted that the main obstacle in this respect is the states' own sovereignty law—by virtue of this impediment, nobody can force the state to change its acts. It should be recognised that any action can be aligned with the ICSID Convention; this is because this convention permits states to use their own jurisdiction for the execution of assets. Second, it has

377 Beharry (n 373).

378 Loukas Mistelis and Crina Baltag, 'Recognition and Enforcement of Arbitral Awards and Settlement in International Arbitration: Corporate Attitudes and Practices' (2008) 19 Am Rev Intl Arb 319, 359.

379 Crina Baltag, 'Enforcement of Arbitral Awards Against States' (2008) 19 Am Rev Intl Arb 391.

380 ibid.

381 Cardosi (n 151) 118.

382 ibid.

been proposed that the World Bank Group's organisations may provide an appropriate recourse of action. This draws attention to a frustrating development in which investors travel in search of assets when states do not satisfy their arbitration expectations. Debates as to how the World Bank can combine investor–state arbitrations with a view to avoiding hollow victories for investors should be understood in this context. As has already been suggested, failing states could be induced to cooperate with awards by the threatened or actual cutting of World Bank loans. From one perspective, this might be viewed as a plausible or practicable solution; however, this is undermined by the foundational principle that underpins the ICSID. This recommendation has been predominantly engaged by scholars but has not yet been practically implemented. The practicalities of politics also militate against this application; the US has not incorporated this deterrent effect into its voting on World Bank loans, to take one example. In addition, it should also be recognised that there is a possibility that states might prefer to withdraw their memberships from the ICSID, as opposed to the World Bank—after all, withdrawal from the latter would be profoundly harmful to the states concerned. It would also mean that they would no longer be pressured by the ICSID's affiliation with the World Bank. Under these circumstances, Article 55 of the ICSID Convention would lose its grounding logic. There is also a third proposal that has not been extensively discussed in the literature. This proposal seeks to establish whether the ICSID Administrative Council can assume a prominent institutional role, assuming responsibility for rejecting applications, made on the part of states and investors, that are made to the institution.

It may be preferable to resolve the issue within the ICSID itself rather than activating the World Bank. If the ICSID was to assume this role, there are clear questions as to how this might be justified under Article 22 of the DARIO, which clearly sets out the respective responsibilities of international organisations. The ICSID does not fulfil the requirements that the article sets out—it will therefore be noted that the ICSID Convention does not set out applicable countermeasures. The ICSID's past and present also militate strongly against its politicisation by the World Bank. By virtue of these strong drawbacks, the aforementioned proposals have not received an extensive consideration. The institution has only, with a view to reducing the sovereign power of investors, has only suggested model clauses and has therefore demurred from taking on an active role. It should, however, be noted that the inclusion of these clauses within BITs and consensual agreements is ultimately upon the bargaining power that is evidenced in reality. In addition to this, it may not be the perfect solution for the enforcement problem but an appeal body can be a step to working on the issue.

As investor–state disputes continue to rapidly proliferate, assuming ever-greater dimensions, the requirement to develop solutions that can be applied to arbitral awards grows in parallel. The ICSID's enforcement mechanism, while more effective than the alternatives, still leaves the last word to states, establishing this as the basis upon which arbitration awards will be honoured. This does not destabilise the ICSID's main principle of depoliticisation and may even ultimately benefit the law of countermeasures. Even though there is theoretically a remedy that can address this issue in ICSID, this still awaits practical confirmation. Ultimately, the best remedy may be to apply the diplomatic protection for non-compliance awards that is set out within Article 27 of the ICSID Convention. It, therefore, appears that the home state can use several countermeasures against the host state, with a view to honouring the award on the grounds of the ICL Draft on state responsibility (2001). This option has, however, not been explored in extensive detail. It may be suggested that it is difficult for investors to receive diplomatic protection, but this is not impossible. In situations of award non-compliance, investors do not have to exhaust all domestic solutions or convince their home state that their case has solid foundations; this has been established by the fact that they have already won the ICSID case. Home states may, by virtue of preponderant economic interests, be reluctant to use countermeasures against host states. However, it should be noted that if they have already redrafted their BITs or investment agreements, then the acceptance of the opposing states is already foregrounded. Upon this basis, it will be recognised that the ICSID is still some distance removed from politicisation. This will not change with the adoption of recourse countermeasures to investment protection rules, which are internalised and reproduced within host state strategies that are directed towards the treatment of foreign investments.[383] In terms of the winning host states, security for costs would be another option to secure compliance of the awards in practice. As highlighted, however, the ICSID articles should be amended accordingly. In addition to the ICL Draft (2001), a further option may be explored through Article 60 of the VCLT.

Bibliography

Schreuer C, 'Investment Protection and International Relations' *The Law of International Relations—Liber amicorum Hanspeter Neuhold* (Eleven International Publishing 2007) 345–358. <http://www.univie.ac.at/intlaw/wordpress/pdf/87_investment_protect.pdf> accessed 10 November 2017

Akinci Z, 'Turkey' in Fouret J (ed), *Enforcement of Investment Treaty Arbitration Awards* (Globe Business Publishing Ltd. 2015) 455–468.

Arangio-Ruiz G, 'Fourth Report on State Responsibility' in *Yearbook of the International Law Commission 1992*, Vol. 2.

Asouzu A A, 'African States and the Enforcement of Arbitral Awards: Some Key Issues' *Arbitration International* 15(1) (1999) 1–52.

Baldwin E, Kantor M, and Nolanmake M, 'Limits to Enforcement of ICSID Awards' (2006) 23 *J. Int'l Arb.* 1.

Balkaya B, 'IBA Recognition and Enforcement of Arbitral Awards- Study on Public Policy' (2015) <http://www.ibanet.org/LPD/Dispute_Resolution_Section/Arbitration/Recogntn_Enfrcemnt_Arbitl_Awrd/publicpolicy15.aspx> Turkey part, accessed 17 February 2016.

Baltag C, 'Enforcement of Arbitral Awards Against States' (2008) 19 *Am. Rev. Int'l Arb.* 391.

Beharry C L, 'Case Comment: *Herzig v Turkmenistan* Requests for Security for Costs in ICSID Arbitrations Involving Third-Party Funded Insolvent Claimants' (2021) *ICSID Review* 1–10.

Berg A J, 'Appeal Mechanism for ISDS Awards: Interaction with the New York and ICSID Conventions' (2019) 34 *ICSID Review* 156–189.

Berg A J V D, 'Some Recent Problems in the Practice of Enforcement under the 308 New York and ICSID Conventions' 2 *ICSID Review* 439 (1987) 449.

Bismuth R, 'Anatomy of the Law and Practice of Interim Protective Measures in International Investment Arbitration' (2009) 26(6) *J Intl Arb* 773, 821.

Bjorklund A K, 'State Immunity and the Enforcement of Investor-state Arbitral Awards' (2008) *Practice* 858.

383 Paparinskis, 'Investment Arbitration and the Law of Countermeasures' (n 209) 277.

Bjorklund A K, 'Arbitration and National Courts: Conflict and Cooperation: Sovereign Immunity as a Barrier to the Enforcement of Investor-State Arbitral Awards: The Re-Politicization of International Investment Disputes' (2010) 21 *Am Rev Intl Arb* 211–315.

Bowett D W, 'Economic Coercion and Reprisals By States' (1972) 13 *Va. J. Int'l L.* 1

Brekoulakis S et al., 'Draft Report of ICCA-Queen Mary Task Force on TPF In 322 International Arbitration Subcommittee On Security For Costs and Costs Daft Report' (November 1, 2015). <http://www.arbitrationicca.org/media/6/09700416080661/tpf_taskforce_security_for_costs_and_costs_draft_report_november_2015.pdf> accessed 06.12.2017

Broches A, 'The Convention on the Settlement of Investment Disputes between States and Nationals of Other States' (1972) 136 *Recueil des Cours* 331.

Broches A, 'Awards Rendered Pursuant to the ICSID Convention: Binding Force, Finality, Recognition, Enforcement, Execution' (1987) *ICSID Review* 318.

Brower C N and Steven L A, 'Who Then Should Judge: Developing the International Rule of Law under NAFTA Chapter 11' 2 (2001) *Chi. J. Int'l L.* 193.

Çalışkan Y and Dülger A, 'Time for the Appeal Tribunal in Investment Arbitration: Lessons from WTO' in Cigdem Nas and Mustafa Erkan (eds), *International Investment and Trade Agreements: Recent Developments and Problems* (Oniki levha 2021).

Cardosi J M, 'Precluding the Treasure Hunt: How the World Bank Group Can Help Investors Circumnavigate Sovereign Immunity Obstacles to ICSID Award Execution' Pepp. L. Rev. 41 (2014) 3

Choi S, 'Judicial Enforcement of arbitration Awards under the ICSID and New York Conventions' (1995–1996) 28 *N.Y.U.J.Int'l Law & Pol.* 175.

Choi W-M, 'The Present and Future of the Investor-State Dispute Settlement Paradigm' (2007) 10(3) *J Intl Econ L* 725–747.

Collier J and Lowe V, *The Settlement of Disputes in International Law; Institutions and Procedures* (OUP 1999) 73

Coop G, Nistal A, Volterra R G, and Fietta V, 'Sovereign Immunities and Investor-State Awards: Specificities of Enforcing Awards Based on Investment Treaties' in Julien Fouret (ed), *Enforcement of Investment Treaty Arbitration Awards* (Globe Business Publishing Ltd. 2015) 67–83.

Crawford J, 'Counter-measures as Interim Measures' (1994) 5 *EJIL* 65.

Delaume G R, 'Foreign Sovereign Immunity: Impact on Arbitration' (1983) 38(2) *Arb. J.* 34, 45.

Dietz T, Dotzauer M, and Cohen E S, 'The Legitimacy Crisis of Investor-state Arbitration and the New EU Investment Court System' (2019) 26 *Review of International Political Economy* 1.

Dolzer R and Schreuer C, *Principles of International Investment Law* (OUP 2008) 4.

Echandi R, 'Non-Compliance with Awards: The Remedies of Customary International Law' (2012) 106 *Am. Soc'y Int'l L. Proc.* 1.

Foster G K, 'Collecting from Sovereigns: The Current Legal Framework for Arbitral Awards and Court Judgments Against States and Their Instrumentalities, and Some Proposals for its Reform' (2008) 25 *Ariz. J. Int'l & Comp. L.* 665, 705.

Franck S D, 'Foreign Direct Investment, Investment Treaty Arbitration, and the Rule of Law' (2007) 19 *Pac. McGeorge Global Bus. & Dev. L.J.* 2, 337–374.

History of the ICSID Convention: Documents Concerning the Origin and Formulation of The Convention, Vol. 2 (1968).

Hodgson M and Campbell A, 'Damages and Costs in Investment Treaty Arbitration Revisited' (14 December 2017) *Global Arb Rev.*

Hueckel J, 'Rebalancing Legitimacy and Sovereignty in International Investment Agreements' (2011–2012) 61 *Emory L.J.* 601.

Hunter J M and Olmedo J G, 'Enforcement/Execution of ICSID Awards against Reluctant States' (2011) 12 *JWIT* 307.

ICSID Secretariat Discussion Paper, 'Possible Improvements of The Framework For ICSID Arbitration' (Washington 2004). <https://icsid.worldbank.org/sites/default/files/Possible%20 Improvements%20of%20the%20Framework%20of%20ICSID%20Arbitration.pdf> accessed 20 May 2021

IBRD, World Bank, Management's Discussion & Analysis and Financial Statements, 55–58 (2012) [hereinafter IBRD MDA], <http://treasury.worldbank.org/cmd/pdf/IBRD_MDA_and_Financial _Statem ents_June_2012.pdf> accessed 22 March 2017

Johnson O T and Gibson C H, 'The Objections of Developed and Developing States to Investor-State Dispute Settlement, and What They Are Doing about Them' in Rovine A V (ed), *Contemporary Issues in International Arbitration and Mediation* (Chapter 14/Fordham Papers 2013) 251–269. <http://booksandjournals.brillonline.com/content/books/b9789004274945_016> accessed 17 October 2016.

Joubin-Bret A and Joubin-Bret C, 'The Effectiveness of The ICSID Mechanism Regarding the Enforcement of Arbitral Awards' in Julien Fouret (ed) *Enforcement of Investment Treaty Arbitration Awards* (Globe Law and Business Publishing 2015) 99–113.

Kalb J, 'Creating An ICSID Appellate Body' (2005) 10 UCLA J. Int'l L. & Foreign Aff. 179.

Kaufmann-Kohler G and Potestà M, 'The Composition of a Multilateral Investment Court and of an Appeal Mechanism for Investment Awards (CIDS Supplemental Report, 15 November 2017) <http://www.uncitral. org/pdf/english/workinggroups/wg_3/CIDS_Supplemental_Report.pdf> accessed 15 May 2019

Kaufmann-Kohler G and Potestà M, 'Can the Mauritius Convention Serve as a Model for the Reform of Investor-State Arbitration in Connection with the Introduction of a Permanent Investment Tribunal or an Appeal Mechanism? Analysis and Roadmap' (2016). <http://www .uncitral.org/pdf/english/CIDS_Research_Paper_Mauritius.pdf> accessed 17 November 2017

Larson G W, 'Default on Foreign Sovereign Debt: A Question for the Courts' (1985) 18 *Ind. L. Rev.* 18 959.

Marcopoulos A J, 'Revisiting the Risk of Undesired Appeal in Investment Treaty Arbitration: Is Deference to the Tribunal's Award Still Less Likely in the ICSID Context?' (2021) *Arbitration International.* <https://academic.oup.com/arbitration/advance-article-abstract/doi/10.1093/arbint/ aiab005/6209780> accessed 2 May 2021

Matute C, 'Forum Shopping in the Execution of ICSID Awards: Is it Time to Revive the UN Convention on State Immunity?' (2016) June 24. <http://kluwerarbitrationblog.com/2016/06 /24/preventing-forum-shoppingin-the-execution-of-icsid-awards-is-it-time-to-revive-the-un -conventionon-state-immunity/> accessed 21 November 2016.

Multilateral Investment Guarantee Agency, World Bank, World Investment and Political Risk 1(2011) [hereinafter WIPR], <http://www.miga.org/documents/WIPR11.pdf> 15 December 2016

Mistelis L and Baltag C, 'Recognition and Enforcement of Arbitral Awards and Settlement in International Arbitration: Corporate Attitudes and Practices' (2008) 19 *Am. Rev. Int'l Arb.* 319, 359.

Murphyt S D, 'The ELSI Case: An Investment Dispute at the International Court of Justice' (1991) 16 *Yale J.Int'l L.* 391.

Nmehielle V O, 'Enforcing Arbitration Awards under the International Convention for the Settlement of Investment Disputes (ICSID Convention)' (2001) 7 *Ann. Surv. Int'l & Comp. L.* 21.

Musa R B H, Polasek M and ICSID, 'The Origins and Specificities of the 315 ICSID Enforcement Mechanism' in Julien Fouret (ed), *Enforcement of Investment Treaty Arbitration Awards* (Globe Business Publishing Ltd. 2015) 13–33.

Nomer E, *Devletler Hususi Hukuku* (20 edn, Beta 2013) 1.

Odumosu I T, 'The Antinomies of the (Continued) Relevance of ICSID to the Third World' (2006) 8 *SDILJ* 345.

OECD, Public Consultation on Investor-State Dispute Settlement (May 16–9 July 2012), paras 62–75. accessed 03 March 2017.

Paparinskis M, 'Investment Arbitration and the Law of Countermeasures' (2008) 79 *British Yearbook of International Law* 264. <https://papers.ssrn.com/sol3/papers.cfm?abstract_id=2377778> accessed 15 February 2017

Paparinskis M, 'The Limits of Depoliticisation in Contemporary Investor-State Arbitration' (2010) 3 Select Proceedings of the European Society of International Law <http://ssrn.com/abstract=1716833> accessed 28 February 2017

Parra A, *The History of ICSID* (1st edn, OUP 2012) 1.

Parra A R, 'The Enforcement of ICSID Arbitral Awards' in D Bishop (ed), *World Bank Group, The World Bank Operations Manual, Operational Policies*, OP 7.40, (2009).

Paulsson J, 'ICSID's Achievements and Prospects' (1991) 6 *ICSID Review* 380.

Pinsolle P, Voisin T, ' Enforcement of Interim Relief In Investor-State Arbitration' in Fouret J (ed) *Enforcement of Investment Treaty Arbitration Awards* (Globe Business Publishing Ltd. 2015) 67–83.

Popov N, 'The Effectiveness of the Grounds for the Annulment of ICSID Awards' (LLM Thesis, Uppsala University 2020).

Puig S, 'Emergence & Dynamism in International Organizations: ICSID, Investor-State Arbitration & International Investment Law' (2012) 44 *Geo. J. Int'l L.* 531.

Puig S, 'Recasting ICSID's Legitimacy Debate: Towards a Goal-Based Empirical Agenda' 36 (2013) 2 *Fordham Int'l L.J.* 465–504.

Reinisch A, 'Will the EU's Proposal Concerning an Investment Court System for CETA and TTIP Lead to Enforceable Awards?—The Limits of Modifying the ICSID Convention and the Nature of Investment Arbitration' (2016) 19 *J Intl Economic L* 761, 772–773.

Roberts A, 'Power and Persuasion in Investment Treaty Interpretation: The Dual Role of States' (2010) 104 *AJIL* 179.

Roberts A, 'State-to-State Investment Treaty Arbitration: A Hybrid Theory of Interdependent Rights and Shared Interpretive Authority' (2014) 55 *Harv. Int'l L.J.* 1.

Rosenberg C B, 'The Intersection of International Trade and International Arbitration: The Use of Trade Benefits to Secure Compliance with Arbitral Awards' 2 (2013) 44 *Geo. J. Int'l L* 503–530.

Schreuer C H, 'Review: State Immunity: Some Recent Developments' (1991) 39 *Am.J.Comp.L.* 213–221.

Schreuer C H, *The ICSID Convention: A Commentary* (CUP 2009) 1.

Schreuer C and Weiniger M, *A Doctrine of Precedent?* (The Oxford Handbook of International Investment Law 2008) 1.

Shihata I F I, 'The Settlement of Disputes Regarding Foreign Investment: The Role of the World Bank, With Particular Reference to ICSID and MIGA' (1986) 1 *Am. U. J. Int'l L. & Pol'y* 97.

Sim C, 'Security for Costs in Investor–State Arbitration' (2017) 33 *Arbitration International* 427–495.

Sinclair, G F, *To Reform the World: International Organizations and the Making of Modern States* (OUP 2017) 1

Subramanian S R, 'BITs and Pieces in International Investment Law: Enforcement of Investment Treaty Arbitration Awards in the Non-ICSID States: The Case of India' (2013) 14 *JWIT* 198–239.

the UNCITRAL Secretariat, Possible Future Work in the Field of Dispute Settlement: Reforms of ISDS (20 April 2017) <https://undocs.org/en/A/CN.9/917> accessed 11 August 2020.

Todd A and Peinhardt C, 'Contingent Credibility: The Reputational Effects of Investment Treaty Disputes on Foreign Direct Investment' (2008) 51 *Urbana* 61801.

Tonova S T, Vasani B S, and Day J, 'Enforcement of Investment Treaty Awards 319 Against Assets of States, State Entities and State-Owned Companies' in J Fouret (ed), *Enforcement of Investment Treaty Arbitration Awards* (Globe Business Publishing Ltd. 2015) 83–97.

Travaini G, 'State 1 – Investor 1: Bring it on!' 1 April 2016 <http://kluwerarbitrationblog.com/2016/04/01/state-1-investor-1-bring-it-on/> accessed 06 December 2016.

Uchkunova I and Temnikov O, 'Security for Costs in ICSID Arbitration' (2015) 326 *Kluwer Arbitration Blog*. <http://kluwerarbitrationblog.com/2015/02/10/security-for-costs-in-icsidarbitration/> accessed 07 March 2017

UNCTAD, 'World Investment Report 2012: Towards a New Generation of Investment Policies' 84–86, U.N. Doc. UNCTAD/WIR/2012, [hereinafter World Investment Report 2012]. <http://www.unctaddocs.org/files/UNCTAD-WIR2012-Full-en.pdf> accessed 12 December 2016

Vannieuwenhuyse G, 'Bringing a dispute concerning ICSID cases and the ICSID convention before the International Court of Justice' (2009) *LAPE* 115–141.

Vicuña F O, 'Changing Approaches to the Nationality of Claims in the Context of Diplomatic Protection and International Dispute Settlement' 15 (2000) 2 *ICSID Review* 340–361.

Proposals for Amendment of the ICSID Rules - Working Paper 4, (vol 1, February 2020) 322.

Wong J, 'The Subversion of State-to-State Investment Treaty Arbitration' 6 (2014) 53 *Colum.J.Transnat'l L.* 1.

World Bank, Disputes over Defaults on External Debt, Expropriation, and Breach of Contract 2012 <https://policies.worldbank.org/sites/ppf3/PPFDocuments/090224b08 231b9e1.pdf> accessed 10 October 2017

CHAPTER 5

Conclusion

5.1 Answering the central research questions

The introductory chapter of this book clearly established the central questions that this book has sought to address, specifically, the origination of the enforcement issue in the investment arbitration field and the question of how the enforcement problem in investor-state arbitration can be overcome in a practical way. This question requires a clear answer if awards granted by the International Centre for Settlement of Investment Disputes (ICSID) are to avoid a tsunami of non-compliance in the future. These hugely important questions invariably raise other important issues: for instance, if there is any proposal to overcome the enforcement issue, and whether they are implied or not. In addition, attention may also conceivably turn to the question of whether there are alternative recommendations to decrease the non-compliance of ICSID and non-ICSID awards within the current system in a practical way.

Arbitration is the most popular dispute resolution system in investor–state disputes because foreign investors are forced to go before host state domestic courts in order to settle their disputes with the host states. Although arbitration is widely accepted as the most favourable method through which to settle investor–state disputes, it still cannot ultimately escape the state sovereignty effect. This feature is most clearly and vividly reiterated at the enforcement stage of arbitral awards. While arbitration protects the foreign investor from state sovereignty, arbitral awardsmay face sovereign immunity from execution and therefore arbitration may not achieve the goal in practice. Foreign direct investment (FDI) is implemented through millions of dollars and it is therefore hardly surprising that few are willing to take a visible risk. Arbitration awards are binding but still have a number of drawbacks, such as the enforcement issue. Ultimately investment arbitration is unable to decisively break with national courts or international tribunals.

The enforcement mechanism of international investment arbitration is afflicted by a number of important limitations, the most important of which is the alleged crisis of sovereign immunity. In recent years, a number of high-profile investment disputes involving similar or identical facts have come up against the same scenario. The state immunity obstacle was not seriously considered when the ICSID Convention was being drafted by the current president of the World Bank. It was also not understood to be a serious problem during the most recent cases. By virtue of the ICSID Convention, and the associated commitment of member states, ICSID awards are voluntarily enforceable in almost 80 per cent of countries around the world.[1] In large part, this can be said to be attributable to Article 54's establishment of a 'system of automatic enforceability of awards,' an

1 Vernon Cassin, 'ITA Workshop on Modern Enforcement of Arbitral Awards—Keynote Address' (2014) <http://kluwerarbitrationblog.com/2014/06/23/ita-workshop-on-modern-enforcement-of-arbitral-awards-keynote-address/> accessed 14 March 2017.

DOI: 10.4324/9781003216919-6

innovation which means that ICSID awards are not subject to judicial review. While this article negates the possibility of collapse in the recognition stage of foreign awards, there still remains the likelihood that this outcome will be evidenced during the process of enforcement in later stages.

As Chapter 1 has extensively demonstrated, sovereign immunity is frequently a problem when a disputing party applies to a responsible state. While a state that submits to arbitration ostensibly waives the right to sovereign immunity, it is obvious that the state may still enjoy immunity from execution. Ultimately this is dependent upon the law of the state where enforcement is sought. While some jurisdictions have doctrine of absolute immunity from execution n, other jurisdictions are too restrictive about immunity from execution. More often than not, this depends on whether the assets are assigned for public purposes. It has previously been observed that most of a state's foreign assets are likely to have public aims. This can make it hard to enforce an award against a foreign state even if the tribunal has decided the state is responsible.

When the foreign investor cannot enforce an award in the host state's territory, they have to search other member countries which hold the debtor state's assets. In addition, the foreign investor also has to persuade the third state to enforce the award. This issue is same as for non-ICSID awards; however, it is important to remember that they may encounter a public policy bar at the first stage of enforcement of a foreign award. If non-ICSID awards pass this first stage, they are likely that it will come against the same obstacle that all ICSID awards meet. By virtue of the fact that the New York Convention is silent about state sovereignty, it is widely accepted that sovereign immunity from execution is a bar to enforce non-ICSID awards. There is not any restriction that impedes the obstacle in the New York Convention. However, the ICSID Convention expressly allows contracting states to assert sovereign immunity from execution as a plea for non-compliance. The main issue is to define the host state's assets, with a view to categorising them as commercial or public. It is easy to manipulate this categorisation because there are no precise guidelines and the categories differ from jurisdiction to jurisdiction. This unhappy circumstance results in forum shopping and the incurrence of great expense for creditor investors in practice.

It is equally instructive to approach the question from the opposing side, with specific attention to the issue of non-compliance. If the losing party was a foreign investor, the host state would receive payment from the investor. A generally accepted premise holds that the foreign investor's property or assets can be seized in the host state's territory. However, if the foreign investor has already withdrawn his or her assets from the state or if the investor has gone into bankruptcy, there is no way that the host state could receive the payment. In the global world, foreign investors are in the position where they can exert considerable influence. In their interactions with developing states, multinational companies have considerable power that can be directed towards the alteration of rules and, therefore, foreign investors are not on the weak side anymore, and they should also provide guarantee to the host states as well. This is the necessity of the time. As has already been identified, Turkey is the main victim in this respect because the government has not yet received ICSID awards payments from foreign investors—this is despite the fact that it has paid arbitral awards made against itself upon a voluntary basis until now. The statistics cited over the course of the preceding discussion suggest that the situation has shifted, with the rate of state victories in investor–state arbitration increasing gradually. Up until now, foreign investors have been understood to be in a position of weakness; as such, they have been protected with bilateral investment treaty (BIT) provisions and also the stipulations laid out in the respective conventions. When the balance of power between the respective parties shifts, the host state requires additional guarantees. In working towards resolutions, it should first be recognised that the protection balance must be achieved and put in place.

In response to the occurrence of non-compliance arbitral awards, several scholars and practitioners have put forward practical proposals. With a view to remedying the execution obstacle, a variety of practical suggestions have been put forward. The essential purpose of practical engagement is not to overhaul the entire investor–state arbitration system, rather it is to identify ways in which this system can be retrieved or recovered. One of the most promising recommendations in this respect has been to create a hybrid sovereign immunity act. From this perspective, the central concern is the enforcement of sovereign law. However, closer examination reveals that the contracting states' immunity acts are more or less similar; while some provide a restricted approach to sovereign immunity, others instead provide for absolute state immunity. In the initial stages of this book, it was observed that the waiver of immunity from execution clause can be drafted into BITs. In this regard, it is instructive to note that the ICSID has a model clause. However, it should also be noted the ICSID Convention has not included the model waiver immunity from execution clause.

Taking the different facts that have been presented into account, it seems likely that it can be difficult to create a hybrid state sovereignty that applies to all member states. States will not allow for their own sovereignty to be orientated from outside. The best example in this respect is the United Nations Convention on Jurisdictional Immunities of States and Their Property (UNCSI), which has not yet entered into force because it lacks the requisite number of member states.

Another popular suggestion holds that the end objective can be achieved by the World Bank cutting the failing state party's loans. The ICSID is an organisation of the World Bank and it therefore seems logical to suggest that non-compliance with the ICSID awards can be addressed by directly cutting the loans. If the debtor state persists in failing to pay the due amount, the World Bank will pay the award from the failing state's capital account. At first glance, this recommendation could provide a significant solution to the execution issue that pertains to arbitral awards. Most countries are members of the World Bank; some of them have capital accounts, while others have loans. In situations of non-compliance with an ICSID award, the World Bank is in a position where it can immediately apply the power of sanction to the losing state. Conceivably, this could have significant implications for the avoidance of unpaid arbitral awards. However, if the World Bank followed this path, it would first require a number of serious amendments. Firstly, the World Bank would be required to amend its own agreement article in accordance—if it failed to thus act, it would be in breach of its obligations. In addition to this, it should also be noted that although the ICSID was established by the World Bank, it is ultimately a self-governing institution. As an independent and impartial platform for the settlement of international investment disputes, the ICSID is predisposed to function in accordance with the principle of depoliticisation. In its aforementioned formulation, the proposed solution could potentially damage or underpin this principle. In addition, it should also be acknowledged that Article 54 of the ICSID Convention establishes that the award will be enforced in accordance with the domestic law of the state in which execution is sought. Upon this basis, the enforcing state has a right to refuse to enforce the ICSID award. It can sustain this refusal by claiming that the attempt to seize state assets is, by virtue of the fact that these assets are used for public purposes, a violation of its sovereign immunity. It is undeniably the case that the losing state cannot construe as derogating from the law in relating to immunity of that state from execution under Article 55 of the ICSID Convention. However, the article will still be ineffective because the enforcing state will determine whether the assets that have been seized serve commercial or public purposes. In addition, there is no superior body within the international field that can object to the state's decision. Nobody is in a position to decide whether the state has manipulated the article.

On the other hand, if the proposal for non-compliance arbitral awards is accepted, the states which are members of both the World Bank and the ICSID Convention can consider withdrawing from the ICSID Convention. This possibility arises as a result of the fact that the losing states will not risk losing their loans or capital account because of an arbitral award. There is a stronger likelihood that these losing states will withdraw their memberships from the ICSID Convention—this is due to the fact that it is more of a burden to withdraw from the World Bank. They have the right to protect their sovereign immunity under the ICSID Convention and resist any intrusion upon their sovereignty. Upon this basis, the ICSID can lose its contracting states.

In addition to these two proposals, it has been debated whether the ICSID can itself avoid non-compliance with arbitral awards. This likelihood is enhanced by the fact that the ICSID administrative body plays a monitoring role. The ICSID can reject the next application made by the failing party, maintaining this position until the ICSID award is paid. The ICSID action could also be justified under Article 22 of the International Law Commission's Draft Articles on the Responsibility of International Organizations (DARIO) but would be conditional upon the conditions in Part Four (Chapter II) of DARIO being fulfilled. If the ICSID action was justified under the DARIO, it would be an effective solution to the execution issue and would not impinge upon ICSID's depoliticisation principle. However, it would still encounter problems in practice. This action cannot be justified because the ICSID Convention does not include the countermeasures in its text. If the ICSID applied this type of countermeasure to the failing party in its next application, the institution would be in breach of the ICSID Convention. The ICSID Convention must accordingly be amended if this action is to be justified under the DARIO. Even if the ICSID Convention had the right to issue these countermeasures, this action would damage the opposing party's rights in some respects.

The discussion of these three solutions illustrates that there has been a sustained engagement with the execution issue in ICSID awards. The ICSID's silence on the proposals is more than likely attributable to the principle of depoliticisation. While it is possible that the ICSID Convention will evolve and develop, its depoliticised character must remain in place. Because the ICSID is a judicial authority, it must be independent and impartial. Taking these various factors into consideration, there is only one option left: countermeasures that are initiated against the state that has failed to pay the arbitral award.

To date, diplomatic protection has been argued to precede the dispute. However, Article 27 of the ICSID Convention allows the investor's home state to sue before the International Court of Justice (ICJ), citing the non-payment of the ICSID award against the host state in the process. Diplomatic protection is preferred as the last remedy to be applied in investor–state arbitration because it is difficult to persuade the home state to defend itself within an international forum. In addition, the investor does not continue to have a voice after it has been protected by its home state in the ICJ. It is acceptable not to request diplomatic protection at the beginning of the dispute for foreign investors; however, it is obvious that diplomatic protection is easier for non-compliance awards. If it is demonstrated that the investor is right in his/her case, it is not necessary to exhaust all domestic remedies. In this instance, home states can apply countermeasures, under the International Law Association (ILA) draft responsibility of state against the host states in the process. This is a more effective way to force the failing state to honour the award. This approach has the additional benefit that it will not infringe upon the principle of depoliticisation that is enshrined within ICSID. In addition, Article 60 of the Vienna Convention on the Law of Treaties (VCLT) provides the injured state with an additional option, enabling it to use countermeasures against the failing state by enabling it to terminate BITs or suspend the treaty protection until payment has been received by the injured state. In this instance, termination of a BIT could be conceived as an overreaction, especially as the object of concern is only one national investor's arbitral award. Taking this objection into account, the suspension of treaty protection may be held to be a more workable solution, especially if trade and investment relations between the states have not broken down. Suspension would have the added benefit of issuing a future warning to opposing states.

Taking the concern of losing investors into account, if the ICSID action regarding rejection of the losing party's next application could be justified under the DARIO, victorious states would not suffer from non-payment. In this instance, the best solution may be the security cost in that field for the states. This point is further reiterated by the Turkish example. Although the investor has not paid three arbitral awards debt to Turkey, the investor is still in a position to initiate a further arbitration proceeding against the state. This is a clear example of bad faith; with regard to the execution issue, the interests of both sides should be recognised and taken into full account.

In conclusion, it should be recognised that international investment arbitration is continually adapting and innovating. This explains why the execution obstacle has arisen so recently; to the same extent, it also explains why the issue has proliferated over such a short time. In addition to considering the proposed solutions, states should recognise that FDI has a reciprocal effect: if a state does not pay the arbitral award, it means that the same state puts its own national investor at risk in other territories. In addition to this, states which fail to comply with arbitral awards are internationally recognised as being risky by international investors. In this regard, it should be remembered that FDI is the main tool that enables states to develop. With a view to avoiding the issue, states should take care to reconsider the drafting of their BITs and investment treaties. To put it slightly differently, if the states have bargaining power, they should take care to draft their treaties in a way that puts in place a proper waiver from execution clause, putting in place countermeasures that enable treaty obligations to be suspended until payments are received. If these measures are in place, the injured investor's state can apply the treaty obligations and the opposing state cannot, by virtue of the fact that it has already accepted the countermeasures, object to the injured state's action. Foreign investors should take care to ensure that their consensual agreements with states take a similar form. Before investing in a state, foreign investors should consider all details before proceeding further.

5.2 Further research

This book has focused on the execution issue that originates within state sovereignty, placing particular emphasis upon the ICSID awards while considering possible solutions, along with their associated benefits and drawbacks. In engaging at each of these points, this book has stressed the need to avoid the further proliferation of the execution issue. Chapters 1 and 2 considered where the issue originated, clearly identifying practical solutions that might be introduced, and taking care to engage them in their full complexity (Chapter 4). Chapter 1 provided additional insight by considering the categorisation of state's assets as commercial or public. An additional degree of complexity was also introduced when it was acknowledged that each state has its own sovereignty act which is applied during the course of this categorisation. Chapter 3 addresses the investment court proposal's potential effect on the enforcement issue and explains why the proposal may not be a good idea for the future investor–state dispute settlement (ISDS). Chapter 4 considered models for international investment arbitration, taking into account options such as the hybrid sovereignty act and a heightened role for the World Bank. Attention invariably converged upon the ICSID's institutional role, with specific reference to international organisations, DARIO, and countermeasures that can be initiated under the state responsibility ICL Draft. In addition, it was also recognised that Article 60 of the VCLT provides another means through which countermeasures can be initiated and applied.

The preceding discussion has served to reiterate the need for the depoliticisation principle of the ICSID to be flexible; if this is not the case, it will be difficult to overcome the execution issue. A preliminary analysis of the most prominent solutions suggested that in the event that this flexibility is evidenced, it will be relatively straightforward to apply the proposed solutions. However, further research is required to identify which of the solutions will work best in practice. In addition, application will only work if the proposed solution is adapted to the interests of both parties. Ongoing research into the enforcement of international arbitral awards clearly reiterate the urgency of this issue. As a first step, the principle of depoliticisation should, with a view to addressing the execution issue, be made more flexible. In addition, as has already been observed, it is also important to consider the reform of the ICSID system, with specific attention to the appeal body and security for costs. These, as opposed to the establishment of a new investment court, are the preponderant considerations. The ICSID is also an established platform for the settlement of investment disputes; even taking into account the limitations and shortcomings that have been hitherto identified, it might be more sustainable to reconsider highlighted parts of the ICSID Convention. Even if countermeasures are also effective solutions in the enforcement of arbitral awards, it cannot be denied that access to diplomatic protection is, while sometimes difficult to achieve, an equally important consideration. In order to offset the possibility of further harm being incurred by the respective parties, the issue of execution in the field must be more closely engaged by the convention's drafters, scholars, and practitioners.

INDEX

www.ingramcontent.com/pod-product-compliance
Lightning Source LLC
LaVergne TN
LVHW080655011026
849160LV00014B/1440
* 9 7 8 1 0 3 2 1 0 7 6 2 2 *